Baroque Churches
of Central Europe

BAROQUE CHURCHES
OF CENTRAL EUROPE

JOHN BOURKE

Photographs by
THOMAS FINKENSTAEDT

FABER AND FABER
3 Queen Square
London

First published in 1958
Second edition (revised and enlarged) 1962
First published in this edition 1978
by Faber and Faber Limited
3 Queen Square, London, W.C.1
Printed in Great Britain by
Whitstable Litho Ltd., Whitstable, Kent
All rights reserved

ISBN 0 571 10689 7

British Library Cataloguing in Publication Data

Bourke, John
 Baroque churches of central Europe. – 2nd ed.
 (revised and enlarged).
 1. Architecture, Baroque – Central Europe
 2. Church architecture – Central Europe
 I. Title
 726'.5'0943   NA5456

 ISBN 0–571–10689–7

Contents

7

CONTENTS

Foreword

This book is not written by an expert or for experts. It makes no claim to be original or learned. It is simply the result of a somewhat extensive study of a subject that captivated me when, some ten years ago now, I went as a lecturer to Munich University and began, in my spare time, to explore Bavaria and the neighbouring lands. My gradual discovery of these beautiful churches proved a source of never-ending delight to me and led me to read all that I could find about them, to reflect on the problems they present and to study the religious beliefs and the aesthetic aims behind them and the means devised to give to these concrete expression. Yet though I revelled in the beauties of line and form, of colour and statue and painting, the attraction that these churches had for me remained something of a puzzle to me until one day I heard a rendering of 'Messiah' in one of the greatest of them whose architect was born in the same year as Handel. An inner relationship then opened up between what I saw all around me and what I was listening to. That a church such as that in which I was sitting should awaken the response it did in anyone as devoted as I had always been to the music of Corelli and Handel and Bach, I saw to be natural and inevitable. It was as if the epoch had spoken with *all* its voices, as if only through their concerted harmony it could breathe its fervour and rekindle its vision.

It was with some surprise that I discovered that, though the great Continental Baroque masters of music and painting have been extensively studied in England, and the secular architecture of the period to some degree, the church art and architecture had been as good as ignored. Some writings on the subject in English there are, of course (see the Bibliography). But either they are very general, or they presuppose knowledge and experience which the average English person cannot be expected to have. I found that there was nothing at all in the way of a handbook that would introduce the ordinary interested and educated but perhaps somewhat bewildered English or American traveller to the subject and point out to him what he ought to see, and where, and why. So, greatly daring, I decided to try myself to compile a book of a kind that repeated inquiries from travellers and an obviously growing interest suggested to me might provide a welcome introduction. The extensive notes that I had already accumulated on numerous visits formed a basis and starting-point.

My aim in offering this book is thus a simple one—to interest English-speaking people in a perhaps unfamiliar but assuredly rewarding and fascinating field of European architecture and art, and, above all, to encourage them to enrich their holidays on the European continent by visiting and enjoying these churches for themselves.

The opening chapters are intended to help the reader to understand certain important aspects of the historical background, something of the spirit of the times in which the churches arose and of the aims which their patrons, architects and craftsmen set themselves to achieve. I have here done my best to put myself in the place of a person approaching the subject with little knowledge and experience. Technical terminology has accordingly been restricted as far as possible, and such terms as occur are explained in a Glossary. The term 'Baroque' itself has been used, and purposely so, in a broad sense to include both the early phase of emergence from the Renaissance and the late development known as the 'Rococo'; the terms 'mannerism' and 'mannerist', as also the phenomena which they are intended to describe, have been ignored. Precisians will no doubt rap me over the knuckles with their rulers; but for the task in hand my concern has been to try to make certain broad distinctions and lines of development clear and encumber the reader as little as was necessary.

In describing the churches themselves I have had primarily in view the actual visitor to them as he moves around and about them. They are dealt with on a uniform plan throughout and in a deliberately terse, guide-book style which I hope will be found to have practical value. For the convenience of travellers not possessed of a car—the ideal means of transport for the purpose, as some of the best of the churches lie very remote—I have added the standard means of access with as much accuracy as was possible. Geographical positions are also given and these the maps will help the reader to locate; a key to the signs used will be found on the map of Austria.

The illustrations have been chosen with the double purpose of doing what justice is possible to the variety of the subject within the limits proposed and of illustrating specific points made in the text. The ground-plans included will, it is hoped, help to make clearer some of the problems of origin and design.

Regarding the versions and spellings of names in text and maps, anglicized versions have been given (or added) where these have become established usage for English-speaking people. Thus the lakes of Constance and Lucerne, the rivers Rhine and Danube and the cities of Munich, Vienna and Nuremberg appear as such and not (or not only) as the Bodensee and the Vierwaldstättersee, the Rhein and the Donau, München, Wien, and Nürnberg. But, in general, anglicization has been purposely avoided. Church-names, for instance, appear in their native form; with names such as Heiliggeistkirche, Kollegienkirche or Theatinerkirche the visitor will familiarize himself easily enough, and it is right that he should (All Saints', Margaret Street, is after all not 'Allerheiligenkirche, Margaretenstrasse'!).

I love dearly Salisbury and Wells, Lincoln and Durham, Tewkesbury Abbey and Beverley Minster—but also Ottobeuren and Weingarten, Diessen and Steinhausen, Melk and Wilhering and Einsiedeln. And if I have at all succeeded in passing on some of my interest and enthusiasm for these beautiful churches which form so notable a part of our European heritage, I shall feel happy and rewarded.

I owe thanks for help and encouragement in more directions than I could name.

FOREWORD

Of my indebtedness to the written researches and judgments of others the Bibliography will give some slight idea. When I was beginning to study the subject I found Heinrich Wölfflin's volume *Renaissance und Barock* particularly helpful and illuminating. Among contemporary scholars I have learnt much from the writings of Dr Hugo Schnell, Dr Norbert Lieb, Professor Hans Sedlmayr, the late Dr Michael Hartig, Dr Hans Tintelnot and Dr Heinrich Decker.

I wish further to express my gratitude—

To my friend and colleague Thomas Finkenstaedt, who took the photographs, for his untiring interest and patience, his skill and his endless journeyings.

To Herr Wolfgang Plapper who drew the excellent maps and reproduced the ground-plans.

To the ecclesiastical authorities of the following churches for kind permission to take interior photographs: the Cathedral Church of St Gallen; the Abbeys of Fiecht, Michaelbeuern, Neresheim, Ottobeuren, Rohr, St Florian, Schäftlarn; the Priories of Birnau and Volders; the Gemeinschaft von den Heiligen Engeln, Angelicum Banz; the Convents of Holzen (through St Josefs Kongregation, Ursberg/Schwaben), Mödingen and Osterhofen; the pilgrimage church of Die Wies (Wieskirche); the parish churches of Diessen, Dischingen, Fürstenfeldbruck (former Abbey Church), Hopfgarten, Irsee, Kleinhelfendorf, Rott-am-Inn, St Wolfgang, Steinhausen.

To the Deutscher Kunstverlag (Munich and Berlin) for their kind permission to reproduce the ground-plans, also for much assistance derived from their varied, often indispensable publications (see Bibliography).

To the authorities of the Würzburg Residenz for having kindly opened the Hofkirche for me on a day when it is normally closed.

To the Right Rev Dr Franz Schreyer, former Abbot of Scheyern, and to the Rev Father Chrysostomus Dierkes, of Scheyern; also to the memory of the Right Rev Dr Angelus Kupfer, late Abbot of Ettal, and to the Rev Father Wunibald Wörl, of Ettal. My visits as guest of these two great Benedictine monasteries were both delightful in themselves and also valuable in affording me some slight insight into the living spirit of a monastic community, the spirit to whose enterprise and devotion in the past most of the greatest of these churches have owed their origin.

To the memory of the Rev Father Dr P. Klingler of Volders, and also to Fr. Karl Pohlmann of Niederaltaich Abbey, for placing time and knowledge at my disposal and for kindly hospitality.

To the Rev Franz-Josef Heldmann, Rural Dean of Geisenfeld, under whose roof I have more than once been generously entertained and in whose car the Rev Georg Deininger first drove me to see Bettbrunn.

To countless other friendly and helpful clergy, sacristans and guides who in one way or another have enriched my visits to their churches.

To my friends Rolf Zitzlsperger, Horst Weinstock, Hermann Neumeister, Heinz Bäuerlein and Ferdinand Stangl, for driving me to see many important churches.

To my friend Hans Strauss, for his exhilarating companionship on so many visits in all three countries and in Rome; and to my friend Toni Bayerl, for a memorable first week-end in Ottobeuren and with whom I first saw Melk and Vienna.

To Professor Nikolaus Pevsner for reading the typescript and for valuable criticism and encouragement; I owe much to his expert comments and suggestions.

To the late Professor Henry Lüdeke, of Basle University, whose guest I was on the occasion of a happy visit with Munich students at the invitation of his Department at Whitsun 1957, and who lent me his car to go to Arlesheim.

To Mr H. D. Molesworth of the Victoria and Albert Museum, for friendly and salutary advice at an early, undeveloped but decisive stage of the book.

Finally, to my publishers, and especially to Mr Richard de la Mare, for unfailing interest, courtesy and skill.

Munich University, 1958   JOHN BOURKE

Note to Second Edition

This book was a modest attempt to fill a gap. That it has not been an unsuccessful one seems to be shown by the fact that a second edition has been fairly soon asked for, which is a source of real pleasure and satisfaction to me.

In the meantime I have myself been travelling about the area with the book as extensively as time would allow to discover errors, omissions and under- or over-estimations; and I now offer it in a corrected, expanded and, I hope, improved form, with the Bibliography also extended and brought up to date.

The original Foreword of 1958 has been revised in several details but otherwise left as it was. This short note, however, is added to introduce the new edition.

To all, reviewers and others—and they have been very many— who have helped me with comments, criticisms and corrections I am very grateful; most of the suggestions offered have been embodied in this new version. In this connection I would mention particularly Professor S. Lane Faison Jr., Chairman of the Art Department at Williams College, Williamstown, U.S.A., and Director of the Art Museum there who, himself on a year's research in Europe also in the field of Baroque, got into touch with me and has been tireless in suggesting improvements and tracking down inaccuracies. My 'church-hunting' expeditions with him and Mrs Faison have been delightful.

Munich University   JOHN BOURKE
Summer 1961

Note to Faber Paperback Edition

Only a limited number of minor corrections have been possible.

My best thanks to the following friends for help on various visits: Otto Klingl, Helmut Fragner, Stephan Scheuerl, Wolf Steigenberger and Stefan Galikowski.

Munich   JOHN BOURKE

Descriptive List of Illustrations

(*Between pages 64 and 65*)

1. *Munich, Theatinerkirche* (1663–90). Façade and dome from N.E.
2. *Die Wies* (1745–54). View of pilgrimage church from N.E. showing rotunda, tower and attached clergy-house.
3. *Steinhausen* (1728–33). Village church from N.W.
4. *Maria Birnbaum* (1661–5). Pilgrimage church from N.E.
5. *Kappel* (1685–9). View of pilgrimage church showing symbolic ('trinitarian') design of three apses and three towers.
6. *Melk* (1702–14). General view of abbey and church from river bank upstream to S.W.
7. *Salzburg, Kollegienkirche* (1694–1707). This façade is an important and influential prototype (cf. Weingarten, Einsiedeln, etc.).
8. *Innsbruck, St Jakobi* (1717–24), with Inn valley and mountain setting, from S.W.
9. *Hopfgarten*, parish church (1715–64). A lively and charming country church façade.
10. *Salzburg*, Cathedral (1614–28). Prototype of Italianate basilica north of Alps.
11. *Vienna, Karlskirche* (1716–29). Façade and dome.
12. *Weingarten* (1711–24). Façade and dome of abbey church from the town.
13. *Einsiedeln* (1719–35). Façade of church and S.W. wing of abbey buildings.
14. *Schönenberg* (1682–95). Pilgrimage church of early Vorarlberg type, on its hill, from S.W.
15. *Munich, Dreifaltigkeitskirche* (1711–14). One of the earliest S. German rhythmical façades.
16. *Berg-am-Laim* (1738–51). Façade from N.W.

15

DESCRIPTIVE LIST OF ILLUSTRATIONS

17. *Ottobeuren* (1748–67). View of abbey church from S.E. showing bold façade, towers, basilical elevation and transept formation.

18. *Vierzehnheiligen* (1744–72). Pilgrimage church from N.W.

19. *St Gallen*, Cathedral (1755–86). E. façade, choir and rotunda.

20. *Volders*, priory church (1620–4). Tower from S.W. looking across the Inn valley, with domed roofing of church.

21. *Dürnstein* (1721–5). Tower of church.

22. *Mödingen*, convent church (1716–18). Pulpit (*Stephan Luidl*, 1720) with symbolic supporting angel, putti groups at corners representing (*left to right*) Faith (anchor), Hope (church) and Love (flaming heart). On sounding-board, symbolic putti around figure of patron saint (Dominic).

23. *Irsee*, parish church (1699–1704). 'Ship' pulpit (1725) with St Michael as figurehead, putti aloft in the rigging, prominent anchor (Faith).

24. *Kleinhelfendorf*. Early stucco ornament (Miesbach school, 1668–9). The Virgin crowned, on crescent moon, between angels. Note echoes of Gothic vaulting and Renaissance panelling, and a general stiffness, despite the good quality of the work.

25. *Diessen*. Later stucco ornament (under organ: *J. M. Feichtmayr*, *c.* 1739). Scroll and rocaille design; putti with symbols of Faith (anchor), Hope (chalice), Love (heart). Note that *both* grip the anchor!

(Between pages 160 *and* 161)

26. *Steinhausen* (1728–33). Interior looking E., showing rotunda arcade, high altar and side altars.

27. *Ottobeuren* (1748–67). Interior with high altar, side altars, pulpit (*right*) and font (*left*).

28. *Diessen* (1732–9). Interior looking E. showing wall-pillars, 'coulisse'-type side altars, high altar and pulpit.

29. *Fürstenfeldbruck*, former abbey church (1701–66). Interior of choir showing high altar with Berninesque columns, and symbolic curtain and clock over choir arch.

DESCRIPTIVE LIST OF ILLUSTRATIONS

56. *St Florian*. Choir stalls, S. side (*Adam Franz, c.* 1700). St Jerome. Note attributes, and cf. plates 44 and 48.

57. *Birnau*. Stations of the Cross (*J. A. Feuchtmayer*), one of four surviving. Note the putti, one with club in defensive posture, the other (head only) looking down on the scene in grief.

58. *St Gallen*. Relief over S. aisle arch in rotunda (*Christian Wenzinger, c.* 1758). St Gallus distributes alms to the poor and crippled. Note the fine restraint, together with the touch of realism in the wooden leg.

59. *Steinhausen*. Window in rotunda of characteristic *Zimmermann* design. Note the stucco ornament, including the whimsical woodpecker!

60. *Dischingen*, parish church. Window in organ gallery, of painted rocaille design (*c.* 1770). Note the tension of curve and counter-curve, the harmony in asymmetry.

61. *Diessen*. Processional staff of bakers' guild; the carved head showing patron saint (St George) and (in cartouche below) a 'bretzel' (*c.* 1760).

62. *Fiecht*, abbey church (1740–4). Pew end in nave (*3rd on right from back, c.* 1743); death of St Joseph, one of series of scenes from his life. Note use of curve and counter-curve; also the carved open-work pew backs.

63. *Osterhofen*. Altar, S. side of nave (*Asam*). Symbolic putto in prayer: 'et oratio mea ascendat ad te, Domine' ('and let my prayer come unto thee, O Lord'). Note the rapt attitude, the rosary, the closed book.

64. *Birnau*. St Bernard's altar, S. side of choir arch. Putto, the famous 'Honigschlecker' ('honeylicker') by *J. A. Feuchtmayer*. He is tasting the honey from the bee-hive at his side that symbolizes the sweetness of the Saint's speech.

65. *Fiecht*. Confessional (*c.* 1744). Death's head putto, symbol of mortality.

66. *Osterhofen*. St John Nepomuk altar. Symbolic putti commemorating the Saint's fidelity in guarding the secrecy of the confessional. The left-hand one, with finger to lips,

points to the words 'secretum meum mihi' ('my secret for myself alone'), the other in jubilation holds aloft the Saint's tongue in a 'glory'.

Cameras used:

Rolleicord IV

Exacta Varex

with the following lenses: *Super Lithagon* 2·5/35 mm., *Tessar* 2·8/50 mm., *Xenar* 3·5/105 mm., *Travenar* 3·5/135 mm., *Xenar* 5·5/240 mm.

MAPS

Southern Germany and Tyrol, pages 72 and 73.

Northern Bavaria, page 101.

Switzerland, pages 184 and 185.

Austria, pages 216 and 217.

GROUND-PLANS illustrating the development of design will be found on pages 288 and 289.

Introduction

We may well be grateful that the last war has left us any works of art and architecture in Central Europe at all. To dwell on the vast and irreparable damage to ancient monuments in Germany would be futile. It is enough to mention what are no doubt the two most serious large-scale losses in the West—mediaeval Nuremberg, bombed to ruins in a matter of hours, and Baroque Würzburg, similarly wrecked in a matter of minutes. Austria escaped more lightly; Switzerland, of course, altogether. Yet much has survived, even in Germany. Southern Germans, in particular Bavarians, and all lovers of beauty with them, have a special cause to be thankful for treasures safely preserved. For throughout Bavaria, and to a lesser extent Württemberg, is spread a wealth of church architecture and art which, alike in its intrinsic quality and in its vivid and vigorous representation of an epoch, has few rivals. That most of these churches have escaped damage is due, no doubt, to the fact that they lie, in the majority of cases, away from the beaten, or rather blasted, track. Many of the finest, like the great abbey churches of *Weingarten* or *Ottobeuren*, stand in otherwise unimportant little towns or, like the 'Wallfahrtskirchen' ('pilgrimage churches') *Birnau* or *Die Wies* or many another, lie remote and isolated; and such as these were spared the fate that overtook those in Würzburg or Munich. Some were lucky; the little Danube town of Donauwörth was largely destroyed, but its imposing Baroque church *Heiligkreuz* survived. Thus it is that still today in Southern Bavaria alone an almost inexhaustible richness of church art and architecture of the Baroque period awaits the visitor. Equally grateful must we be that so many beautiful Baroque buildings have been preserved also in Austria and, though here their

21

safety was never threatened, in Switzerland, *Salzburg Cathedral* was hit and Innsbruck's churches suffered considerably; but *Melk* is still there untouched, and *Wilhering*, and in Vienna the *Karlskirche* successfully survived the blast of seven bombs that landed around it. And on Swiss soil we can still rejoice at *Einsiedeln* and *St Gallen* and *St Urban*.

The area chosen here for study—Southern Germany, Switzerland and Austria—has certain unifying elements of artistic tradition that seem to justify the choice. In the first place, it is, of course, an area permeated throughout by influences from Italy, the home of Baroque. Italian architects and artists, whether from Italy proper or from the Italian-Swiss districts of Tessin and Graubünden, we find working everywhere; native architects and artists studied Italian ideas and models. The Jesuits, the chief early ecclesiastical patrons of the style, built churches alike in Munich and Dillingen, Innsbruck and Vienna, Lucerne and Solothurn on the pattern of *Il Gesù* in Rome, the mother-church of the order, designed by *Vignola*. Secondly, within the area itself important cross-influences can be found. In Southern Germany and in Switzerland architects of the influential Vorarlberg school were active as builders; and more than one church owes a debt to the ideas of the Austrian architect *J. B. Fischer von Erlach*. On the other hand, artists from Bavaria—the *Asam* brothers, for example, and stucco-artists from *Wessobrunn*—were called in to decorate churches in parts of Austria and Switzerland. It is sad, let us add in passing, that Czecho-Slovakia, on whose soil the Bavarian family of the *Dientzenhofers* chiefly lavished their architectural talents, is still inaccessible to the ordinary traveller from the West. But so it is, and for our present purpose there is little practical point in doing more than referring, as we shall do, to buildings there for the sake of comparison.

That a Baroque church leads many (and not only English) people on to unfamiliar ground and confronts them with problems of understanding and appreciation that are at first bewildering I fully realize. What these problems are and how they may be approached I have tried to suggest in the chapter entitled 'The

Spirit of Baroque'. I shall be content if I succeed in encouraging others to go and see these churches for themselves on their Continental holidays and helping them, when they do, to understand and enjoy what they find. During the past few years, in which I have been living and working in Bavaria and crossing over for visits into Austria and Switzerland, I have devoted an increasing amount of my spare time to a study of the churches and have experienced them, great and small, in the most varying conditions of weather and lighting and worship. To *Neresheim* I first came in a thunderstorm. In the great white church, that rose proudly against a leaden sky, a funeral service was nearing its end—a member of the Abbey community was being brought to burial amid the chanting of his brothers and the clamouring of the heavens. No less unforgettable was a performance of Handel's 'Messiah' in *Die Wies* one radiant summer Sunday afternoon when everything, sunlight and music, architecture and art, seemed to be working together in a great paean of harmony and colour and glory. Some churches I have visited and been alone there in a deep silence broken only by a distant cow-bell from an upland pasture, or the fluttering of a butterfly around the haloed head of a saint. Others I have seen on the occasion of some great pilgrimage with thronging thousands cheerfully pious and gay in costume, festival banners and crosses high uplifted. I have been present at countless services in these churches from the simplest village devotion to a Haydn Mass in all its splendour. I have seen them, too, in the most varied natural settings—*Birnau*, delicate and lonely, on the sloping grassy northern shore of the wide Lake of Constance; and across the water *St Gallen* clustered thickly about by the houses of the old town, or *Engelberg* far up in its mountain valley at the foot of the snowy Titlis. Some contrasts remain with me vividly. Twin-towered *Banz*, throned on its windy hill, seen from afar; and twin-towered *Ottobeuren*, no less throned in its ample valley, waiting to be discovered. On the Danube, *Weltenburg* huddled low on its shingly spit of land in the tight embrace of the river as it sweeps round in a sharp curve to break through a deep gorge; and 250 miles downstream, in Austria,

Melk up on its rock, vast and majestic. One and all, my visits to the churches have, in this way or that, been memorable; and I have taken every opportunity that presented itself of understanding them more fully in their various aspects—artistic, historical, symbolic, liturgical.

Before passing on to a more detailed consideration of the subject there is one general question that I would like to deal with here at the outset. Some readers, with pictures to hand or, it may be, memories in their minds, of Schönbrunn and Nymphenburg, may feel inclined to ask why the secular architecture is not also included. Why only the churches and not the palaces too? Is this not an artificial procedure, above all in regard to the Baroque era in which the religious and the secular were so closely interconnected? This would be a perfectly justifiable question. In reply to it I would make the following points. First, to deal with the secular architecture would greatly increase the bulk and complication of this little book without raising any questions fundamentally fresh for those unfamiliar with Baroque art. The undoubted fact that the religious and the secular aspects of the Baroque era were interwoven can, I believe, be explained only if it is realized that the Baroque outlook was essentially a religious one. As I shall try to show later, the devices employed by Baroque architects and the artists who co-operated with them were aimed ultimately at producing effects of religious or metaphysical significance, in particular at the apparent overcoming of spatial limitations so that the eye of the beholder is led on from the part to the whole, from the finite to the apparently infinite. And these characteristic aims, though present everywhere, can of course be followed most clearly in a Baroque church. Secondly, the English reader has in fact the chance of studying Baroque secular architecture in his own country—at Blenheim Palace, for instance—even though it be a Baroque modified by other influences; whereas the real Baroque church is unknown in England. Thirdly, the secular buildings have mostly long lost their original functions and are thus in a sense no longer living witnesses of their time. It is of course true that in many cases the great monastic buildings have also been turned to secular uses; but very many, and among them some of the greatest (*Weingarten, Ottobeuren, Neresheim, Melk, St Florian, Einsiedeln*, to mention but a few), are still playing their ancient part. The churches themselves, monastic or otherwise, though a few have passed into Protestant hands, are still performing the function for which they were built.

1. The Historical Development

The period which saw the creation of these churches lies roughly between 1650 and 1780. In these years the Baroque emerged from the Renaissance and reached its greatest achievements on the European continent, passing over, about 1720 and under French influence, into the decorative elaboration of the Rococo. The whole development touched England relatively lightly. To consider in detail why this was so would take us too far afield, but certain facts of importance must be recalled. There was, for example, no consolidated revival of Catholicism in England from the late sixteenth century onwards; whereas, as we shall see later, the so-called 'Counter-Reformation' on the Continent imparted a most powerful fresh impulse to church building and church art. Indeed, the Baroque began to flourish at a time when in England the puritan spirit with all its austerity was rising more and more to prominence and an atmosphere developing that was not merely unfavourable but actually, and actively, hostile to religious art. A second Cromwell arose to continue the deplorable iconoclasm of his earlier namesake. Again, it was after all the classicist rather than the Baroque spirit, Palladio[1] rather than Bernini or Borromini, 'that, first through Inigo Jones and then through Wren and his followers, determined and inspired the new architecture of the period in England. And this fact, in its turn, cannot but reflect the temper and taste of the people.

The Baroque is sometimes thought of and treated as if it were merely a phenomenon in the history of style. Such a view, however, is superficial and inadequate, for a style is the expression of

[1] His architectural work *I quattro libri dell' architettura* was published in Venice in 1570 and appeared in an English translation in 1715.

an age and a spirit and can be understood only as such. We shall not understand the soaring of the early Gothic architecture, as we find it at Amiens or Salisbury, unless we see it as the expression of the religious aspirations of the age that created it; nor, again, the later development of the Gothic except as the reflection of change and decline in those aspirations. The symmetry and severity of a 'Queen Anne' house reflect architecturally the rational clarity and balance of the age of Pope and Addison, and must be so considered. Again, the revival of the Gothic style in the architecture of the nineteenth century in England and elsewhere, regarded by itself, will be inexplicable; it can be understood only as the architectural expression of that revived interest in the past, especially in the Middle Ages, which was one of the legacies of Romanticism. So it is with the architecture and art that we have come to term 'Baroque'. These also must be considered, studied and judged, not in isolation, but in their wider context as aspects of a period of human history and culture.

The historical events and influences that brought about the close of the Middle Ages and led on to the Renaissance and the Baroque are, no doubt, too well known in general to need more than brief outline here.

It is in the fourteenth century that we first find signs of a stirring of that spirit of enquiry, criticism and humanism that announced the breakdown of the mediaeval order. The scene is first Italy, then England. The new spirit found its first important literary expression in the work of Petrarch and Boccaccio in Italy, in that of Chaucer and of the author of *Piers Plowman* in England. In the religious field it is reflected first in the activities of Wyclif in England and Huss in Bohemia. The fifteenth century brought a further deepening and widening of its scope. In 1453 Constantinople fell to the Turks, and Greek scholars fled westwards over Europe taking their learning and their writings with them. About the same time the invention of printing (Gutenberg in Mainz in 1453, Caxton in England in 1476) came to facilitate the spread of the new learning and the new spirit. By 1550 the 'Renaissance' was in full flood and making itself felt in all fields of life and art and thought. The older theocentric conception of the universe, the awe of the supernatural and transcendent, was gradually replaced by a view in which Man, newly conscious of his faculties and powers, became, rather than God, once again a focal point. The authority of the individual conscience and taste began to rival that of the Church; questions of ethics and politics, as we see most clearly in the work of Nicolò Macchiavelli, became dissociated from those of religion. In art and in literature we find an increasing intermingling of Christian tradition with pagan myth, of Christian with pagan figures and symbols. The former religious and ecclesiastical ideals and sanctions yielded to humanistic or aesthetic standards. A fresh access of uninhibited delight was felt in the world of sense with its colours, its forms and its movements—a delight that easily and often took on exaggerated expression. Asceticism vanished, and the beauty and welfare of the human body became again of as much interest and importance as those of the human soul. Even the Papal court itself became a centre of humanism and adapted itself to the new spirit.

The sixteenth century, however, though it saw the culmination of the Renaissance, also brought fresh turning-points. Older traditions and allegiances, though in new forms, began to reassert themselves. At first, indeed, we find not only an intensification of the humanistic spirit but also Luther's demand for reform within the Church and his subsequent break with Rome. Thus the seed sown by Wyclif and Huss now bore fruit in the 'Reformation' movements which spread in central and northern Europe and by which, in an important sense, the spirit of independent thought that had been awakened in the fields of art and letters was carried over into those of religion and theology. But hardly had this new challenge to the old order been thrown down than it was seriously and vigorously taken up by the Roman Church itself which began setting its own house in order; and the second half of the century witnessed a widespread and powerful return to its authority.

The driving forces behind this return were principally two. The first emanated from the personality and work of a strange and remarkable Spanish soldier, and subsequently regular priest, Ignatius Loyola, who with a band of followers in 1534 in the church of Montmartre at Paris founded the Society of Jesus (Jesuits). The new Order, organized with a military strictness and selflessness and dedicated to the support of the Roman Church in its struggle with the reformers and to the preaching of the Gospel, placed itself unreservedly at the disposal of the Pope against whatever dangers or adversaries he might send its members. Authorized by Papal Bull in 1540 and fortified in its inner life by the '*Spiritual Exercises*', a manual of instruction for meditation and conduct completed by Loyola in 1548, the Society spread rapidly and widely. The first Jesuits to appear in Bavaria arrived in Ingolstadt in 1549 and made that town a centre of their missionary activities. By 1556 they were in control of the university of Dillingen. The beginning of the building of the great Jesuit church *Il Gesù* in Rome in 1568, which was to become the mother church of the order, formed a landmark alike in the development of Roman church architecture towards a richer style and in the renewal of the architectural influence of Rome in Italy and beyond. One of the earliest and most important examples of this influence outside Italy is to be found in Bavaria. In 1583 the foundation stone was laid of the Jesuit Church of St Michael (the *Michaelskirche*) in Munich. This building, modified in various respects by local taste,[1] is more restrained and less ornate than is the *Gesù*. Yet in the general conception of its ground-plan and its elevation, as also in the central position in the city assigned to it and its adjoining collegiate buildings, the Italian influence is unmistakable. St Michael's, in its turn, as prototype, came to exert upon the churches that arose north of the Alps in the following two centuries an influence that can hardly be over-estimated. Upon this pioneer church followed other Jesuit churches, in Bavaria at *Altötting* in 1591, at *Dillingen* (begun 1610) and *Mindelheim* (1625), in Austria at *Vienna* and *Innsbruck* (1627), in Switzerland at *Lucerne* (1666) and *Solothurn*

---

[1] Notably in the rejection of the characteristic but apparently uncongenial full dome with drum (see p. 34).

(1680), which with individual variations reflected the design of the mother church just as they bore witness to the aims of its founders.

The second decisive influence was that of the Council of Trent (1545–63) convoked by the Pope of the time, Paul III, with a primary aim similar to that of the Jesuit Order, namely, the re-establishment of the unity of Christendom under the leadership of the Roman Church. Its importance for the development of Baroque church art lay not merely in its general aims but also in its special provisions that in the services of the church the pic-torial arts were to be—not banned, as the extreme Reformers desired—but enlisted and protected for the portrayal of events in the lives of Christ and the Saints. That the Council was also con-cerned to ensure dignity of treatment and avoid exaggeration is as clear as the fact that later on exaggeration in many forms crept in. This later development was no doubt due to an increas-ing tendency to concentrate on the depicting of suffering, which led at times to tastelessly gruesome representations of torturings and martyrdoms. The recommendations of the Council, however, were in themselves but a reasonable recognition of the important part played by the senses in worship and devotion. If we consider them, as we should, in connection with the methods of contem-plation prescribed in the *Spiritual Exercises* of Loyola we shall realize that both alike are aspects of the same underlying mis-sionary appeal and movement, a movement to which the name of 'Counter-Reformation' has been given. There is no doubt that the Counter-Reformation was the main driving force in the development of Baroque church architecture and art.

That in the following century the tension between the forces of Reformation and Counter-Reformation threw Europe into serious convulsion will surprise only those who forget how closely the religious and political issues of the time were interconnected. It was in Germany, the land of the Reformation, that the strug-gle, the so-called Thirty Years' War (1618–48), was principally fought out, distracting the country from end to end and leaving a legacy that is still having its effects. And yet, utterly calamitous though the war was for the development of the country as a whole and on a long view, it acted as a spur to immediate architectural enterprise. After the long years of destruction and ruin the urge to build and beautify was again felt strongly everywhere and nowhere found more persistent and devoted expression than in the churches that in the following decades began to arise in Southern Germany.

In thus stressing the importance of the Jesuit Order and the Council of Trent for the development and spread of church architecture and art in the early Baroque period I am anxious to avoid a misunderstanding. I am in no way contending that Baroque architecture and art in themselves had their origin in, or were the products of, the Counter-Reformation. Such a view, though it has been held, would be quite unhistorical and neglect facts that cannot be just set aside in the interests of theory. It would neglect the fact that the Baroque spirit is found straining for expression in works of art and architecture created before the Counter-Reformation was ever heard of—works, for example, by *Correggio* (1494–1534) or by *Michelangelo* (1475–1564), to mention no other names. It would also neglect the further facts that the leaders of the Counter-Reformation were not primarily concerned with creating works of art at all, and that in certain ways their severity and asceticism stood in remarkable contrast to the richness and magnificence of even the earliest Baroque art.[1] Nevertheless, there seems to me no doubt that the reforming movement within the Catholic church so quickly perceived and utilized the possibilities offered by the contemporary development in art that now, when we think of the church art and architecture of the period, the terms 'Baroque' and 'Counter-Reformation' are inseparable.

In Central Europe this passion for church building showed itself nowhere with greater richness and exuberance than in *Bavaria*. Certain reasons may be suggested for this fact.

(1) The close contact with Italian architects, especially those from the Italian-Swiss cantons of Tessin (Ticino) and Grau-

---

[1] J. Braun (in his work *Die Kirchenbauten der Deutschen Jesuiten*) points out that in their earliest churches in Germany the Jesuits conformed carefully to existing local architectural style.

bünden (Grisons) gave a powerful impetus in the years after the long war and the accompanying impoverishment of native talent. One of the earliest Bavarian Baroque churches, the *Jesuit Church* at *Dillingen* on the Danube (1610–17), was built by the Graubündener *Hans Alberthal* (=*Giovanni Albertalli*). Later the great and influential church of *St Kajetan* (*Theatinerkirche*) in *Munich* (1663–90) is almost entirely the work of two Italian-Swiss architects *Enrico Zuccali* and *Agostino Barelli*. Zuccali also drew up the plans for and began work on the abbey church at *Ettal* near Oberammergau (begun 1709). Other notable examples of this influence on Bavarian church architecture of the period are the *Dreifaltigkeitskirche* (Holy Trinity) in Munich and the monastic churches at *Neustift* near Freising and *Fürstenfeldbruck* (begun 1701) to the west of Munich—all the work of *Antonio Viscardi* from Tessin. To the north, in the upper Main valley, *Antonio Petrini* brought the Italian style to Franconian Bavaria with his monumental church of *Stift Haug* in *Würzburg*. Farther west, in Württemberg, we find the Italian *Donato Giuseppe Frisoni* decisively shaping the great abbey church at *Weingarten* (1715–24). The influence of Italy was, of course, not confined to architecture. The art of painting ceilings and domes with frescoes as we find it in Bavaria and elsewhere north of the Alps was of Italian origin and continuously influenced from Italy. We need think only of three great names in this connection, of *Correggio*, whose fresco of the Assumption in the dome of Parma cathedral (begun 1527) is the earliest forerunner of its type; of *Andrea Pozzo* (1642–1709), the early master, and literary exponent, of that technique of perspective illusion upon which the art relied for some of its most characteristic and greatest effects; and of *Tiepolo* in the eighteenth century, whose frescoes in the Residenz at Würzburg were of great importance for the later development of the art in Bavaria.

We must not, however, exaggerate these Italian influences. They provided a powerful initial stimulus and left a permanent heritage of form and detail. But they were also quickly adapted to, and modified by, local spirit and tradition; and as we pass into, and on through, the eighteenth century we find many Italianate features disappearing. A striking example of this process is the fate of the Italian type of dome (i.e. dome surmounting a cylindrical drum). The *Gesù* in Rome has a dome of this type. *St Michael* in Munich, though otherwise modelled on that church, has no dome at all, and though the form reappears in later churches that show Italian influence (*Munich Theatinerkirche, Weingarten, Ettal*) it was evidently felt to be alien not only in Bavaria but throughout Southern Germany. An interesting transition stage can be seen in the church at *Ottobeuren* where the dome has shrivelled to a kind of pyramidal roof over the crossing. Nor, again, must we forget the influence of France in lightening the rigidness of the Italian Baroque tradition. If Italy was the home of Baroque proper, France was the home of that more delicate, more fantastic later development of it that we know as the Rococo and which began to make itself felt in Bavaria from about 1720 onwards.

(2) A second reason for the intense development in Bavaria we may see in the relatively unified and consolidated character, alike in geographical, political and religious aspects, of the core of the region, the original state of Bavaria (Altbayern). Geographically, the lands between the Danube and the hills flanking it to the north, the Alps to the south, and the rivers Lech to the west and Inn to the east, formed a compact, secured, self-contained area. Politically this area had, since the end of the twelfth century, formed the Dukedom, later the Electorate, of Bavaria and indeed been under the rule of a single reigning house, that of the Wittelsbachs. In religion, despite a certain spread of Protestantism in the western (Suabian) districts, Bavaria, and especially Old Bavaria, emerged from the religious struggles of the sixteenth century with its devotion to the Catholic faith in essence unimpaired. At the end of that century (1598), on the threshold that is to say, of our period, this religious and political solidarity found combined expression in the strong and devout personality of the first Elector, Maximilian I, whose first act as a ruler was to make a pilgrimage to the much-revered shrine at Altötting.

(3) The mention of the House of Wittelsbach, that guided the destiny of Bavaria as a political power from 1180 to 1918, brings us to a third reason—the lavish patronage given by these rulers throughout to the promotion of the arts. In this respect no ruling house in Europe has done more. Yet here again we must not forget the other side of the picture. The support did not all come from princely quarters. Equally enthusiastic and active as patrons were the bishops and abbots who, with few exceptions, came from the ranks of the townsfolk and peasants. How ambitious these sometimes were may be piquantly illustrated by the case of the abbot of Schussenried who was forced to resign because his new pilgrimage church at Steinhausen cost in the end four times the estimated amount!

(4) Finally, we must not forget the character of the Bavarians themselves and its influence upon their art. This is a complex matter, for the Franconian Bavarians of the north differ from the Suabian Bavarians of the west, and both from those of the south and east. Yet certain general observations seem justified.

(a) The Bavarian, broadly speaking, is what has been called an 'Augenmensch', a 'man of the eye'; one, that is to say, for whom the eye is the primary channel by which he establishes contact with, and draws significance from, the world around him. His attitude is essentially sensuous, perceptive, intuitive. He is a sharp and fascinated observer of nature and of his fellows. Like the Austrian he has much of the Southerner's delight in the variety and fulness of the world of sense in its pageantry of shape and colour, light and shade. Even where his approach is intellectual or reflective his thought tends to be of a strongly pictorial cast in which the 'inner eye' is quite as much at work as the intellect. We think, too, of his fondness for play and drama which shows itself alike in a love of the formal ritual of theatre and opera and in a sense of the dramatic in ordinary human intercourse which often saves him from taking himself and his life too seriously. The connection between these characteristics of the people and the markedly sensuous, pictorial, dramatic nature of their Baroque art is not hard to see.

(*b*) Though the capital of Bavaria is the third largest city in Western Germany the Bavarians are at heart a peasant people. In extent Bavaria is the largest state of Western Germany, yet it possesses only three towns with a population of over 100,000. Even Munich itself, despite its size, has retained its 'country town' atmosphere to a remarkable degree. One may travel with peasant women in the Munich tram, their heads in scarves and their baskets with them, or share a table in a beer hall in the city centre with peasants, perhaps in costume, come up from the country. The Bavarian has, indeed, something of the healthy vitality and directness of the peasant which give him a naturalness and a lack of sophistication that, to one foreigner at least, are refreshing and endearing. He has also, especially the South Bavarian, the conservatism of the peasant. He is a traditionalist, clings tenaciously to his forms of life and work and supports them with vigour against outside attempts to encroach upon or alter them.

If now to these reflections on the character of the people we add the fact that in Bavaria the Baroque in all its forms was not merely a pre-occupation of princes and prelates but penetrated right down among the people, above all among the country people, we shall perhaps understand better why Bavarian church Baroque developed so richly and why the language it speaks is so intimate and buoyant.

When we turn to *Austria* we find that many of the above considerations hold good for the situation and development there also. And yet there are important differences.

(1) Early contact with Italian influences was no less inspiring and vitalizing than in Bavaria. The imperial court at Vienna sought, and could command, the best at a time when Austria herself was weak in architectural talent. The way had been prepared in the field of civilian and military architecture. In the year 1529 the Turks had with difficulty been repulsed before Vienna, and the decision was taken to carry out a radical reconstruction of the city's obsolete fortifications. This work was completed by 1590,

and the leading architects responsible for it were Italians. It was the solidity of this system of fortifications that eventually, in 1683, made possible the decisive victory over the Turks, established the position of the Habsburgs in the eyes of Europe and stirred a wave of national feeling throughout the country. This Italian achievement in military architecture was soon followed up in the ecclesiastical field. By 1628 there had arisen in Salzburg a church of uncompromisingly Italian character, *Santino Solari's* new cathedral, the first of its kind north of the Alps and destined to exert an influence as great as that of *St Michael* in Munich. Italian influences were also coming in with the increasing activities of the Jesuits even though some of the earliest Jesuit churches, such as that at Innsbruck (completed 1640), were not actually the work of Italian architects.

Here the first difference between Austria and Bavaria in this connection may be noted. The formal, rigid spirit and indeed the individual architectural forms of Italian Baroque maintained themselves in Austria to a degree not found in Bavaria. We have already referred to the fate of the Italian dome in Southern Germany; when we have named the *Munich Theatinerkirche*, *Stift Haug* in Würzburg, *Weingarten*, *Ettal*, *Fulda Cathedral* and *St Blasien* we have named all the important examples. Yet in Salzburg alone there are as many as this, not to mention Vienna or Innsbruck or individual churches such as *Melk*.

There are other differences in the nature of the Italian influence. The Italian-Swiss architects, who played so decisive a part in Bavaria after the Thirty Years' War, are scarcely heard of in Austria. *Giovanni Gaspare Zuccalli's* two churches in Salzburg stand almost alone. The Italians who worked in Austria came almost entirely from North Italy. Again, though Italian architectural influences were more permanent in Austria than in Bavaria, the actual activities of Italian architects seem to have come to an end earlier than was the case with the Italian-Swiss architects in Bavaria. The latter exercised important influence up to about 1720, whereas even before the end of the seventeenth century the supremacy of the Italians was being challenged in

Austria by native architects. In 1690 we find *J. B. Fischer von Erlach* defeating Italian rivals in a competition for the erection of a triumphal arch in Vienna, and in 1716 his winning design for the far more important project of the *Vienna Karlskirche* again involved the defeat of an Italian competitor.

(2) A second point of general similarity between the situations in Austria and Bavaria lies in the fact that the Austrian lands, though without the geographical compactness of Bavaria, also experienced for many centuries (1253–1918) the political continuity afforded by a single ruling house, in this case that of the Habsburgs, in whose hands also the imperial crown remained from 1438 to 1806 and whose residence was Vienna. To this continuity and to the presence of the imperial court as an incentive to architectural activity must be added, in a degree not known even in Bavaria, the unbroken unifying and vivifying influence of Catholicism whose bishoprics and monastic foundations in the Baroque period rivalled the Court in the magnificence of their projects, patronage and achievements. Yet here again differences meet us. The influence of the Court and of the higher clergy seems to have lain heavily upon the development of church architecture and art in Austria. The lightness and joyousness of Bavarian Baroque is found in Austrian churches of the period only in those areas open to Bavarian influence. Even in the later years such shining examples as the *Stadtpfarrkirche* (parish church) in *Wilten* (Innsbruck) or as *Wilhering* abbey church (five miles upstream from Linz) are rarities in Austria. In Vienna there is nothing like them—the nearest approach is the *Piaristenkirche*, perhaps the brightest church in the city.

(3) Two further points of contrast between the two regions may be added in support of the last observations. In Austria the Baroque was never taken to the hearts of the countryfolk as it was in Bavaria, nor was it in its later (Rococo) forms allowed to enter the churches to the same extent. The wealth of fascinating, if sometimes slightly uncouth art of the middle and later Baroque periods that we find in Bavarian village churches has no real counterpart in Austria. Let us take three areas of Austria in

which the peasant element is predominant and where we might expect to find something of the Bavarian development—Tyrol, Vorarlberg and Carinthia. Tyrol has beautiful Baroque churches, large and small, to show; yet it is not a Baroque country as Bavaria is. Far less so are the other two areas, paradoxical though this may be in the case of Vorarlberg whose architects in Baroque times contributed so greatly to the adornment of Southern Germany and Switzerland.

The historical development of *Switzerland* presents certain well-known features that mark it off distinctively both from that of Bavaria and from that of Austria, and reflect themselves in the architecture of our period. Of these, two above all must be borne in mind.

The first is the long political opposition to the central power of the Holy Roman Empire, an opposition which resulted eventually in complete independence and neutrality. The effective beginning of this development was the foundation in 1291 of the 'Everlasting League' between the people of Schwyz, Uri and Unterwalden to preserve their independence in a defensive alliance against the encroaching power of the Habsburgs. As a result of successful battles against the latter the League had by 1386 grown to include Zürich, Lucerne, Zug, Berne and Glarus. The way then led through further wars to a second League (1513) which comprised in all thirteen districts and implied the *de facto*, if not yet the *de jure*, separation from the Empire; to the legal recognition by the Emperor of independence at the Peace of Westphalia that closed the Thirty Years' War (1648); to the settlements of 1798 and 1803 by which the republic was finally set up; and to the guarantee of perpetual neutrality by the Congress of Vienna (1815). Thus we see that independence of central political control was achieved just at the beginning of the period in which we are here interested.

The second feature of importance was the Protestant Reformation movement of the early sixteenth century, originating in Zürich in 1519 with the work of Zwingli and continued in

Geneva from 1533 by Calvin. This broke the supremacy of the church and led to the denominational split which, despite the missionary campaign in 1570 by the archbishop of Milan, Charles Borromeus, and the intense work of Jesuits and Capuchins throughout the land, has remained to this day. It also, as elsewhere, spread a severe spirit most unfavourable to the growth of church art.

Thus by the time our period opens a situation had developed in Switzerland which it is important to keep in mind. On the one hand, unlike the cases of Southern Germany and Austria, all the links of control with the central political power of the Empire had been broken. On the other, a religious cleavage had arisen to which, though paralleled in Germany as a whole, even in Southern Germany, there was little similarity in Bavaria and none at all in Austria. Accordingly in Switzerland we shall find throughout this period little patronage of building on any scale —none of a political and relatively little of a religious origin. We shall find no great residences or palaces. The secular architecture of the time is confined to municipal buildings such as town halls (e.g. those at Zürich, Lausanne, Lenzburg, Thun, Bischofszell, Zofingen), the town houses of citizens (many good examples in Zürich, Basle, Geneva, Berne and Fribourg) and occasional modest country mansions such as those of *Waldegg* (Canton Solothurn), *Oberdiesbach*, *Thunstetten* or *Hindelbank* (all Canton Berne). Great monastic foundations there were. But when we have named *Einsiedeln*, *St Gallen*, *St Urban*, *Rheinau* and with these *Disentis* (in Graubünden) we have named them all; and of these the conventual buildings of St Urban and Rheinau have passed into secular hands. There are, however, in addition to a few smaller monastic churches, a considerable number of interesting, often beautiful, parish churches up and down the country, though mostly in Catholic districts.

2. The Spirit of Baroque

The visitor to one of these Baroque churches, however he may arrive and however unprepared he may be, can hardly remain insensitive to the richness and the energy of what confronts him. And as he looks at it, inside and out, at first perhaps in no little bewilderment, he may become aware that it breathes a message; that from tower to tabernacle, from swinging arch to painted dome, from the most charming putto to the most magnificent altar it breathes a message which, in itself timeless, is in some way the message of an epoch. Perhaps then he may become interested to know more of the message and of the epoch which could express itself in such remarkable forms. These pages are written to try to help him.

The first difficulty which the English visitor will meet lies probably in the word 'Baroque' itself. Some general terms of art and architecture will convey to him more or less familiar notions. When he hears a building described as 'Gothic' he will no doubt have a very fair idea of what it looks like and could probably give some account of the characteristics of the Gothic style. Even the (to English ears) less familiar term 'Romanesque' he may be able to connect with 'Norman' as a style of thick walls, massive columns, small windows and round arches. But 'Baroque' will probably arouse either no response or misgivings. The visitor need not worry himself unduly. The problem involved is far from simple. Even specialists have only relatively recently begun to consider it seriously, and they are by no means agreed. Further, the term has been detached from its historical background, narrowed and depreciated in meaning; and this has not helped matters. The 'Baroque', as we have already pointed out, has come to be thought of simply as a rather dubious phenomenon of style; but such a view is quite inadequate.

THE SPIRIT OF BAROQUE

The derivation of the term is uncertain. Several theories have been put forward.[1] The most usual explanation is that it comes from a French adaptation of a Portuguese word *barocco* which means a rough, irregular, misshaped pearl. This agrees at least with the widespread use (and fate) of the term to describe something exaggerated, outlandish or grotesque and with the consequent disfavour that has attached to it. But in point of fact all the suggested derivations agree in concentrating on the notion of oddness or irregularity. If then we interpret the Baroque style on these lines it appears as nothing more than an exaggeration or degeneration of the Renaissance style out of which it grew. In truth, however, these linguistic derivations do not get us very far. Suppose we do call the Baroque odd or exaggerated. These are but relative terms. The Gothic, after all, as the name reminds us, originally signified something outlandish; and indeed, one can think of Gothic churches compared with which many Baroque ones appear sober and normal. The important question is not what name was given to a particular style and what the derivation of that name is supposed to be; it is why a particular age found expression in a particular style and what message it passes on to us in this way. Above all in the case of the Baroque we must be prepared to look behind the outward pomp and pageantry at the life and spirit of the times. The fact that one's own land may have been touched by the characteristic spirit of the Baroque less, little or not at all should not cause trouble or arouse prejudice.

We should not try to apply standards where they do not apply or to force comparisons which should not be made, to judge the Baroque by the Gothic or Romanesque to which we may be accustomed and attuned. We may indeed complain that English scholars have not overstrained themselves to help the ordinary student or traveller to a better understanding of these things. The literature on the subject in English is sparse.[2] The term 'Baroque' has been eschewed like a faked coin or a thing unclean. Even the

[1] See the discussion in Gilbert Highet's *The Classical Tradition* (Oxford 1949), pp. 289–92, 646–8.
[2] See Bibliography.

latest edition (sixteenth, 1954) of so comprehensive and widely accepted a handbook as Banister Fletcher's *History of Architecture* devotes to European Baroque, apart from cursory references, about three pages out of 960; and, except for *Borromini, Vignola* and a few other Italians, the index does not give the name of a single great European architect of the time. *Balthasar Neumann* and *Fischer von Erlach* might never have existed. The *Adams* get a good look in: the *Asams* not a mention.[1]

There are perhaps two main reasons why English students and scholars have fought shy of the Baroque. To the first I have already alluded. The Baroque spirit, and so the Baroque style, touched England but lightly and sporadically. Let us think of a few examples of English architecture of the period—St Paul's Cathedral, for instance, or Vanburgh's palaces of Blenheim and Castle Howard, or the churches of Hawkesmoor or Gibbs' Radcliffe Camera at Oxford. I personally would hesitate to describe any of these as truly Baroque and I would give two reasons for my hesitation. First, I do not find in them the characteristic Baroque relationship of parts to whole, that of subordination to a central effect. The main façade of Blenheim Palace is to me a co-ordination of component parts that is essentially classical in spirit. Secondly, I do not find in them the other arts (painting, plastic ornament, sculpture) working in concert with architecture towards a central effect; the other arts indeed are often hardly in evidence at all. Architecturally, some of the work of Hawkesmoor and Gibbs seems to me to reflect the Baroque spirit more nearly than that of other English architects of the time (the façade and tower of St Anne's, Limehouse, or of Christ Church, Spitalfields, for instance, or in its way the Radcliffe Camera). There are also, of course, isolated outbursts like the south porch of St Mary's at Oxford and large numbers of monuments in churches and elsewhere up and down the land which show Baroque influence in

[1] Other examples: Short, Ernest: *History of Religious Architecture,* London, 1921, has just over 2 pp. on Baroque (Austria not mentioned); Russell, A. L. N.: *Architecture,* London, 1927, has 7 pp. on Baroque (out of 260); Statham, H. H.: *A History of Architecture,* London, rev. ed. 1950, has 1½ pp. on German Baroque.

design and ornament. In painting, the only English Baroque artist on the grand scale was Sir James Thornhill (Greenwich painted hall, his best work; the sombre paintings in the dome of St Paul's; a ceiling at Hampton Court which compares favourably with the others by the Italian Antonio Verrio), though along with him may be mentioned his forerunner Robert Streater (1624–80) who painted the ceiling of the Sheldonian theatre at Oxford. The sculpture of the period in England is of no great significance, small in scale (monuments, busts), the best of it by foreign artists (Rysbrack, Roubilliac) who cannot be claimed as English merely because they settled in England any more than can the composer Handel. Stucco ornamentation is fairly plentiful and widespread, mostly in secular buildings, mostly ceilings, much of it fine, but again much of the best of it by foreign (Italian) craftsmen. Finally there must be added the furniture (especially the mirror-frames) of the style associated with the name of Thomas Chippendale. Thus we may say that the Baroque in its various phases makes itself felt in English architecture and art. But we cannot, all in all, say more than that. Compared with the impacts made by the Renaissance and by Classicism that of Baroque and Rococo was slight.

A second reason for this neglect of the Baroque lies undoubtedly in the English tendency to think of and describe periods of English art and literature principally in terms derived from national history and tradition. Thus in architecture 'Romanesque' becomes 'Norman', 'Early Gothic' and 'Late Gothic' become respectively 'Early English' and 'Perpendicular', 'Renaissance' tends to become 'Tudor' or 'Elizabethan'. And 'Baroque' becomes—well, what does it become? In literature it becomes 'Miltonic', 'Metaphysical', 'Caroline', 'Restoration' and the like. In architecture it becomes (to the more Europeanly, or humanistically, minded) 'Renaissance' or 'late Renaissance'; to others 'the age (or school) of Wren', 'Georgian' or just 'Seventeenth Century' or 'Eighteenth Century'. This is all perfectly understandable, in certain respects inevitable and even justifiable, and up to a point has its counterpart in the usage of certain Continental lands. Yet it must also be recognized that the extent to which this tendency has developed in English thought is in many ways unfortunate; for the great cross-connections with the Continental sources of English culture have thereby become blurred and even lost to sight.

Let us return now to our subject and try to examine the matter a little more closely. We are concerned here with churches, and so it seems natural and best to begin by considering the spirit of Baroque in its religious aspect, and by tackling here at the outset what is no doubt the central difficulty for very many. Although, as has been emphasized, Baroque art did not originate in and with the Catholic Counter-Reformation, the fact remains that these churches and their art are the creations of Catholicism, indeed of a militant and missionary Catholicism. This fact must be admitted and faced. What then is the non-Catholic to do who lacks in a greater or lesser degree the requisite religious and devotional background? How is he to approach and appreciate all this pageantry and symbolism? (I may add that I am here assuming an open-minded interest on the part of the reader and visitor; upon the special difficulties to which prejudice of one kind or another may give rise I shall have a word or two to say later.)

To these questions perhaps I may venture a personal answer. Though I myself am also not a Roman Catholic it has yet seemed to me that during the years in which I have been studying these churches with ever-increasing interest I have glimpsed something of their inner meaning. A first requirement is some knowledge of the historical background, and this I have tried to give in the previous chapter. But the real beginning has to be made in the churches themselves. My own first experience of the kind was in 1949 when a German friend took me to see the great abbey church at *Ottobeuren*. I remember being immensely impressed at the massive, shapely exterior with its bold lines and overwhelmed at the pageant of colours and statuary within. The visit was rather short, and I came away with a somewhat confused mass of pictorial impressions, and a great desire to return. This first step was soon followed up by regular visits to churches within easy reach of Munich. In these I used to sit and wander round for an hour, helped at first by a little book which put me wise on certain fundamental things. I found everything of great, if unusual and unfamiliar, beauty and was led to inquire further into the nature and cause of this beauty. I do not, of course, mean that in a study of this kind the purely aesthetic aspect should be separated and considered in isolation. This would be a quite false way of approach, one which would divide what should not (and in the last resort cannot) be divided, and one which the Catholic, and rightly, would condemn. But I feel quite sure that the aesthetic approach can, for the uninitiated, open the way to an understanding of the deeper religious meaning, and so to an experience of the church as a unity with all that it is, and has, and reveals. Further, I believe this approach to be one, possibly the only one, which the creators of the church themselves would have entirely approved. For everything about a Baroque church is symbolical, and deliberately so. The purpose is to attract the senses of the beholder and to lead him on beyond the world of sense.

One or two illustrations may make this clearer. The structural principles that underlie the planning of a Baroque church in its ground-plan and elevation—the relation of straight line to curve, of circle to oval and rectangle, of longitudinal to transverse axis, of the various parts one to another—unite to produce effects of beauty and harmony which we feel even though we may not be able to analyse. Yet, as we shall consider more in detail later, their spatial, geometrical character subserves symbolic purposes. If, when we enter such a church, our eye is caught irresistibly by this or that, or led irresistibly in a certain direction, this is no accident but the result of careful placing and carefully planned perspective with an ultimate aim in view. Again, when we look up at one of the great visionary ceiling frescoes and see the heavens thronging with figures of angels and saints and martyrs, rank on rank, far up into the height where amid a blaze of light the Godhead is, we marvel at the artistry of perspective, of colour, of grouping; and in doing so we experience aesthetic satisfaction. But we find in fact that we cannot stop there. We realize that here is intended a great representation of the union of the visible and the invisible worlds in which earth and heaven are brought together in a rich pageantry of colour and symbol, of worship and communion. A festival upon which Baroque Catholicism laid particular stress was indeed that of All Saints. And this great festival, whatever the particular interpretation that we may care to put upon it, is surely one that may endear itself to Christians of all shades of belief, one that even for others may express the idea of a great spiritual union transcending distinctions of creed and race.

Of the main impressions that a great Baroque church of, say, the middle period will make upon the visitor as he wanders around it and studies it, two will, perhaps, be the strongest.

The first and more immediate will be that of an almost over-whelming wealth of decorative detail alike in the paintings, the stucco ornamentation and the statuary, massed in seemingly end-less profusion. He looks up at the frescoes on the ceiling and is dazzled by the rich colouring and by the hosts of angels and saints and prophets crowding away into infinite perspective depths. For relief he turns to some particular, more limited object, let us say a representation of the Holy Trinity crowning one of the great altars (that over the high altar at *Aldersbach*, for example) and even there feels almost lost in the multitude of angels and cherubs, sacred signs and rays of light darting out, that surround the central figures. Or he looks at some individual pillar capital (say at *Steinhausen*) and again is almost bewildered at the wealth and variety of line and tint, curve and volute and moulding with which even so small an area is adorned. The richness and variety in general are, indeed, so great that many visits to any single one of the greater of these churches are needed before he can discover the inner unity and order of what he sees.

For unity and order there are. And it is only when these have become apparent that the second main impression is received, an impression which bides its time but which brings him still closer to an understanding of the spirit of Baroque. The visitor will gradually realize that despite and behind all the variety, complica-tion and exuberance certain principles of order are rigidly ob-served. That this is so, and in what ways it reveals itself, will become clearer the greater the number of churches studied and comparisons made. Ground-plans and elevations, even where seemingly simple, will be found on closer attention to conceal planning of a subtle, indeed mathematical character aimed at producing definite effects of a partly aesthetic, partly symbolic character. We shall find, for example, frequent structural use of certain numbers that have come to have sacred and thus symbolic associations, especially 3 (the Trinity), 5 (the wounds of Christ), 7 (the words from the Cross, the sorrows of Mary), and 12 (the Apostles); steps will be found grouped in flights of three or seven, pillars or windows in groups of three (*Weltenburg* lantern has twelve windows). Even the often remarked asymmetrical element in Baroque church decoration is here of importance and will be found to be in some way balanced and compensated. At *Steinhausen*, for example, the side altars flanking the choir arch are individually asymmetrical in design, but taken together in pairs they counterbalance each other and in so doing lead the eye towards the all-important high altar (plate 26). Again, the representations of holy figures in statuary are given, for all the dramatic pose and ardour that breathe from many of them, in certain prescribed groupings and with certain traditional attributes.[1] The great visionary frescoes, too, where there is a series of them, will be found to be united by a single theme (e.g. the life of Christ or of a saint, or, more abstractly, as at *Einsiedeln*, the Redemption of Man). And in individual frescoes the figures, for all their seemingly arbitrary crowding and thronging, will be seen to be grouped in some order that reappears again and again, portraying, for example, a hierarchy of status—the peasant and the citizen, the noble and the prince, the clergy and the bishop, the prophets and martyrs and saints, and above all, crowning and sustaining all, the Deity.

For it is at this level that we must see the basic conception of the Baroque outlook, the conception not merely of order but of a divinely ordained order pervading and uniting earth and heaven. This notion of order and of harmony based upon order was cen-

[1] See Appendix I, and Plates 28, 36, 37, 44, 47, 48, 51, 56.

tral. The harmony is preserved only as long as the order is observed. We may also appropriately recall here that the philosophical system of the great European thinker of the period, *Gottfried Wilhelm Leibniz* (1646–1716), was based on the notion of a 'pre-established harmony' in the universe. The outlook is, of course, an authoritarian one in the sense that the source of order and harmony was sought in a ruling principle from above; and we know that politically the Baroque era was the era of actual or attempted absolutism. But it cannot be over-emphasized that for the religious mind this order was thought of as proceeding from and ordained by God. For Baroque Catholicism the world-order is a theocentric order. Until this is realized the architecture and art of these churches cannot be understood in their deepest sense.

In a manner, then, the Baroque took up and continued the mediaeval outlook; in the visionary frescoes of its churches Gothic aspiration finds an echo. Yet there was, of course, an important difference between the two. For between them lay the age of the Renaissance in which attention had shifted to man, human powers and human institutions; and this inheritance could not be denied or escaped. Thus in the Baroque the earthly order of human society acquired a prominence unknown in mediaeval times. Faith, it was believed, had been lost and must be restored. And the manner in which Baroque Catholicism sought to restore it lay, not in disparaging or rejecting the world or human experience and society, but in accepting and using it at once as symbol and as approach. On the one hand, the earthly order was to be shown as a reflection, however faint, of the heavenly, so that men, by studying and reflecting upon the one, might be more easily led beyond it to a contemplation of the other. Parallels were drawn and stressed between the two. The status and authority of the earthly prince, above all of the Pope conceived as vice-gerent of Christ on earth, became symbols of the authority of the heavenly King. Ignatius Loyola himself seems to have thought of the heavenly society as a kind of heavenly court with God as King surrounded and attended by a great company in their appointed stations. On the other hand, the earthly world of sense was to be enlisted to the full as a means of approach to the invisible world. Thus we find all the arts being called into action in a concerted appeal to the senses; a visible world of figure and colour, grouping and symbol was created to lead the mind and heart of the worshipper onward and upward to transcendent, invisible realities. The visitor to a Baroque church will indeed find himself surrounded by a host of figures and objects and designs which constitute, as it were, a massed challenge to his faith—figures of the Persons of the Trinity in prescribed grouping; figures of angels and saints, prophets and martyrs; emblems of sanctity and martyrdom; symbols of religious doctrine and dogma. He will not for one moment be alone but in the presence of a great company, each member of which has a message.

Up to now we have been thinking of the Baroque primarily in its religious aspect, of the aims of Baroque Catholicism in its efforts to reawaken religious faith. We must now turn, or return, and glance at the developments in architecture and art which the Catholic revival found already in progress and used for its own ends.

It may well be that too much emphasis has been put on the suddenness and completeness of the break with the past that set in with the Renaissance. Had this break been as complete as is sometimes suggested, the Baroque could never have recaptured as much of the religious spirit of the past as it did. The problem of the relation between Baroque and Renaissance is a complex one. Yet a fundamental break there was, and we can think of it in a twofold aspect. A cleavage arose between the Renaissance world as a whole and the mediaeval; and a divorce occurred between the religious and the secular elements in life. The latter was the cause of the former.

At first the new spirit was marked in architecture by restraint, repose and clearness of perception—characteristics of the classical feeling of which it claimed to be the revival. In the work of *Bramante* (1444–1514), for example, there is a clarity and a balance, a moderation in size and an attention to individual forms and their grouping that give no impression of tension. This early calm, however, gave way to increasingly greater restlessness. The spirit born at the Renaissance increased in power and self-aware-ness and sought expression in the dynamic, the colossal, the magnificent. The first important figure in this later development is probably *Michelangelo* (1475–1564) in whose work we can de-tect a certain tension arising from the will to subordinate indi-vidual parts to a single whole, a dynamic urge towards monu-mentality. We see this in the great Last Judgement fresco in the Sistine Chapel, we see it too in the façade of the Palazzo dei Conservatori on the Capitol and in his modifications of Bramante's plans for St Peter's.

To these tendencies a further one was added in the architecture of the first half of the following century. In 1638 *Francesco Borromini* completed his little church *San Carlo alle quattro Fon-tane* in Rome. The event was epoch-making, for a new principle was seen to be at work. Hitherto, though the views of architects on the relation of the parts of a building to each other and to the whole had undergone change, one element had remained un-questioned in its stability—the material. But now it seemed as though the very material were submitting itself to the will of the architect. Walls previously thought of as static masses or surfaces to be moulded or decorated began themselves to acquire move-ment (plates 15, 33). In the play of curve against curve, convex against concave they took on rhythm at the architect's design and behest. In this way a building comes to develop a unity and balance that depends no longer on mere static interrelations but on a dynamic tension and interplay between its parts. Spatial form becomes more important than the material that bounds it. This discovery of rhythmical movement and the ideal of a har-mony derived from diversity and tension were taken up also in matters of decoration and lighting. Thus in a developed later Baroque interior we find not only lines curving, surfaces swinging and perspective merging and shifting but also figures clustering and light and shade varying in such diversity and complexity that the eye is urged ever onward in an effort to compass the whole.

Objects are constructed and shaped and grouped in such a way that they present themselves and claim to be viewed in many and varying aspects and patterns.

Nothing is more characteristic and significant of this development than the emergence and exploitation of one particular spatial form—the oval or ellipse. Borromini's little church is in essence oval on plan; and in the works of the greatest Baroque architects of Central Europe—above all *Fischer von Erlach* and *Kilian Ignaz Dientzenhofer*, but also *Balthasar Neumann, Dominikus Zimmermann* and *Johann Michael Fischer*—the oval takes on central importance as a structural form (see ground-plans). Now the oval is the very symbol of dynamic tension. It is, as it were, a dislocated (though not misshapen) circle; a form in which, as we shall mention again later, two axes, a longitudinal and a transverse, seek fusion with difficulty and whose harmony rests on this fact.

It was doubtless this dynamic, apparently irrational element in Baroque architecture and art, this conscious urge towards totality of experience that rendered them eloquent means for the expression of the religious feelings and aims that we have mentioned. The interior of a great Baroque church such as *Einsiedeln* or *Melk* or *Vierzehnheiligen* is so constructed and decorated that the eye can never take it in completely as a spatial whole although, and this is the point, it is ceaselessly driven to try to do so. Such an interior thus takes on a symbolic character. It unifies endless diversity; and it keeps us in mind of the infinite.

Let us now leave these general reflections and pass on to try to illustrate them by some of the main characteristics of the churches themselves.

First, the purely architectural features—the ground-plans and elevations. It is often said that the primary problem of the Baroque church architect was to unite and fuse two diverse spatial elements, that of the longitudinal or lengthways axis, on the one hand, and that of a central space on the other. He aimed, in other words, at retaining the 'drive' from west to east with which the

Romanesque and Gothic ground-plans made us familiar and yet at giving the interior as a whole greater centrality and compactness. This is a perfectly fair way of putting the matter, and most of the churches do in fact show varying attempts to solve this problem (see ground-plans). Yet this is also to state it merely as an *architectural* problem. We must enquire further why the architectural problem arose at all—just as we are entitled to ask why the ground-plans of mediaeval cathedrals took the forms they did.

It will be useful here to consider for a moment what the main effects were which it was intended that these churches should produce on the worshippers individually and collectively present in them. Two were of chief importance. First, the sacrament of the altar was to be given a more central place than ever in the services of the church. This meant that the attention of the worshippers must be directed and fixed with greater certainty than ever upon the high altar.[1] Now clearly the main *architectural* device to secure this effect will be an adequate retention of the longitudinal axis, so that the high altar is appropriately 'distanced'. Other contributory devices, as we shall see, were added. The high altar itself was given increasingly monumental dimensions and a commanding position, the mensa itself raised on a series of steps (plates 28, 29, 35, 36). Side altars were so placed as to help to lead the eye inevitably towards the high altar—either by being set transversely in series on either side of the nave so that they stand to the high altar as the successive 'side-scenes' or coulisses of a stage to the backcloth (plate 28), or by being placed in pairs flanking the choir arch, but obliquely, so that again the gaze of the beholder glides off them and on to the high altar (plates 26, 27). Secondly, a sense of community was to be inculcated among the congregation joining together in worship, a feeling of union among those on earth and with those in heaven.

Now the geometrical forms which have this 'embracing' or

---

[1] The term 'altar' will in this book be used to refer to the entire complex of holy table proper (mensa), with tabernacle, and reredos or superstructure.

'binding' effect, and thus express and symbolize union and community, are (in the ground-plan) the circle or oval and (in the elevation) the round arch and the dome. We can now perhaps better understand why the architectural problem of merging longitudinal axis with some kind of 'central' (circular, oval or even polygonal) space or rotunda arose at all. It was intended that the worshippers should be led *both* to focus their attention upon the high altar as the liturgical and devotional centre of the church *and* that at the same time they should in their worship feel a sense of togetherness and communion.

Let us return for a moment to the oval or ellipse. The importance which it acquired in determining the ground-plans of Baroque churches has been mentioned. It will now perhaps be clearer why this came about. The (longitudinally set) oval combines in itself *both* the desired characteristics of which we have just been speaking. As a form of spatial expression it fuses (as the circle does not) both the 'embracing' effect of the circle and the 'thrust' of an axis directed upon the altar. It both *binds* and *points*. It is, moreover, a very elastic form in respect of the relation between its lengthways and its transverse axis and is thus applicable to very varying plans and sites.

There were other considerations present in the minds of the architects of the time as they sought to give expression to their twofold aim. In the true Baroque church we find no arcades of columns or pillars impeding the view eastwards and the sense of spatial community. Pillars, if present, are set well away from the central field of vision. Either they stand withdrawn in the curve of a central rotunda (*Steinhausen*, *Wies*), or they take the form of 'Wandpfeiler' (wall-pillars) which are really internal buttresses projecting at right-angles from the side walls.[1] In the latter case they either form 'backs' for side chapel altars or are pierced by arches with resulting shallow side aisles (often in churches of

[1] A church built on this principle is known in German as a 'Wandpfeilerkirche', or 'wall-pillar church'. I shall use this direct translation of the German term to describe the type which, though unfamiliar in England, is frequent among these churches. For illustrations of it the reader is referred to plates 23, 28, 32.

Vorarlberg type). This piercing of the wall-pillars, it should be pointed out in passing, raises an interesting further question. In those (mainly Swabian) areas where in Gothic times the hall-church type with its lofty detached columns had been a tradition it seems almost as if the attached wall-pillars of the new style were felt to be in some way an alien import. For there appears a tendency, early noticeable, to make them look as if they too were detached—either by piercing them with arches (*Weingarten*, *Weissenau*, the extreme case being *St Gallen*); by emphasizing their capitals and entablature (*Obermarchthal*, *Rheinau*, *St Urban*); or by applying pilasters or half-columns to them (at *Arth*, fluted pilasters on three sides; at *Zwiefalten*, doubled half-columns). There are indeed churches of the period in which, contrary to Baroque feeling, the hall type has held its own (*Schöntal*, *Isny*; cf. also *Sachseln* and *Sarnen*. Do we perhaps find an echo of it in *Steinhausen* and *Die Wies*?).

There is, of course, one case in which pillars or columns may be present in a manner alien to Baroque feeling and intentions— that of a mediaeval church that has received later Baroque decoration while retaining its original architectural structure (a few examples: *Freising Cathedral*, *St George* at *Amberg*, *Rottenbuch*, *Andechs*, *Kremsmünster*, *Beromünster*). Such a case, however, will, at least to a practised eye, betray itself at a first glance, not merely by the obviously greater age of the arcades and the church as a whole (*Freising*, *Beromünster*) but also by a clear discrepancy between the architectural proportions and the requirements of the decoration (*Andechs*; *Solbad-Hall*, parish church).[1]

Again, a Baroque church has no transepts that project to any extent beyond the nave walls, for these would interfere with the sense of a centralized space. Sometimes we find slight external projections of transeptal character containing side chapels, as in most churches of the 'Vorarlberg' type, e.g. *Obermarchtal*, *Schönenberg* (plate 14), *St Urban*. Sometimes the appearance of a

[1] Some of the chief churches of this type are considered separately on pp. 147 ff.

transept is given in the interior by the fact that the bays in which the principal side-altars stand are of greater span or greater height than the others (*Zwiefalten, St Katherinenthal, Melk*— where this effect is greatly increased by the dome over the 'crossing'). But in neither of these cases is there any real transept formation. Nor can the projection of the rotunda, e.g. at *Die Wies* or *St Gallen*, or of the central section of the church as at *Rott-am-Inn* or *Neresheim* be called a transept. The nearest approaches to transept formation are found in those churches which either have, or are influenced by, basilical form (*Salzburg Cathedral, Ottobeuren, Weingarten, Fulda Cathedral, Munich Theatinerkirche*). But in the first three of these cases the transepts are apsidal in character, which reduces their independence; and in the latter two they are so shallow as to be of little consequence.

We find similar 'centralizing' tendencies in the planning of side chapels. Many devices are employed to minimize their separateness and emphasize their organic connection with the main building. The main one was to place them so that their altars are optically subordinate to the high altar; the two chief methods of doing this have already been mentioned (page 53). A further device for reducing the independence of side chapels was to curve their lines and surfaces. At *Osterhofen*, for instance, only the floors of the niche-like side chapels are flat; the ground-plans are oval, the ceilings slightly domed. These conditions are repeated even in the upper storeys of the chapels at gallery level (plate 32).

Many of the interiors, indeed, after about 1720 show few straight lines or flat surfaces at all. Arches swing in all directions. Wall surfaces seem in rhythmical movement. Concave curves interplay with and set off convex ones. Altar steps or rails are curved (*St Katherinenthal*). Altar columns are often spiral in form (*Osterhofen*, plate 35). Choir-stalls are found set in curves or semi-circles (*St Gallen*). This rhythmicality is echoed even in small objects and designs (plates 59-62). Some of the significant aspects of curves have been mentioned. Another may be added. Curves vitalize a building; and in worship there should also be joyfulness. That the swinging, dancing play and interplay of curves has a certain evocative function in this respect will be easily realized. This delight in curved lines and surfaces finds expression also, of course, to some extent in the exteriors of the later churches, above all in the façades. The façades of the following churches offer in this respect interesting comparisons and contrasts: *Salzburg Kollegienkirche*, *Weingarten*, *Einsiedeln*, *Berg-am-Laim*, *Zwiefalten*, *Ottobeuren*, *Melk*, *St Gallen* (see plates 6, 7, 12, 13, 16, 17, 19).

From the architecture we pass to the decoration of the churches. Apart from its beauty and motionless drama this has the important function of forming the symbolic link between earth and heaven. A naïve or preoccupied visitor to, let us say, *Steinhausen* on a sunny day might be forgiven for thinking at the first moment that the church into which he had come had no roof, that he was still looking up into a brilliant sky, but one in which now some extraordinary pageant was being enacted (plate 39). This, of course, is exactly what the Baroque painter intended he should think! And if he went on to try to find out what was happening and who this great crowd of people could be, he would be further fulfilling the painter's hopes. The flat, dome-shaped vaults and the vast frescoes that cover them in these churches are so conceived and executed as to give the impression that the ceiling, and with it the barrier between earth and heaven, is riven asunder and dissolved. To the aspiring soul and the struggling sinner are opened up visions of the saints in light and the Godhead in glory. The Church Militant here on earth looks upward and sees portrayed the shining splendour of the Church Triumphant. And indeed the effect of the greatest of these paintings, seen in favourable lighting, is overwhelming—the richness and variety of the colouring, the marshalling of the figures in their groups and ranks, the illusion of great depth and height produced by a combination of subtlest perspective drawing and skilfullest gradation of colour from full and glowing reds, blues, greens and browns at the base of the picture to the fine, intense blends of white and yellow in the mystical blaze at the summit. Often the experience of illusory height and depth is attained, or at any rate attempted, by the introduction of architectural motifs (predominantly an Italian and an early tradition: plates 26, 30, 40). Columns and colonnades, domes and pyramids rise up into heaven like an upward extension of our own world. Here the risk of destroying the illusion is, of course, much greater; and sometimes the treatment is so heavy (e.g. *St Florian, Kreuzlingen*) as to convince no one. But often, by infinitely skilful perspectival drawing and gradation of colour, incredible illusory effects are produced, effects not only of height and depth but of objects in the fresco regrouping themselves and changing their sizes and directions as the beholder moves from one position to another. The most extraordinary example known to me, and one painted on an entirely flat ground, is the huge ceiling fresco in *St Maria Victoria* at Ingolstadt, by *Cosmas Damian Asam*.

The link between the visions in these frescoes and the worshipper in the church is formed by the statuary and the altar paintings.

A great multitude of figures and groups surrounds the visitor in one of these churches. He sees saints and prophets and Fathers of the Church at decisive points of vantage, significantly poised and with their appropriate attributes[1] (plates 44, 47, 49). He sees angels and putti flying, sitting, leaning, supporting, listening, adoring, pointing, reproving, on altar and pulpit, organ and confessional, making jubilant music, bearing emblems of the Betrayal or the Crucifixion, bringing messages from on high, in charge of the mounting horses of Elijah's fiery chariot, attending the crucified and awaiting the risen Saviour, up-bearing the Virgin at her Assumption (plates 22–3, 35–7, 54, 57, 63–6). He sees symbols of dogma and doctrine—of the Trinity (a triangle, plates 35, 36); of the all-seeing eye of God (an eye, usually framed in the triangle), of the self-sacrificing love of Christ (a lamb or a pelican), of his wounded heart (a heart clasped by a crown of thorns), of the Annunciation of the Virgin (a lily) or of her sorrows (a sword or swords piercing her bosom), of the revela-

[1] See Appendix I.

tion of divine mysteries (a curtain over choir arch, altar or pulpit drawn aside by putti, plates 29, 37); of the transitoriness of mortal things (a clock, plate 29), and of much else.

A few groups of statuary may be mentioned as, perhaps, typical examples. At *Osterhofen*, on the St John Nepomuk altar (south side of nave) are two charming putti who commemorate the saint's faithful keeping of the secrecy of the confessional. One, with solemn, warning gesture and expression, holds a tablet bearing the words *'secretum meum mihi'* to which he is pointing; the other, with face upturned in rapture, holds aloft a representation of the saint's tongue framed in a flaming halo (plate 66). At *Diessen*, flanking the high altar, are four magnificent, more than life-size figures of the Latin Fathers of the Church. The right-hand lower figure (St Jerome) stands holding in one hand a book and a crucifix upon which he is gazing, in the other a staff and a skull. Kneeling at his feet is a playful little putto trying the cardinal's hat of the saint on his own curly head—symbolizing, what? Presumably the truth that human greatness lies in the soul and not in rank, secular or ecclesiastical! (plate 44, cf. 51). At *Osterhofen*, again, on the north wing of the high altar is a larger, highly dramatic group in which a female figure, standing above a large globe (the world) and holding aloft a cross, with vigorous gesture and drapery swirling is casting down another figure upon whom she has placed her foot and round whom a serpent (sin, doubt) is coiling, with fanged jaws vainly raised to strike—the victory of Faith over Unbelief (plate 46). At *Einsiedeln*, on St Joseph's altar (north side of nave) we find a seated female figure in a rapt attitude with eyes blindfolded and a telescope in her hand, symbolizing the saint's blind faith in God. In the *Jesuit Church* at *Vienna*, if we look at the base of the pulpit, we shall find another fascinating pair of symbolic putti struggling fiercely, one of whom has horns and hoofs and a tail!

In many of the great altar compositions we find earth and heaven linked in a thematic unity that extends from the altar painting to the statuary above and even to the fresco on the ceiling overhead. That this unity should originate where the altar itself is has symbolic significance; for according to Catholic belief the altar is the place where, by the real presence of Christ in the sacrament at the consecration, heaven and earth are veritably linked at the supreme moment of worship. One or two examples of such compositions must suffice as illustrations. At *Diessen*, at *Schäftlarn* and at *Fürstenfeldbruck* the high altar paintings represent the Assumption of the Virgin through the clouds to heaven; above them, and crowning the whole altar in each case, is a group of statuary of the Trinity surrounded by angels and clouds and rays of light, the Son looking tenderly downwards towards the painting with outstretched hand in a greeting of welcome to His mother as she ascends (plate 37). At *Steinhausen* the altar painting shows the Descent from the Cross; but the Cross itself is bare. The theme is continued both in the pietà on the tabernacle immediately in front of the painting (the dead Christ rests on His mother's knee) and in the upper painting of the altar which shows the risen Christ, and even in the ceiling fresco above in which the Father in the glory of heaven is awaiting His Son. At *Wilhering*, too, we find altar and fresco linked in this way. The high altar painting again depicts the Assumption of the Virgin, above which we see in statuary the Holy Trinity preparing a crown for her supported by angels, while the ceiling fresco overhead shows an angel choir (and indeed full orchestra!) celebrating her arrival. In all these examples it is an upward movement by which earth and heaven are symbolically linked. Sometimes the reverse is found. At *Einsiedeln* the fresco in the main dome shows the Manger at Bethlehem as the centre of a great pageant of adoration with shepherds and their sheep below on the ground, angels and saints in the sky; while at the apex of the dome God the Father is looking down upon the drama that is unfolding itself. At a lower level than this painting, in the spandrels of the arches and on the cornices sculptured figures of angels and putti are flying down to earth with scrolls and streamers inscribed with the good news for mankind. Here the church itself, not merely an altar, is the point of union between earth and heaven. In each of these examples, then, and in many others, architecture, painting, and sculpture mingle their powers in a grand unison of symbolic representation.

Very careful thought was devoted to the effects of colour and of lighting in a Baroque church interior.

The use of colour for aesthetic and symbolic purposes was a matter of complexity and subtlety that would need a treatise to itself, and we cannot here do more than point out a few tendencies. The treatment of the walls and wall-pillars varied a good deal in practice. South German feeling seems to have preferred a white or cream-white background colour against which the furnishings, especially the altars, would stand out conspicuously. In interiors showing Italian influence, on the other hand, the walls are usually coloured by being faced with marble or stucco or gilded. This is one reason for the much greater lightness of South German churches and others influenced by them. *Melk* and the slightly later *Weingarten* are both huge, massive churches; but whereas in the former the prevailing colour of the walls is dull gold, in the latter it is white. The effect of *Melk* is much richer but also much more sombre. The interior of *Weingarten*, equally majestic, is lighter and more radiant. In general there is a tendency to enrich and intensify colour in an upward direction (a process which culminates in the frescoes on the ceiling) and often also in the direction of the high altar (for this *Die Wies* is a good example). In the frescoes themselves, as we have already mentioned, the subtle grading and lightening of the colours from the base of the picture towards its apex adds powerfully to the illusion of depth and height (plates 41, 42). Frequently recurring symbolic uses of colour are a reddish tint in altar compositions (the blood of Christ shed) and the association of particular colours with particular figures (the Virgin's robe usually blue—the colour of constancy).[1]

The lighting of a Baroque interior posed its own problems. In a Gothic church the stained glass windows with their figures and scenes were themselves part of the great picture-book by which the faithful were taught by their Church. In the Baroque church

[1] See Appendix II.

the windows served only to let light in onto the picture-book displayed inside the building; what was important was that they should do this with the adequacy and subtlety required. They were thus of plain glass and devoid of tracery and other impediments to the flow of light. There were two main conditions to be fulfilled. First, that the light should fall as and where desired; that is to say, that it should blend with the architecture and the decoration to contribute to the total effect of the interior, and that it should especially illumine certain important areas (above all, frescoes and high altar). Secondly, that it should not dazzle the beholder, diverting his attention and blinding him to what he ought to see. The chief method of securing this double aim was that of indirect or concealed lighting. Important windows are hidden behind pillars or in side-chapels or transepts, or placed high up (sometimes in the lantern of a dome) or in the west wall behind the worshippers. Again and again we may enter one of these churches and be surprised to find it filled with light though not a window is to be seen at first. Churches that consist principally of a rotunda offer interesting experiences in the matter of lighting. Some (the *Karlskirche*, and others, in Vienna; or *Ettal*) have a drum-dome over the rotunda; some (*Steinhausen*, *Die Wies*) have not. Theoretically one might suppose that any church of rotunda type would offer unique lighting possibilities, and especially if it had a dome; and it is indeed always worth while on a bright day devoting time to such a church to watch the varying effects as the sunlight moves round from window to window. But as regards the presence of a dome as a source of lighting, all depends on the position and size of the windows. Large windows skilfully placed lower in the body of the rotunda may produce more brilliant and diversified effects than smaller ones set high up in a dome. Yet again, we must avoid false comparisons. 'Brilliance' by itself is but one characteristic, and one that might well be felt to be out of place in, say, *Weltenburg* or *Melk*.

If the question of lighting was of central importance for the architect of one of these churches it is hardly less so for the visitor. Anyone who wishes to experience the finest light effects in a

Baroque church interior must take account of weather and time of day. In general, the duller the weather, the less satisfactory will be the impression. Further, the orientation of the church, together with the position of its windows, must be studied. A church that lies on a north-south axis and is lit from both sides should be visited either fairly early in the day or later in the afternoon when the sunlight is coming in through the windows of one or other side of the building. On the other hand, a church that lies on an east-west axis will almost certainly offer its finest lighting during the middle hours of the day. The height of the sun and the character of its light will also be of importance. The golden sun of an early autumn afternoon, for instance, will give effects of great richness and mellowness but at the expense of a certain clarity of detail.

At this point we will pause and sum up, and do so by way of introducing a comparison which will probably not come as a surprise to the reader. He will have noticed that in referring to various aspects of a Baroque church interior we have used expressions drawn from the theatre. We have just been thinking of the general 'lighting' effects of such an interior. Elsewhere we have spoken of side altars set in pairs for specific optical effects like the 'side scenes' or 'coulisses' of a stage leading up to the high altar and its painting that form the 'backcloth'. We shall later find at least one church (*Diessen*) in which this back scene (that is, the high altar painting) can actually be shifted and replaced according to the festival celebrated. And indeed, in the Baroque age a church was felt, and described, as a 'theatrum sacrum', a place where sacred mysteries are 'enacted' and holy rites 'performed'. We shall find it illuminating, and need think it in no way unnatural or shocking, to think of these church interiors in this way. The 'stage' of the 'sacred theatre' is thus the sanctuary with the high altar as the central focal point of liturgical 'action'. The choir and nave then form the 'auditorium' where the congregation-audience, the worshipper-spectators watch as well as pray.

A few words may be added on the subject of the exterior of a

Baroque church in relation to the interior. The exterior is usually severe, sometimes (as with the churches of *J. M. Fischer*) extremely so, and with little ornament. Such ornament as there is will be found confined to the façade and to the tower or towers. Façade ornamentation takes the form of volutes on the gables, pillar or pilaster capitals of a certain richness, more or less elaborate cornices perhaps with stretches of balustrading above and statuary in niches or crowning the gable. Tower decoration, apart from features shared with the façade, consists principally in the more or less intricate and lively shape of the cap or helm (good examples are those of *Munich Theatinerkirche*, *Aldersbach*, *Vierzehnheiligen*, *Melk*, *Fulda* (see plates 1, 6, 18)). A tower may even be crowned by statues at its corners (*Salzburg Kollegienkirche*; *Dürnstein*; plates 7, 21). Outstanding in beauty and richness is the tower of *Dürnstein*. Windows are for the most part very plain, though the characteristic designs of *Dominikus Zimmermann* have great charm. The exterior colour of a church will depend on whether the stone is left uncoated or is coated with plaster and, if the latter, what the treatment is. *Vierzehnheiligen* has an ochre stone facing that glows richly in the sunset. *Einsiedeln* is greenish-grey. Others are washed over in white, with pilasters and bands of a second colour. Sometimes the ground-colour is an ochre with pilasters of white (*Maria Birnbaum*) or even dark red (*Günzburg*, *Waldsassen*). Very great care was taken to fit and adapt a church to its surroundings.

This external plainness is not the result of accident or indifference. It has a twofold reason. First, the monastic churches, and it is these that are externally the plainest, seldom stand free and open to view but are enclosed on more than one side, often on three sides, by the monastic buildings. There would in these cases have been little point in lavishing great craftsmanship upon the exterior. With the 'pilgrimage churches' the case is somewhat different. They stand normally in isolated positions and exposed to view from all sides; and we do in fact find that their exteriors have been designed and carried out with a greater eye to refinement of line and detail (*Steinhausen*, plate 3; *Birnau*). It might

1. *Munich*, Theatinerkirche (see pp. 134–5)

2. *Die Wies*, pilgrimage church and clergyhouse (see pp. 89–91)

3. *Steinhausen*, parish church (see pp. 87–8)

4. *Maria Birnbaum*, pilgrimage church (see p. 166)

5. *Kappel*, pilgrimage church (see pp. 103–4)

6. *Melk*, abbey and church from the river (see pp. 213–15)

7. *Salzburg*, Kollegienkirche (see pp. 241–2)

8. *Innsbruck*, St Jakobi, with Inn valley mountains (see pp. 246–7)

9. *Hopfgarten*, parish church (see pp. 257–8)

10. *Salzburg*, cathedral (see pp. 239–40)

11. *Vienna*, Karlskirche (see pp. 203–5)

15. *Einsiedeln*, façade of abbey church (see pp. 178–80)

12. *Weingarten*, abbey church; façade and dome (see pp. 120–2)

14. *Schönenberg,* pilgrimage church (see p. 131)

15. *Munich*, Dreifaltigkeitskirche (see pp. 136–7)

16. *Berg-am-Laim* (near Munich), St Michael (see pp. 78–9)

17. *Ottobeuren*, abbey church (see pp. 81-2)

18. *Vierzehnheiligen*, pilgrimage church (see pp. 113-15)

19. *St Gallen*, cathedral (see pp. 188–90)

21. *Dürnstein*, tower of church (see pp. 221–2)

20. *Volders*, tower of priory church, with view of Inn valley (see pp. 251–2)

23. *Irsee*, 'ship' pulpit (see pp. 127–8)

22. *Mödingen*, pulpit (see p. 167)

24. *Kleinhelfendorf*, parish church, ceiling stucco ornament, 1669
(see p. 165)

25. *Diessen*, stucco ornament, *c.* 1736 (see pp. 76–8)

perhaps be thought that the same considerations would have applied to the many smaller churches built purely as parish churches which can be viewed freely from all sides but which nevertheless are in general very plain externally. But these would probably not have had the importance nor commanded the wealth to justify greater expenditure on the exterior. Where in such cases we do find greater attention lavished on the outside of a church it often takes the form of painted decoration of walls or tower or both (*Mittenwald* and *Götzens* are notable examples). There is, however, a second and more fundamental reason for this general external plainness. The exterior of a Baroque church is relatively *unimportant*. The secret of the church does not lie in outward embellishment. The outer walls are simply a cloak, decent and often austerely beautiful, thrown around what is all-glorious within. This contrast between exterior and interior is thus seen to have a symbolic character of its own. It is to remind us of the deeper contrast between the outer and the inner life, between the material and the spiritual, the body and the soul.

Before closing this chapter and passing to an account of the churches themselves, I cannot refrain from adding a few remarks upon certain objections which, whether from prejudice or from a seeming confusion of thought, are sometimes levelled against the religious art we are here considering. It is criticized by some as false, by others as dramatic or theatrical, by others even as idolatrous and superstitious. Let us shortly consider these three charges.

Some persons appear offended at the 'illusory' character of Baroque church art and architecture. The portrayal or suggestion of non-existent perspectives, the 'posing' of figures and groups at certain significant points and with certain significant gestures, the 'placing' of altars to achieve certain effects of direction and composition—all this, they seem to feel, is a 'build-up', a deliberate creation of elaborate illusions, and to be condemned as such. Those who take such a view, however, seem a little unclear in their thoughts. The term 'illusion' is ambiguous. On the one hand, it may be used to indicate some phenomenon which (like a mirage) is in fact not what, or how, we believe it to be, or which (like a hope) does or may not represent things quite as they are. Now either we discover this discrepancy, or we do not. Even if we do not, an illusion in itself need not be harmful to us; it might (as in the case of the hope) even be beneficial. On the other hand, the term may be used to suggest that a deliberate deception is being practised upon us—with the tacit further insinuation that the deception is in some way harmful. Here what is implied is that we have been not only led, but also in some way *mis*led, into thinking something. Someone has deceived us.

Let us now imagine a person who goes into a church of the high Baroque period resplendent in its pageantry of art and symbolism. As he sits, he looks upward, perhaps, and seems to see a vision of the heavens opened and saints in glory praising God in infinite realms of celestial light. Or his gaze wanders eastward, guided here and there by a pointing hand or an altar set obliquely across a corner, until it comes to rest on the high altar tabernacle where a red lamp flickers, statues of saints stand keeping their watch for ever, and wonderful angels bend low in adoration. And by all that he sees he is led, perhaps for a few moments only and even in spite of himself, to reflect upon spiritual things, even to worship. He has clearly been *led* to certain thoughts and experiences. Has he been *misled*? If so, in what way, and in what does the deception consist? Again, has anyone deceived him? If so, who? The painter of the fresco, the designer of altars and statuary, the architect himself—or all together in a subtle and shameless conspiracy? But the Baroque architects, painters and craftsmen were not of this kind, they were not deliberate deceivers. They were men of vision, talent and piety whose only mistake lay in having their own clear conceptions of heaven and earth and portraying these with technical brilliance and uncommon majesty for the help and inspiration of others. They sought to keep us in mind of the eternal. Have they in this offended, or been guilty of falsity?

To the objection that Baroque church art is theatrical, one is tempted to reply by asking when the association of religion with drama became something unusual or unjustifiable. The great Passion Play at Oberammergau, a Baroque creation in the heart of Baroque Bavaria, offers a three-hundred-year-old refutation of such an idea. It is in fact a very ancient association, one that goes back to the origins of religious expression. We may suspect that there is an unconscious confusion in the minds of those who express their distaste in this form. Perhaps they mean simply that this art is over-elaborate, over-loaded, excessive in detail. Now it may readily be admitted that in an art so rich and so self-confident as the Baroque a tendency to exaggeration in this or that respect is the besetting sin. But it must also be pointed out that 'exaggerated', 'ornate' and 'over-elaborate' are terms that are relative in their reference. An object that appears exaggerated in design when taken in isolation will probably, when viewed in its total context or as representing some idea symbolically, lose its 'exaggeration'. In a Baroque church we must never lose sight of the total effect or of the symbolism at work throughout. Aesthetic and symbolic considerations interpenetrate so closely that a hasty judgment is likely to miss the essence of the matter, even be hopelessly astray. It may, however, also be that those who express themselves in this way really mean that for them Baroque church art is in some way 'false' (this point we have just been considering) or that it is 'idolatrous', a point to which we now in conclusion pass.

There are those who are repelled by what they see in these churches not so much because they think it false or theatrical as because they think that it ought not to be there at all. God is a Spirit, they hold, and they that worship Him should do so in spirit only without the harmful distractions of paintings and graven images. This raises an ancient, complex and controversial question that cannot be even adequately stated in a few lines. The objection here referred to strikes, of course, at religious art as such; but it strikes with special force at an art so consciously sensuous in character as the Baroque. I am thinking here not of those for whom (as for myself years ago) a Baroque church interior was an unfamiliar and somewhat bewildering experience, but of those who for dogmatic reasons deplore and reject what they see. Confining ourselves to the problem of worship we may surely reply that not everyone finds it easy, or even possible, to worship in spirit only. Many need some visible object to help them focus such powers of spiritual concentration as they possess. For many, indeed, worship is in any case an act not of the mind or spirit alone but of the whole being, one in which mind, spirit, heart and senses can and must respond in union. Again, we surely do well not to be over-ready with expressions such as 'idolatrous' or 'superstitious'. They carry an accusation which those who make it are seldom in a position to justify or substantiate. They, too, are relative in their reference; 'idolatry' and 'superstition' appear in many forms in the world. It is unfortunately possible to be scorchingly austere on the subject of statues and candles in churches and yet to idolize one's belly or one's bank-account and be painfully superstitious about one's dreams or one's horoscope!

3. The Churches

We turn now to the churches themselves which, it is hoped, will become the goal of those who read these pages. Before doing so, however, it will perhaps be well to pass in bird's-eye review the development of the era as a whole as reflected in the main phases of its church architecture and art.

The earliest phase (c. 1650 to c. 1710) lacks both the more exuberant imagination and the more delicate craftsmanship of that which followed. We feel the restraint and rationality of the Renaissance and the formal Italian influence. Ground-plans are clear, interiors easily 'experienced'. Stucco work, though often of fine and rich quality, is thick and static, in lines or panels with rather stiff leaf and fruit motifs predominating. Frescoes, if present, are small, like enamel plaques or medallions set in the stucco with which they were not at first of equal decorative importance. Examples: in S. Germany *Benediktbeuern* (1683–6), *Holzen* (1696–1704); in Austria, *Garsten* (1677–93), the *Vienna Dominikanerkirche* (1631–4); in Switzerland, *Muri* (rotunda, 1694–8), *Rheinau* 1704–11).

The second phase (c. 1710 to c. 1770) shows gradual but striking sophistication of design, lightening of treatment, elaboration of detail. Whether we call it late Baroque or Rococo does not ultimately matter; we have here not a distinct style but a further imaginative development of existing tendencies. Curving, rhythmical movement invades ground-plans, structures and furnishings. Stucco work becomes more delicate, fanciful, feathery; frescoes become larger, looser and 'airier' in their figure grouping, more dynamic and asymmetrical in their composition; statuary takes on greater dramatic tenseness and abandon. Examples:

in S. Germany *Die Wies, Vierzehnheiligen, Birnau*; in Austria, *Wilhering* and *Wilten Pfarrkirche*; in Switzerland, *Einsiedeln, Ittingen, St Gallen*. The visitor whose way leads him thither may take object-lessons in comparing and contrasting these two phases at *Steingaden*, if he studies first the decoration in the choir (*c.* 1663), then that in the nave (1740–50), or at *Benediktbeuern*, if he passes from the main church (1683–6) into the Anastasia chapel (1750–8); in Austria, at *Wilten*, if he first examines the *Stiftskirche* (1651–5) and then crosses over the road—and over a century—to look at the *Pfarrkirche* (1751–5); or in Switzerland, if, after visiting the church at *Arth* (1695–6), he will make the short journey to *Schwyz* to compare the *Pfarrkirche* (1769–74) there.

Finally, towards the close of the eighteenth century we find a return to a greater restraint and calm and a revival of classical form and feeling. In Bavaria there are signs of it already at *Rott-am-Inn* (1759–63). It is clear enough at *Rot-an-der-Rot*. A casual observer of this latter church might be led into assigning to it quite an early date; its dates in fact are 1781–6. In Austria the classicist revival made itself felt only in Vienna, but hardly at all in church architecture. Examples in Switzerland are numerous —we may select the parish churches of *Cham* (1783–6) in Canton Zug and *Gersau* (1807–12) in Canton Schwyz.

These, outlined very broadly, are the main phases in the development. We find, indeed, local variations and deviations, some of them surprising. A few may be mentioned. At *St Florian*, for instance, large-scale frescoes are met with as early as 1690–5. At *Ochsenhausen*, on the other hand, or again at the *Lucerne Jesuitenkirche* the frescoes are remarkably small for their dates (1725–7 and 1749–50 respectively). Again, I doubt whether even an experienced visitor to the Carmelite church at *Reisach*, with its total absence of frescoes and stucco decoration and its general pronouncedly classicist austerity and serenity, would readily guess its date—1737–9, contemporary with *Diessen* and almost with *Wilhering*. And it was with surprise that I found the elegant, lively pulpit at *Asbach* to be of a date as late as 1780.

SOUTHERN GERMANY

The story of the building of the S. German Baroque churches is in the main the story of the work of a few eminent architects and families of architects assisted by painters, stucco workers and sculptors of no less distinction. We shall group the churches here under their respective architects and deal with each group chronologically. This will enable the reader to study the individual buildings, to trace in them the development of the styles of the various architects and to make cross-references for purposes of comparison and contrast.

The architects and groups of architects of importance are the following:

JOHANN MICHAEL FISCHER. Born 1692 in Burglengenfeld (Oberpfalz); 1723 settled in Munich where he became city and court architect; died 1766 in Munich. Some seventy churches in S. Germany are wholly or partly his work or show his influence.

DOMINIKUS ZIMMERMANN. Born 1685 at Wessobrunn, the home of one of the most eminent schools of stucco workers in Europe; 1708 settled in Füssen, 1716 in Landsberg-on-the-Lech where he later became mayor; died 1766 at Die Wies. Works few in number and confined to S.W. Bavaria and E. Württemberg. His brother *Johann Baptist*, with whom he often co-operated, equally distinguished as fresco-painter.

THE ASAM BROTHERS. *Egid Quirin* (b. 1692 Tegernsee) and *Cosmas Damian* (b. 1686 Benediktbeuern), sons of Hans Georg Asam, himself a distinguished architect and artist; 1711 studied in Rome; 1724 court appointments in Munich; *Egid Quirin* died 1750 at Mannheim, *Cosmas Damian* 1739 at Weltenburg. Co-operated constantly, *E.Q.* as stucco artist and sculptor, *C.D.* as fresco painter, and both as architects. Major works few in number but include the decoration of *Einsiedeln* and *St Jakobi* in Innsbruck. Strongly influenced by Italian forms and feeling, especially by Bernini and Borromini.

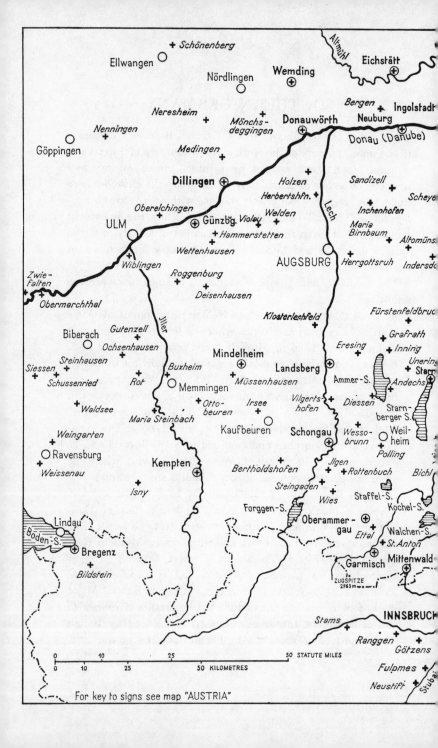

For key to signs see map "AUSTRIA"

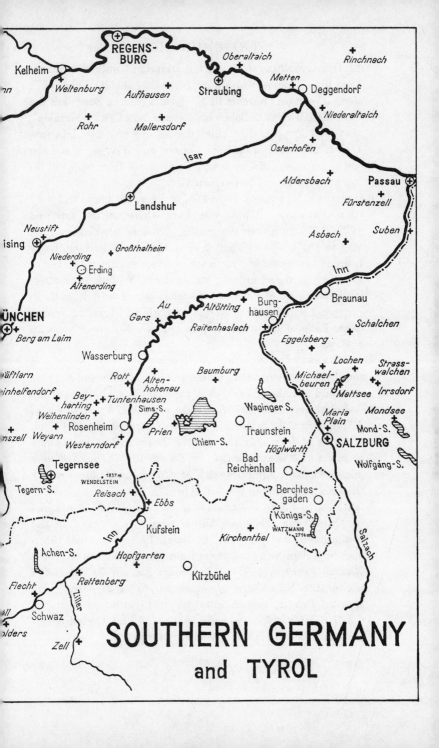

THE CHURCHES

THE DIENTZENHOFER FAMILY. A Bavarian family of architects from the district of Bad Aibling (near Rosenheim), who built some important churches in N. Bavaria (*Fulda, Banz*) but did most of their work in Bohemia (Böhmen, now Czecho-Slovakia), above all Prague. The chief figures are six, five brothers, *Georg, Christoph, Leonhard, Johann* and *Wolfgang*, and the son of *Christoph, Kilian Ignaz*. The work of *Christoph* and his son not represented in Germany.

BALTHASAR NEUMANN. Born 1687 at Eger. His name and work connected above all with Würzburg where he first appeared 1709; 1714 ensign in the guards of the prince-bishop; 1723 visit to Paris, also to Vienna; died 1766 at Würzburg. Early training many-sided (in mathematics, engineering, town-planning, civil and military architecture). Wide field of activity, from *Trier* (*St Paulinus*) to *Vierzehnheiligen* (N.E. of Bamberg) and southwards to *Neresheim* (N.E. of Ulm) and *Meersburg*, Lake of Constance (palace chapel). No major work in S. Bavaria.

THE VORARLBERG SCHOOL. Architects and craftsmen from a number of intermarried families from the area round Bregenz at E. end of Lake of Constance. Especially notable those of the *Moosbruggers* (*Caspar Moosbrugger* 1656–1725, architect of *Weingarten* and *Einsiedeln*), the *Beers* (*Franz Beer* 1660–1726, architect of *Irsee, Holzen*) and the *Thumbs* (*Michael Thumb* architect of *Wettenhausen, Peter Thumb* 1681–1766 of *Birnau* and *St Gallen*). Affinities with *St Michael* in Munich rather than with the Italian basilical type.

ITALIAN AND FRENCH ARCHITECTS. (Architect of *St Michael* in Munich was *Friedrich Sustris* who, though born in the Netherlands, had grown up in Italy). Later important influence of Italian-Swiss architects from Tessin and Graubünden: *Antonio Viscardi* (1645–1713), *Enrico Zuccalli* (?1642–1724), also of the N. Italians *Agostino Barelli* (1627–?1687) and *Antonio Petrini*; French influence chiefly through *François Cuvilliés* (1695–1768) who between 1730 and 1753 directed the architectural plans of the electoral court.

Johann Michael Fischer

Of all S. German architects of the Baroque *Johann Michael Fischer* was the most productive and, after *Balthasar Neumann*, the greatest. His churches, in general, show certain characteristic features which it may be of interest to note briefly here. They are:

(1) An unmistakable predominance of the architectural over the decorative element. Even about his minor works (e.g. the reconstructed choir at *Niederaltaich*, the parish churches at *Aufhausen* and *Unering*) there is a certain monumentality. His exteriors are solid, compact, austere, of a shapely vigour. In his interiors, richly decorated as they have mostly been, there is no tendency for the walls, pillars and arches, even when subjected (as at *Osterhofen* or *Zwiefalten*) to a severe test, to 'dissolve' into decorative areas.

(2) A continuous pre-occupation with problems of spatial relationships and proportion, especially with the characteristic Baroque problem of how to fuse longitudinal axis with central space. He seems here to have been guided in the main by two principal ideas, which he employed repeatedly, sometimes separately, sometimes in combination. One of these is that of a central octagon with 'open' sides giving on to other sections of the church (nave, choir, side chapels, etc.); the other that of a series of intersecting sections oval or circular on plan. The former idea is prominent in the ground-plans of *St Anna am Lehel* in *Munich* and *Aufhausen* parish church; the latter in those of *Diessen*, *Zwiefalten* and *Ottobeuren*; while the combination appears in those of *Berg am Laim*, *Rott am Inn* and *Altomünster*, the last two being his two latest churches (see ground-plans).

In one or two cases the extent of his participation is doubtful. He made a design for *Wiblingen*; but how far this was carried out is not clear. At *Schäftlarn* he may have helped in the façade.

His principal churches are the following:

Osterhofen, 1726–40 (S. bank of Danube between Deggendorf and Vilshofen, from which, as also from Regensburg and

Passau, rail and bus connections). Convent church (Premonstratensian foundation *c.* 760) forming N. side of monastic buildings. Replaces a former Gothic church. The architect to some extent bound by existing ground-plan and remains of earlier choir. A wall-pillar church with 3-bay nave, narrower apsidal choir and slender built-in W. tower.

Noteworthy features. Exterior: calls for little comment. The treatment of apse and choir roof should be noted as anticipating *Diessen. Interior* (plate 32): (1) The wall-pillars characteristic of this type of church with side-chapels between. (2) The rhythmical vigour of the nave and the predominance of curved lines: all interior corners rounded off, balconies swinging convexly outward (cf. later *Zwiefalten*), the arches with double movement upwards and inwards (cf. *Diessen*), the side chapels oval on plan and slightly domed. (3) The immensely rich decoration is by the *Asam* brothers (altars, stucco ornament and statuary by *Egid Quirin*, frescoes and paintings by *Cosmas Damian*); note especially (*a*) the high altar (plate 35) with its spiral columns (recalling Bernini's baldachino in St Peter's at Rome), the fine angels flanking the tabernacle, the putti precariously astride the garlands swung between columns and walls, the symbolic figure of the Paschal Lamb silhouetted against the window with the Trinitarian triangle as background, and on the N. wing the symbolic group of Faith trampling Unbelief underfoot (plate 46)—all this highly characteristic of the imaginative and daring art of the Asams; (*b*) the St Anne altar on right of choir arch, the seated figure of St Anne, in my opinion one of the most deeply human creations of Bavarian Baroque; (*c*) the great nave fresco depicting scenes from the life of St Norbert, founder of the Order; (*d*) the St John Nepomuk altar in S. nave chapel with symbolic putti (plates 63, 66) of wonderful charm in attitudes of adoration and commemorating the Saint's fidelity as confessor.

Diessen, 1732–9 (S.W. shore of the Ammersee, 25 m S.W. Munich; rail connection Munich–Herrsching and boat across, from Augsburg and from Weilheim; on Augsburg–Landsberg–

Weilheim road with bus connection). Formerly collegiate church of Augustinian canons (eleventh century foundation), now parish church, forming N. wing of conventual buildings. Fischer's first major independent work with one of his finest interiors, indeed one of the stateliest in S. Germany. A pronouncedly longitudinal wall-pillar church with entrance bay under organ loft, 4-bay nave, choir and narrower apsidal sanctuary and single S.W. tower.

Noteworthy features. Exterior: (1) The early, not very imaginative façade makes an interesting comparison and contrast with Fischer's next (*Berg-am-Laim*) and with the others that follow it. (2) The treatment of the choir apse recalls *Osterhofen*. (3) The truncated tower, till recently with steeple, is a poor 19th-century rebuild after lightning damage (1846) and now awaiting the replacement of the original fine Baroque helm.

Interior (plate 28): (1) The proportions should be studied and the firm, majestic effect of the whole composition. (2) The incurving of the lunette arches to take the vault are characteristic and recall *Osterhofen*. The 'horseshoe' form of the choir-arch (emphasized by the cornices from which it springs) lends a particularly fine, vigorous poise. (3) Though the church is long in proportion to its breadth, any excessive eastward thrust is held in check by the dominant high altar and the effect of the circular saucer dome over the choir. (4) This interior offers an excellent example of the *theatrum sacrum*; we have the 'side-wing' altars, varying in size and design, leading the eye by stages on and up to the high altar; and the 'back scene' itself (i.e. the high altar painting) can actually be shifted and replaced by others for the different festivals. (5) The decoration and furnishings are by various hands and all first-rate. To be noted especially: the brilliant frescoes, the masterpieces of *Johann Georg Bergmüller* (scenes from the history of Diessen and Andechs; over the choir, Christ surrounded by a host of saintly figures of the line of Diessen-Andechs); the delicate stucco ornament by *Franz Xaver* and *Johann Michael Feichtmayr* and *Johann Georg Übelherr* (plate 25); all the altars,

especially the superb high altar (*François Cuvilliés*) (plate 37)
with its four finely and dramatically conceived figures of the
Fathers of the Western Church, St Gregory and St Augustine
(N. side), St Ambrose and St Jerome (S. side, plate 44), probably
by *Joachim Dietrich*, and the second nave altar on S. with painting (St Sebastian) by *Tiepolo*; and the fine pulpit (*J. B. Straub*).
The high artistic standards for which the Augustinians were
noted were nowhere attained more nobly than in this interior.

Berg-am-Laim, 1738–51 (S.E. outskirts of Munich, terminus of
tramline No. 4 from city centre). Built on a commission from
Clemens August of Bavaria, Archbishop and Elector of Cologne,
as collegiate church for the Brotherhood of St Michael. Lies
enclosed by, though its façade protrudes through the W. wing
of, the conventual buildings. A wall-pillar church with octagonal nave, narrower octagonal choir and transversely elliptical
sanctuary of the same width, and twin-towered W. façade.

Noteworthy features. Exterior: (1) The rhythmical façade
(plate 16) with its imposing two-storeyed, convex, niched central section and the lively upper cornices to its towers, is both
monumental and elegant and a great advance in design on that
at *Diessen*. (2) Not very satisfactory or attractive, on the other
hand, is the squat roof like a truncated pyramid; one feels it as
a poor substitute for the dome that in Austria or Italy the
church would probably have had. *Interior:* (1) Here we see the
results of deeper reflection upon spatial problems, and the
typical Baroque question of how to merge a central space with
a lengthways axis finds one brilliant solution. The feeling of
centrality is inescapable, the nave octagon dominates, the high
altar seems nearer than in fact it is. Yet the sense of length is
equally unmistakable, the high altar is also sufficiently 'remote'. The secret lies in the following facts. The thrust eastwards is imparted by the length of choir and sanctuary (in fact
equal to the diameter of the nave!) Yet this thrust is optically
retarded (*a*) by the fact that the E. limb as a whole is composed of two sections, the design of each of which on plan—a
small octagon, followed by a transverse oval—takes up the

centralizing effect of the nave; and (*b*) by the foreshortening effect produced by the massiveness of the high altar and the apparent continuation of the main cornice across it (see ground-plan). (2) Note the part played by the nave side altars in their transeptal niches in emphasizing the effect of breadth. (3) Decoration and furnishings (1743–67) are all excellent; the frescoes (note especially that of the vision of St Michael in the nave saucer dome) are brilliant works of *Johann Baptist Zimmermann*, the delicate stucco ornament also by him; the altars and statuary by *Johann Baptist Straub* (cf. those at *Ettal*) with altar paintings by various hands. Note the angel on the pulpit with the blue-and-white Bavarian flag in his hand!

Fürstenzell, 1739–48, towers not finished until 1774 (7m. S.W. Passau). The building of this church had a somewhat clouded history. Josef Mattäus Götz began it but was dismissed for alleged incompetence. Fischer was called in and continued the work, but after an unfortunate sinking of the choir walls which led to increased costs and to tension with the monastery he withdrew before its completion. Yet he gave the church its decisive character and it may with propriety be reckoned a work of his. A wall-pillar church with 4-bay nave, slightly narrower apsidal choir and twin-towered W. façade.

Noteworthy features. Exterior: the façade, with slightly convex central section and happily proportioned towers, has nobility and stands in line between *Berg-am-Laim* and *Ottobeuren*. *Interior*: (1) Recent restoration has greatly enhanced it and brought back its brilliance. (2) Signs of the discontinuity in construction referred to above are visible at the E. end—the provisional appearance of the wall behind the high altar, the apparently unfinished pilasters, the abrupt stopping of the stucco round the arch. (3) The galleries over the side chapels are convex frontally but less so than those at *Osterhofen*. (4) The frescoes are fine, delicate works by *J. J. Zeiller* (1744–5), especially that over the nave which shows, in thematic connection: below, Satan defeated; middle, Faith, Hope and Charity personified; above, Mary as intercessor. (5) The high altar, a good work of *J. B. Straub*, is not in its original condition; last century arch-shaped side pieces were removed.

Zwiefalten, 1740–65 (Danube valley, 30 m. S.W. Ulm, 4 m. from N. bank of river; station Riedlingen, bus connections from Tübingen and Urach). Parish church; former Benedictine abbey church (foundation 1089) forming N. arm of monastic buildings; beautifully situated in wooded, hilly country. A wall-pillar church with 4-bay nave, developed transeptal bay and long E. limb containing monks' choir and sanctuary and flanked by twin towers. The ground-plan recalls a mediaeval pattern and it may be that Fischer deliberately kept close to that of the older church that his replaced.

Noteworthy features. This church and *Ottobeuren* are Fischer's two largest and most imposing; if *Ottobeuren* must be given the palm, *Zwiefalten* has much grandeur and beauty. With its length of 315 ft. it actually exceeds its rival. (1) The façade, in the manner of *Diessen* but more important and imaginative, has yet something of a seventeenth century heaviness and is inferior in brilliance and organic unity to *Berg-am-Laim* and *Ottobeuren*. (2) Compare the position of the beautiful towers with that of those at *Benediktbeuern, Holzen* and *Rot*. (3) The little flat-gabled transeptal chapels recall the Vorarlberg design (cf. *Obermarchtal, Irsee, Schönenberg*). *Interior:* (1) The low-pitched, rather tunnel-like effect of the interior as a whole is surprising in view of the high pitch of the roof and due no doubt to several causes—the great length, the actual relative lowness of the ceiling and the scale and rich colouring of the frescoes which make the ceiling seem still nearer. (2) The convex galleries recall *Osterhofen* and have a slightly narrowing effect (unimportant here, as the nave is so wide; for the opposite, broadening effect of concave galleries cf. *Weingarten* and *Donauwörth Heiligkreuz*). (3) The double pilasters impart a note of stability much needed in so decorative an interior. (4) At the fifth bay, though there are no real transepts, the effect of a 'crossing' is produced by the bay being double the width of the others, by the four prominent transverse arches overhead (the only ones in the church) and by the circular saucer dome. (5) The decoration is almost excessively rich but magnificent in quality. Of the frescoes (*Franz Josef Spiegler*, see p. 276) note especially that over the nave (a vision of the human race led by St Benedict in homage before the Holy Trinity and the Virgin), the painter's masterpiece, wildly ecstatic and in its rapture and transport seeming to overflow all bounds and to whirl us up too into its depths. The highly delicate stucco ornament is by *Johann Michael Feichtmayr*; the best of the statuary by *Josef Christian*—note especially the pulpit and the group opposite (vision of Ezekiel).

Ottobeuren, 1748–67 (8 m. S.E. of Memmingen, 15 m. N. of Kempten; rail and bus connections from both). Abbey church (Benedictine foundation 764). Of eight plans submitted Fischer's was carried out; many would consider the church his crowning achievement. A wall-pillar church of basilical type (compare and contrast *Salzburg Cathedral* (plate 10) and *Weingarten*), with 2-bay nave, developed apsidal transepts with conical roof over crossing, 2-bay square-ended choir and twin-towered façade.

Noteworthy features. Exterior (plate 17): (1) The beauty, vigour and compactness of the building as a whole are striking, the thrust of the roof towards the façade gable counteracted perfectly by the massive transept and the strong verticality of the towers. Viewed from half-way down the attractive, wide street of old houses it presents a most noble sight. (2) Its situation is, for a monastic church, unusual, projecting from one wing of the conventual buildings and exposed to view on all sides save that of the choir wall (*Obermarchtal* and *Fulda* stand similarly). (3) The splendid, soaring façade reflects several influences, partly from Fischer's own past work (cf. with *Berg-am-Laim* and *Zwiefalten*), partly Fischer von Erlach's *Kollegienkirche* in *Salzburg*. (4) The conical roof over the crossing, and its finial, certainly form a more shapely substitute for a dome than the devices at *Berg-am-Laim* and *St Gallen. Interior* (plate 27): (1) The first impression is overwhelming; possibly no other church of the period presents such massive and majestic architecture combined with such rich and delicate decoration. It is, however, possible to feel precisely in this combination of the colossal and the elegant a certain discrepancy, especially when a comparison is made with other contemporary interiors (e.g. *Die Wies* or *Vierzehnheiligen*). The tendency of later Baroque (Rococo) decoration was towards lightening and loosening, and some may feel that here architecture and decoration are not quite in step. (2) The elevation should be noted; the form is basilical inside as well as outside. Yet wall-pillars are present, and there are no real side-aisles—only openings through the wall-pillars. (3) Transepts and crossing are fairly fully developed, the transepts projecting considerably; the ground-plan is most definitely cruciform, though their apsidal character reduces the independence of the transepts. (4) Decoration and furnishings are all fine. Of the frescoes (*Johann Jakob Zeiller*), that over the crossing (the coming of the Holy Ghost at Pentecost) shows clearly the looser, airier character of the later Baroque treatment (clearer still in *Christian Wenzinger's* frescoes at *St Gallen*). Stucco-work and most of the statuary are by *Johann Michael Feichtmayr*; note especially the statuary on the high altar, and the font with group of Baptism in Jordan. The carved and inlaid choir stalls (*M. Hormann* and *J. Christian*) and especially the contemporary choir organ (*Karl Josef Riepp*) are notable; the organ should be heard if at all possible.

(The visitor should not fail to see those parts of the huge monastic buildings open to the public, especially the *Library* and the *Kaisersaal*.)

Rott-am-Inn, 1759–63 (W. bank of Inn between Wasserburg and Rosenheim, from both of which rail and bus connections; easily and quickly reached from Munich by rail with change at Rosenheim). Formerly abbey church (Benedictine foundation late eleventh century), now parish church. A form of wall-pillar church of complicated ground-plan (q.v.). To a central, slightly projecting octagon are added two narrower quadrilateral E. sections (sanctuary and former monks' choir) and two similar W. sections (bay of nave and entrance hall) flanked by side chapels. The actual interior of the church however consists only of three of these sections, the octagon and the sections E. and W. of it (sanctuary and nave), the monks' choir being hidden behind the high altar, and the entrance hall under the organ gallery.

Noteworthy features. Exterior: Of a forbidding plainness, the façade even more undistinguished than *Diessen*, the flanking towers (in their lower halves twelfth century, survivals from older church) unequal in height and never completed. Of some interest is the fact that, though the central interior saucer-dome is relatively at least as developed as those at *Berg-am-Laim* or *Ottobeuren*, this is not reflected externally in the form of the roof, the line of which is unbroken throughout. *Interior:* Surprises as one of the most beautiful of all. (1) The pervading restraint is noticeable (compare the balconies and arches with those at *Osterhofen*. (2) Of central architectural interest is the octagon in which and through which three lines of movement meet and cross—the longitudinal movement from W. to E., the 'centralizing' movement of the octagon itself and the circular dome above, and the 'centrifugal' thrust of the four diagonally opposite corner chapels. The interplay of these movements, upon which the optical effect of the octagon rests, can be seen in the ground plan, to which the reader is referred (on p. 288). (3) The decoration is mostly of superb quality owing to the cooperation of two great artists, *Matthäus Günther* (his fresco in the central dome, of the Benedictine Order in glory, full of glowing colour and vitality—note the defeat of the dragon by the archangel Michael—as also of mystical depth and light) and *Ignaz Günther* (statuary on high altar—especially fine and expressive the Empress Kunigunde; and on the transverse nave altars—note the figure of Cardinal Peter Damian on N. altar, plate 51). Fine also the pulpit (*Josef Götsch*, pupil of *Ignaz Günther*). (4) If a criticism of this interior is allowed it is, perhaps, that its scale is too small for its basic conception, with the result that the dome is felt as slightly oppressive and some of the other parts (e.g. the diagonal corner chapels) as somewhat dwarfed.

Altomünster, 1763–6 (15 m. E. of Augsburg, 12 m. N.W. of Dachau; from both, as also from Munich, rail and bus connections). Abbey church (Benedictine foundation eighth century for monks and nuns: since 1485 Brigittine). The last of Fischer's churches, he died before its completion. A type of wall-pillar church of complicated design; to a large octagonal nave are added three eastward sections—a 2-storey section quadrilateral on plan, an apsidal choir and (above and behind) a second choir. The Brigittines being a double Order of monks and nuns, the problem was to construct a church in which three groups (monks, nuns, and lay brothers) could take part in the services unseen, and so undisturbed, by one another; to which had to be added and accommodated the lay folk. Fischer's solution produced, not an oddity as might be thought, but an interior which combines certain well-known features of his churches with other surprising and beautiful vistas.

Noteworthy features. Exterior: The tower and its helm are very shapely. The greatly extended E. limb should be noted. *Interior:* (1) The arrangement to meet the accommodation needs can be clearly made out. We enter the main octagon (with two tiers of galleries), immediately E. of which is the 2-storey section with lay-brothers' choir below and nuns' choir above, then the apsidal sanctuary, then (above and behind the high altar, now used as the parish altar) the monks' choir with stalls and altar. The whole lay-out of the greatest interest as an attempt to meet unusual monastic requirements in a way satisfactory both practically and aesthetically. (2) The decoration is of varying quality. The delicate and restrained stucco work by *Jakob Rauch* (1773), the frescoes by *Josef Mages* (1768), especially fine in the drawing and colouring, that in the nave saucer dome depicting scenes, actual and legendary, from the history of the Order; the two chief altars by *J. B. Straub*, late and fanciful but good.

Other churches of J. M. Fischer

Altomünster was Fischer's last great work; he died, as we have seen, while it was being completed. Of his other, lesser but always interesting and beautiful churches, attention is directed to the following. The first four all show variations of the central octagon theme of which we have spoken and which found its perfect expression at *Rott-am-Inn*.

Rinchnach, 1727–9 (12 m. N.E. Deggendorf, on the Regen-Passau road). The nave is a new construction; choir and tower were taken over from the fifteenth-century church and baroquized. Fine stucco work (artist unknown) and frescoes by *Andreas Heindl*.

Unering, 1731 (4 m. N.W. Starnberg on isolated hill) with interior of great charm; good harmonious contemporary furnishings and nave fresco.

Aufhausen, 1736–51 (12 m. S.E. Regensburg, 16 m. S.W. Straubing). One of Fischer's strongest interiors, its appeal predominantly architectural. Here (as at the contemporary *Ingolstadt Franziskanerkirche* before its total destruction by bombs) the narrow sides of the octagon are pierced by arches at ground and at gallery level so that the diagonal axes thrust through to the outer walls, as later at *Rott*.

Bichl, 1751–3 (just N. *Benediktbeuern*) with frescoes by *J. J. Zeiller*, and high altar with a notable group of St George and the Dragon by *J. B. Straub*. Side altars 1709. No stucco.

Dominikus Zimmermann

In *Dominikus Zimmermann* we have a figure who differs in certain important ways from *J. M. Fischer*. Fischer was an architect pure and simple and his churches were decorated by a variety of artists. Zimmermann, having been trained and achieved distinction as stucco artist and designer of altars as well as architect, united in his own person the practice of several arts. Again, he worked in frequent co-operation with his brother, the painter *Johann Baptist Zimmermann*, who contributed the frescoes to all his greater churches. These two facts together lead us to expect (what indeed we find) in his interiors a greater unity of design and execution and a closer harmony of architecture with decoration than is often the case in those of Fischer. A third difference lies in a greater lightness and buoyancy of treatment, everywhere apparent and hardly paralleled elsewhere. In place of the massively architectural manner of Fischer we have a greater delicacy and slenderness. This is not to say (as might be said of the *Asam* churches) that the architectural element tends to get submerged or dissolved. Nothing could be architecturally more emphatic than the pillars in *Steinhausen*; they are *there*, and they *function*. Yet strength is so fused with beauty that the effect is at once architectural and decorative. Along with this delicacy goes also a gaiety, an almost primitive fancy that make us feel in his work the touch of the merry peasant.

His works are few and his fame rests on fewer still—on three, in fact, the churches at *Steinhausen* and *Günzburg* and the pilgrimage church known as *Die Wies* or *Wieskirche*. It is to these that we shall confine ourselves here, though, for those who wish to study his work further, attention is drawn also to the following lesser works: *Mödingen*, near Dillingen (monastic church 1716–21, his earliest church); *Buxheim*, near Memmingen (parish church, 1725); *Siessen* (15 m. S.W. Biberach, 1726–33); *Landsberg* (1741–52), Johannis-Kirche (with brilliant altars, especially high altar with statuary by *Johann Luidl*); *Eresing* (parish church, 1756–7, a reconstruction), near Landsberg, and *Gutenzell*, N.E. of Ochsenhausen, also a Baroque reconstruction (1755–6, see p. 151). Some believe, myself included, that he may also have been the unknown architect of the very elegant pilgrimage church *Maria Steinbach* (1746–53) near Memmingen (see below).

The three major churches show, apart from the general characteristics referred to above, certain others. (1) They represent successive stages in the working out of a single architectural conception which finds its full expression in *Die Wies*. (2) The basis of this is a predilection for an oval ground-plan; the *Steinhausen* church consists of a central oval with small rectangular E. and W.

sections added, that at *Günzburg* of a nave of concealed oval character with deep apsidal choir attached, while *Die Wies* unites the
essence of both these designs (see ground-plans). (3) The great
attention given to questions of lighting, together with the design
and disposition of the windows, gives these churches a quite
remarkable brightness and brilliance.

Steinhausen, 1728–33 (20 m. W. of Memmingen, 30 m. S.W. of
  Ulm, 6 m. S.W. of Biberach; nearest station Schussenried 3 m.;
  bus connections irregular). Pilgrimage church (pilgrimage
  since fifteenth century). In 1727 the Abbot of Schussenried
  commissioned Zimmermann to plan a new church. Owing to
  miscalculation the church in the end cost four times the estimated amount, with the result that the abbot had to retire and
  Zimmermann's later request to spend his last days in the abbey
  was refused. A 'round church' with central oval rotunda set
  lengthwise (the sides squared off externally in transeptal
  fashion), small rectangular sections in E. (sanctuary) and W.
  (entrance with organ gallery over) and single slender W.
  tower. Stands in open, wooded country and rises with graceful
  pride above the village roofs. A jewel of dignity and beauty, a
  'first, fine, careless rapture' which, to one person at least, has a
  greater perfection than the later masterpiece *Die Wies*. A most
  fascinating church.

Noteworthy features. Exterior (plate 3): (1) The impression of
size given by a relatively small church is surprising (actual
dimensions: length 150 ft., height to roof ridge 106 ft., of
tower 205 ft.). (2) The union of compact strength and elegant
poise in the whole composition is notable. (3) The details are
fine—the upward thrust of the front gable which, echoed in
the tower cornices, helps the graceful tower to soar; the side
gables with an almost Renaissance flavour; the pairs of volutes
rolling together with binding effect at significant points; the
firm yet finely moulded main cornice running right round the
building; the characteristic and charming tripartite windows.
(4) The squared and gabled sides and intersecting roofs, suggesting transepts and a crossing, almost conceal the oval form

of the interior, though the curved wall sections give a hint of what will be found inside. *Interior* (plate 26): (1) Lightness of treatment, gaiety of spirit and firmness of structure unite marvellously; note especially the fine pillars that with their widely projecting imposts so confidently catch and sustain the rhythmical dance of the arches. (2) Here again the Baroque problem of merging length with centrality is well solved; the longitudinally set oval together with the shallow sanctuary afford the twofold impression desired. (3) Highly instructive is the relationship between side altars and high altar. The two side altars are placed obliquely, thus leading the eye on; they are also unsymmetrical in design, each requiring supplementation by the other, and both by the high altar. (4) The rotunda offers a good example of apparent 'rooflessness', increased by the balustrading round which figures are grouped. The fresco itself (depicting a favourite theme of Baroque theology— Mary, surrounded by angels and saints in glory, as Queen of Heaven and gateway to the New Testament after the loss of Paradise) is of great brilliance, depth and movement (plate 39). (5) The thematic unity of the high altar paintings and pietà with the fresco above has already been mentioned (see p. 60). (6). The stucco work is everywhere of fine and fanciful quality. Note particularly the rich pillar capitals with their motifs of leaves and fruit and animals' heads. Here and there on windows and capitals we find birds perching (plate 59) and insects crawling with delightful whimsicality. (7) Of the statuary attention is specially drawn to the figures of the apostles Peter and Paul (plate 47) on the high altar, the quaint, vigorous, peasantlike figures of apostles sitting (in symbolic position) above the pillars at the springing of the vault and the putti on the altars (plate 26).

Günzburg, Frauenkirche, 1736–41 (on the Danube, 15 m. downstream from Ulm; on the main line Stuttgart–Ulm–Augsburg–Munich). Parish church replacing fourteenth century building destroyed by fire 1736. In 1754 still without altars and pulpit, and consecration not until 1781. The design consists of a nave externally oblong, internally oval with slightly projecting side chapels, a narrower choir whose square-ended outer walls enclose an inner polygonal sanctuary and single tower flanking choir. The church stands in a commanding position above the river.

Noteworthy features. Exterior: Monotonous compared with the other two churches but relieved by the warm ochre and brick-red colouring and by the situation in which it groups picturesquely with the roofs of the old houses and the old town wall tower. *Interior:* Beautiful in itself and important as the link between *Steinhausen* and *Die Wies*. (1) The nave, despite its outer rectangular appearance, gives the impression of being oval, a result attained (*a*) by the rounding-off of the corners, (*b*) by the slight concave recesses in the side walls, (*c*) above all by the oval construction of ceiling and fresco. (2) The columns here are set well to the sides, yet still detached and so placed that they too emphasize the oval. (3) The design of choir and sanctuary with gallery round and two-storey altar, hinted at at *Steinhausen*, appears here further developed and will be repeated with still greater elaboration at *Die Wies*. (4) In this church the architect was not helped by his brother. Frescoes (remarkably small in size for date) and also altar paintings are by *Anton Enderle*, stucco decoration by *Thomas Gering*, Günzburg artists of talent. As already mentioned, the altars were added later, the statues on the high altar (*Ignaz Hillebrand*) not till 1757. (5) The glazed gallery below the organ was once the nuns' choir of an adjacent convent later dissolved.

Die Wies, 1745–54 (12 m. N.E. of Füssen, 12 m. N.W. of Oberammergau; no rail connection, nearest station Lechbruck, $5\frac{1}{2}$ m.; bus connections from Garmisch-Partenkirchen, Oberammergau, Füssen, Steingaden). Pilgrimage church (pilgrimage since mid-eighteenth century); present church replaced a (still existing) small chapel that could not accommodate the numbers. The design consists of an oval rotunda with narrower, sharply convex façade, at the opposite end a deep apsidal choir against which is built a single tower and against this in turn the clergy house. The building stands in flowery meadows, to the south a picturesque skyline of undulating, wooded Alpine foothills. In Bavaria its praises are sung so loudly and so much as a matter of course that there is a risk of sober judgment being swamped in the chorus of adulation; and I do not apologize if I am a little heretical in this or that respect.

Noteworthy features. Exterior (plate 2): (1) That the church as a whole is Zimmermann's maturest work and that the interior is of unique beauty is true. That the exterior with its heavy, hump-like roof, over-slender tower and dwarfed clergy house is as harmonious as it might have been, one may take leave to doubt. It is usually said that Zimmermann tried to shape the roof-line to conform to the ridge-line of hills in the background; but this, if true, would produce an effect only from one angle. (2) Unlike *Steinhausen* the exterior here reveals the general nature of the interior design. (3) The design and the grouping of the windows are characteristic for Zimmermann and should be compared with *Steinhausen*. (4) The position of the tower (undistinguished in itself) is symbolic, at once connecting and separating the sacred and secular buildings. (5) The use of the columns to bind, as it were, the façade on to the rotunda is interesting. *Interior:* Here we find, indeed in a heightened degree, most of the general characteristics that astonish at *Steinhausen*—the lightness, the brilliance, the porcelain-like delicacy, the unearthly serenity. Here, too, the brothers co-operated and we have again the saucer dome of the rotunda adorned with a single, vast, visionary fresco by *Johann Baptist* (representing the Last Judgment, or rather, the moment just before it, for Christ is still on the rainbow, we see, and has not yet taken His seat on the judgment throne). (1) Here the designs of *Steinhausen* and *Günzburg* blend and we have the deep choir of the latter with its gallery and its two-storey high altar linked in a masterly way with the rotunda of the former. (2) The firm single pillars of *Steinhausen* have given way here to pairs of slender columns with fillets and separate capitals though linked in entablature and base, an arrangement which, together with the further fact that they bear statues and other ornamental objects, lessens the architectural element of the interior. Columns, however, have an effect of their own upon lighting in that light glances off them as it does not off pillars. (3) The choir merits close study—note the continuation of the nave side aisle at a (symbolically) higher level in the gallery, the intensification of colour, the architecturally daring openings piercing the walls above the arcades for extra light. (4) The dynamic pulpit (*D. Zimmermann*) seems blown into ecstasy, as if the wind of Pentecost were passing through it, greeted by the exquisite and innocent putto in his cave beneath. (5) Very fine are the four figures of the Latin Fathers of the Church (*Anton Sturm*) with all the nervous, almost impatient movement, the tense and dramatic gestures of the Rococo (plate 48).

*　　　*　　　*

Maria Steinbach, 1746–63 (right bank of the Iller, 6 m. S. Memmingen, whence rail connection to Lautrach and 20 mins. uphill walk). Parish and pilgrimage church. Included in this section with some reservation as the architect is not documentarily known. Important authorities, however (Michael Hartig, Hugo Schnell, Ernst Gall), incline to attribute the church to *D. Zimmermann;* and indeed anyone coming from *Steinhausen* and *Die Wies* can hardly fail to be struck by many similarities —the lines of the exterior, the rhythmical façade (cf. *Wies*), the form of the windows, the double high altar with side galleries and characteristic colouring, to mention no others.[1] In any case, a notable and beautiful building without and within. A wall-pillar church recalling the Vorarlberg type, with 4-bay nave, slightly projecting gabled transept and similar secondary W. transept, apsidal choir and single, built-in W. tower.

Noteworthy features. Exterior: (1) Altogether most pleasing, the elegant, if robuster, compactness of the whole design offering, in

[1] See Epplen, H.: *der Baumeister der Wallfahrts-Kirche zu Maria Steinbach* (Memminger Geschichtsblätter 1954–6).

its way, a challenge to *Steinhausen*. (2) The highly dynamic façade, to which I hardly know a parallel, with its two steeply upsurging cornices, one above the other—as if to give the slightly over-sturdy tower a 'hoist'. (3) The tower itself, firm, four-square, a little squat perhaps by reason of the depressed cap, contrasts interestingly with the slender tapering of the *Steinhausen* tower. (4) The slight gable-crowned transeptal projections find an echo in the apse—the five little gables joining with the great façade gable to 'clamp' the roof, as it were, firmly in place. *Interior:* Everything of fine quality, architecture, decoration, furnishings. (1) The rhythmical gallery swinging obliquely across the corners gives the nave a great, embracing sense of unity; the organ and loft on high-pitched arch form a majestic composition; the lighting everywhere most skilful. (2) The admirable stucco ornament (especially note the pilaster capitals and the putti above the niched statues flanking the choir arch) is by *F. X. Feichtmayr* and *J. G. Übelherr*—the latter's last, and in my opinion most sensitive and exquisite, work (he died at Steinbach 1763). (3) Frescoes and altar paintings are by *F. G. Hermann*, especially colourful and powerful (though not of great perspective depth) the nave fresco representing the favourite theme of Mary as mediatrix of divine grace. (4) The imposing two-tier high altar strongly recalls that at *Die Wies* both in its (symbolic) reddish tints and in other respects; note that the columns of its lower portion are linked architecturally with the ceiling. (5) At first sight a pulpit seems lacking; then we discover that there are twin pulpits (one each side of nave) formed by enlarged gallery bays of somewhat greater projection, but without sounding-boards or religious symbols other than the supporting angels—a unique design, as far as I know.

The Asam Brothers

In certain ways the brothers *Egid Quirin* and *Cosmas Damian Asam* resemble the Zimmermanns. We saw that Dominikus

Zimmermann was an architect who was also an artist and a craftsman. The same is true of Egid Quirin Asam. Again, Dominikus Zimmermann co-operated in his work with his painter brother Johann Baptist. So did Egid Quirin Asam with his painter brother. But the differences between the two cases are great. The co-operation between the Asams was more constant and intimate. In that both brothers in fact were trained as architects it is not possible to say, in the case of one of their original churches, that either was solely or even chiefly responsible for the architectural plan. These are joint works in the fullest sense of the word, and all that we can safely attribute is the work in which each is known to have excelled, Cosmas Damian in fresco painting and Egid Quirin in stucco work and statuary.

These considerations raise another, and more fundamental, one. Both brothers were at heart not architects at all but decorators. They never learnt, nor practised, the architect's craft thoroughly. The churches that they themselves built as well as decorated are very few—two, in fact, and neither large. And even in these we cannot but feel that the architecture as such was of secondary importance and that it was upon the ornamentation that they expended their gifts and energies. The art of both brothers alike was, in essence, pictorial rather than architectural. Their interest lay in creating atmosphere and vision, in deliberately undermining the limitations of matter and bursting the bonds of space by all the devices of perspectival illusion and fanciful lighting. Indeed, we may even think of their art as in a sense hostile to architecture, in that they deliberately aimed at diverting attention from architectural elements as such, at 'dissolving' the surfaces and masses of walls and pilasters and vaults so that the effect of the visionary and mysterious atmosphere should be unimpaired. We may well feel that the Asams, more than any other of the architects that we shall be considering, recapture something of the mediaeval spirit. Certainly the two churches that are peculiarly their own, *Weltenburg* and *St John Nepomuk* in Munich, have a mystical and mysterious atmosphere that is unique. It must also be remembered that both brothers worked almost exclusively for the Church. Cosmas Damian was occasionally commissioned for secular work,[1] his brother never.

The genius of the two as decorators was in wide demand, and they decorated the churches of other architects over a wide field. We shall here let four churches represent their work, those four in which they worked also as architects. But attention is directed in passing (we shall return to them again) to their greatest achievements in the field of ornamentation proper. It is to be found in the churches of *Weingarten, Einsiedeln, St Jakobi Innsbruck, Fürstenfeldbruck, Osterhofen, Freising Cathedral, St Maria Victoria Ingolstadt, Aldersbach.*

Rohr, 1717–25 (18 m. S.S.W. of Regensburg, 18 m. N.W. of Landshut, 25 m. E. of Ingolstadt; no rail connection—nearest stations Langquaid and Abensberg, each 6 m. Bus connections from Munich, Rottenburg, Abensberg). Abbey church (since 1946 Benedictine; originally foundation of Augustinian canons). The decision to rebuild was a result of the effects of damage done in the Thirty Years' War. The architect was almost certainly *Josef Bader* working under the supervision of *Egid Quirin Asam* who intervened principally to secure the conditions he needed for his choir and high altar. A church of wall-pillar type with 3-bay nave, slightly projecting transepts, apsidal choir and single W. tower.

Noteworthy features. Exterior: Plain and uncouth and calls for no comment. The tower (lower storeys Gothic, upper storey and cap seventeenth century), massive and dumpy, unimaginatively covering a third of the already undistinguished façade. *Interior:* The proportions are imposing, the lines clear and strong, the Italian influence unmistakable. But only one feature need claim our prolonged attention, the Assumption group above the high altar. We see it at once in the distance as we enter. It is the greatest of *Egid Quirin's* works and one of the most remarkable and, in its way, superb creations in

[1] E.g. Schloss *Schleissheim* (near Munich; staircase fresco); Schloss *Alteglofsheim* (near Regensburg; fresco in Oval Room).

Europe (plate 36). The modest mensa itself of the altar is set
well forward in the sanctuary; behind it, the dark brown semi-
circle of the choir stalls; and behind these again and on a higher
level is set the group of statuary flanked by massive brown
columns bearing a broken triumphal arch. Round an empty
tomb out of which grave-clothes are showing are ranged a
group of Apostles in attitudes varying from incredibility to
utmost ecstasy, with gestures sweeping and dramatic. The
moment depicted is that when they have opened the Virgin's
tomb to show the body to Thomas who was not present at her
burial, and they find only grave-clothes and flowers. In the air
above them, upborne by angels, is the more than life-size
figure of the Virgin ascending to heaven, apparently hovering
in mid-air as she goes up towards the clouds where the Holy
Trinity await her with a crown. The whole composition is beyond description and almost beyond praise. Note particularly
(*a*) the treatment of the individual apostles, their attitudes,
gestures and expressions (plate 45); (*b*) the great hovering
group, the Virgin herself appearing as a Baroque 'grande
dame' of great magnificence yet great humanity (the hands and
drapery particularly fine); (*c*) the scene in heaven above with
the faces of cherubs among the shafts of light; (*d*) the simple
and effective colouring (tomb reddish-brown and green, figures
white, backcloth green, gilding overhead). Note also the lack
of colour decoration in the church itself, no frescoes, pale tinting, restrained gilding; whether intended or not this certainly
leaves the eye free to concentrate on the central group undisturbed.

Weltenburg, 1717–21 (on the Danube mid-way between Regensburg and Ingolstadt, 6 m. upstream from Kelheim; station
Kelheim; no regular bus connection, but summer coach and
river excursions from Regensburg and Kelheim. Particularly
recommended, the rapid downstream trip Weltenburg-Kel-
heim through most impressive gorge scenery). Abbey church
(Benedictine foundation early seventh century, one of the
oldest in Bavaria). Like *Rohr* the abbey suffered severely in the

Thirty Years' War and began to recover only about 1714. The ground-plan shows three rectangles, the central one much larger, each containing an oval, the ovals forming respectively central rotunda, on W. entrance hall (with organ gallery over), on E. sanctuary with apsidal extension behind high altar. Over the rotunda is a high cylindrical drum with dome-like roof. There is a single tower. The situation is of great and romantic beauty, low down in a loop of the river as it sweeps round to break through a wild, deep, rocky gorge.

Noteworthy features. Exterior: (1) Church and abbey buildings are huddled closely together, no doubt because of the site; the tower rises oddly through the roof of one wing of the quadrangle. (2) A glance at the arrangement of windows will prepare us for unusual lighting effects inside, though hardly for what we actually find. Except in façade and apse there are no lower windows at all; the rotunda has twelve (a symbolic number) but all just below roof level and all very small. (3) The otherwise pleasing façade suffers somewhat from the remarkable heaviness of the cornice. *Interior:* The attention is at once arrested by two connected features, the mysterious lighting, and the high altar. (1) More even than we suspected the rotunda is lit almost entirely from above, the organ blocking much of the western light. As we suspected, light radiates onto and from the high altar. The result is a distinction between a mysterious, earth-bound gloom below and an unearthly radiance above and to the east. We feel in some strange borderland between the earthly and the heavenly; we are very conscious of atmosphere, but at first hardly at all of objects. This feeling repeats itself in *St John Nepomuk* in Munich where conditions are similar. (2) Looking up, we find that we are looking through an 'open' cupola (surely a reminiscence of the Pantheon in Rome) up to the fresco many feet above, and that the twelve windows admitting the light are between the two. This two-level device (repeated at Munich) of creating a separate heavenly sphere *into* (and not merely *at*) which one looks increases both the visionary character but also the remoteness of

96

what is seen. On the S. side of the open cupola *Cosmas Damian* has set a half-length figure of himself looking over the cornice, and we must in piety notice him in passing! (3) As at *Rohr*, the high altar is the dramatic focal point, though the effect is achieved by other means. Behind the altar itself and at a higher level rises a great structure like a triumphal arch through which St George on horseback comes riding towards us out of a blaze of mystic light to kill the dragon and rescue the maiden— the whole group of figures seen in silhouette against the light. A *tour de force*, but a brilliant and effective one. (4) In general, the decorations are strongly Italianate in conception and colouring. Fine is the figure of St Martin on the N. corner of the high altar. The dome fresco has as its theme the coronation of the Virgin before the Holy Trinity and amid the Church Triumphant.

Ingolstadt, St Maria Victoria (1732–6). Built as prayer and meeting room for the Jesuit congregation; since 1804 chapel of the Brotherhood 'Maria vom Sieg'. Designed perhaps by *E. Q. Asam* though the ascription seems uncertain. Rectangular, aisleless building with turret over W. façade.

Noteworthy features. Exterior: compact and very attractive; the facade with its flanking volutes to upper storey strongly Italianate; the decoration (fine and elaborate white scroll ornament on a pink ground) as elegant as it is unusual on an exterior. *Interior:* in no way a 'typical' Asam interior, as are those of Weltenburg or St John Nepomuk in Munich, and, it may be felt, too low for its length and width, yet of great quality. (1) Notable above all the vast fresco (130 ft. by 49 ft.) by *C. D. Asam* covering the entire flat ceiling and offering the most remarkable perspectival illusions to the visitor as he moves about. The general theme is the favourite one of Mary as mediatrix between Man and Christ. Thin shafts of light symbolize the significant connections between the different figures and groups (from God Father to and through Christ and Mary, from Mary to the groups representing the Four Continents). As we move up the church we should notice the way in which the architectural elements in the picture (especially the pyramid on the right and the tower in the far left corner) 'shift' their positions and directions. (2) The shapely and beautiful altar with stucco baldachin imitating brocade has four good figures that seem to show the influence of *Ignaz Günther*. (3) Rich and exquisite the carving on stalls, doors and organ gallery. (4) The paintings on the walls are by various hands, those over the doors flanking the altar by *G. B. Götz* (*c.* 1749). (5) In the sacristy is a celebrated and magnificent monstrance by *Johann Zeckl* of Augsburg (1708) with a representation of the naval battle of Lepanto.

St John Nepomuk, Munich, Sendlingerstrasse; 1733–5. Designed and built by the Asams at their own expense, adjoining the house bought as a dwelling by Egid Quirin, to be their private chapel. Stands now between this house and the priest's house which they also provided but which, unfortunately for the symmetry of the group, was raised a storey in the nineteenth century. Suffered superficial damage in the last war.

Noteworthy features. Exterior: As only the façade is visible there is little to be said. (1) The wide, heavy, outward-swinging gable gives a sense of breadth and helps to divert attention from the extreme narrowness of the building in proportion to its height. (2) The symbolic blocks of rock, upon which the church appears to be built, should be noted on each side of the porch. *Interior:* (1) A number of the general features of the *Weltenburg* interior repeat themselves here, in particular (*a*) the management of the lighting to give the symbolic contrast between gloom below and radiance above, the darkness of earth and the light of heaven; (*b*) the construction of the ceiling in such a way that the eye passes through a lower level (here, owing to the narrowness of the church, merely indicated in the form of a projecting cornice) to a higher realm above and beyond; (*c*) the placing in the upper part of the high altar of a symbolic group of statuary as focal point of devotion—here the Holy Trinity in the traditional German form of the 'Gnadenstuhl' (Mercy Seat), a composition of great beauty poised daringly at the verge of the parapet, the crucial point between darkness and light, the frontier between earth and heaven. (2) The large relief of the Saint at gallery level above high altar (a copy of an original in Vienna) replaces since 1960 a previous painting and probably corresponds more closely to Asam's intended design. (3) The great ceiling fresco is unfortunately the part of the church that has suffered most from the last war; it is badly in need of restoration at the moment (July 1961), and in places its design is already unrecognizable. (4) Before leaving the church we should reflect with what amazing success this unpromising site (90 ft. long and only 28 ft. wide) has been utilized to produce a great effect. Indeed, the very architectural difficulties have been turned to account as a foundation for decorative and atmospheric possibilities, and probably only the Asams could have succeeded here. We see perhaps what Mr Sacheverell Sitwell means when, describing another City church on a constricted site, James Gibbs' St Mary-le-Strand in London, he writes that 'the interior of the church is too cramped and narrow to give him scope. Perhaps only the brothers Egid Quirin and Cosmas Damian Asam of Bavaria could have made the most of it.'[1]

Straubing, Ursulinenkirche, 1736–41 (Danube, between Regensburg and Passau; from both main line rail and bus connections). The Asams' last church; Cosmas Damian died before it was finished. A tiny 'round' church with quatrefoil groundplan; to the central rotunda are added a W. bay internally apsidal, externally square-ended with façade, two shallow, flatly apsidal side chapels and a deeper apsidal sanctuary.

Noteworthy features. Exterior: The façade and its setting recall, and may be compared with, *St John Nepomuk* in Munich. *Interior:* Despite unfortunate later alterations to the W. gallery a light, charming and characteristic interior. (1) The intersection of the four internally apsidal side arms with the rotunda adds firmness to variety in the design; the slightly greater depth of sanctuary (and indeed also of the W. bay) emphasizes adequately the longitudinal axis (cf. in this respect *Bernhard-*

[1] *British Architects and Craftsmen* (see Bibliography), p. 108.

zell in Switzerland). (2) Characteristic for the Asams is the (symbolic) lighting from above, especially in the sanctuary where the sharp cornice (as at *Weltenburg* and *Munich*) separates the 'heavenly' from the 'earthly' realm. (3) The favourite Berninesque altars reappear here; interesting and beautiful the windows replacing a superstructure in the side altars and, in all three altars, the great crowns supported by angels. As I think back on the magnificent achievement of the brothers Asam in all these three countries—in *Weingarten*, in *Innsbruck*, in *Einsiedeln*, to mention no other places—I salute this tiny church in gratitude and admiration. Whether they knew it or not, it was their gentle farewell.

The Dientzenhofer Family

Both the Vorarlberg and the Italian-Swiss church architects of the Baroque period, as we shall see, lavished their talents outside their own home districts. The Bavarian family of the *Dientzenhofers* offers a certain parallel. They came from around Bad Aibling, now a pleasant little watering place between Munich and Rosenheim. Yet their greatest achievements were on Bohemian (now Czecho-Slovakian) soil, above all in Prague itself. Southern Bavaria, their home, owes them almost nothing; Northern Bavaria a few fine churches which we shall here deal with. The important figures are six: five brothers, *Georg*, *Christoph*, *Leonhard*, *Johann* and *Wolfgang*, and the son of *Christoph*, *Kilian Ignaz*. Of these, the two most distinguished, *Christoph* and his son, are not represented in Germany.

The real contribution of the Dientzenhofers to Central European church Baroque, though it finds expression in only one of the Bavarian churches (*Banz*), is clear and can be briefly stated. It was they, especially Christoph and his son, who took up and applied the new style of Borromini and Guarini in which, as we have already tried to show (p. 51), the curve rather than the straight line became the fundamental unit in plan and elevation, which considered the space rather than the material as primary,

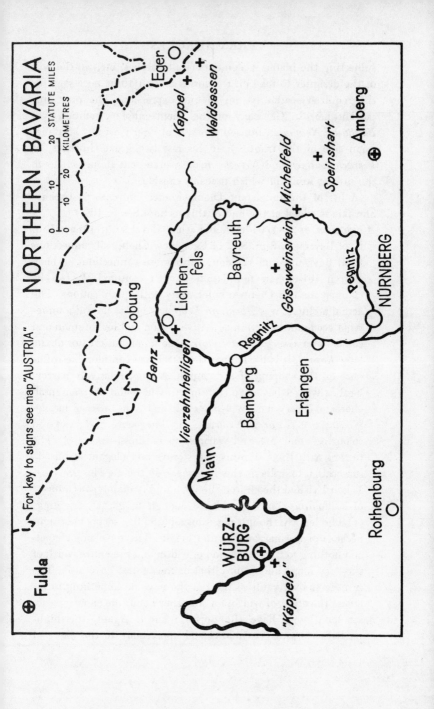

NORTHERN BAVARIA

Fulda

Coburg

Eger

Keppel

Waldsassen

Speinshart

Amberg

Michelfeld

NÜRNBERG

Pegnitz

Gössweinstein

Bayreuth

Lichten-
fels

Banz

Vierzehnheiligen

Regnitz

Bamberg

Erlangen

Main

WÜRZ-
BURG

"Käppele"

Rothenburg

For key to signs see map "AUSTRIA"

STATUTE MILES
0   10   20
0   10   20
KILOMETRES

subjecting the material elements (walls, arches, etc.) to the will of the designer to take on the forms and rhythms necessary for the required spatial system to find expression. The most important heir in Germany of the Dientzenhofer tradition was *Balthasar Neumann*, himself a native of Eger (just on the Bohemian side of the frontier); in his last two great churches, at *Vierzehnheiligen* and *Neresheim*, he worked out its principles to the utmost limits of which it seems capable.

(A list of the important Dientzenhofer churches in Czecho-Slovakia is added at the end of this section. See p. 109.)

Waldsassen, 1681–1704 (close to Czecho-Slovakian frontier, 35 m. E. of Bayreuth, 8 m. S.E. of Eger, now Cheb; rail connections from Bayreuth and Weiden; various bus connections). Abbey church (Cistercian foundation twelfth century). It can be claimed for the Dientzenhofers only with qualifications. The actual architect was *Abraham Leuthner*; but as he was a somewhat academic and unimaginative person and his foreman and collaborator *Georg Dientzenhofer*, the ingenious creator of the later *Kappel*, it is likely that the latter had considerable influence on the shaping of the church. A long, relatively narrow basilica with 4-bay nave (the fourth wider and of 'transeptal' character), very narrow 4-bay choir and twin-towered façade. *Noteworthy features. Exterior:* (1) The ochre and brick-red colouring lend life and warmth to its massiveness. (2) The towers with their diminishing storeys and elegant helms do something to relieve the heaviness of the façade. *Interior:* When I visited the church the nave unfortunately was a forest of scaffolding, but I could see enough to gather essentials. (1) The length, though not unusual (280 ft.), seems enormous because of the narrowness and height. The nave side chapels add nothing to the impression of width, and the entire width of the very long choir is only that of the central nave aisle. The transverse oval vault-sections of the nave do something to increase the effect of width; on the other hand, the choir frescoes set lengthwise have the opposite effect. Again, the high-pitched 'clerestory' windows add appreciably to the effect of height. (2) Like that of *Speinshart*, this interior has more in common with the Vorarlberg type than with the most characteristic Dientzenhofer work. (3) The rich stucco work and statuary (*Giovanni Battista Carlone*) are notable; especially good the figures of the Latin Fathers in symbolic position on the crossing pillars, and the putti on the pillar cornices at the springing of the arches. (4) The choir stalls (*M. Hirsch*, a native of Waldsassen) are among the best and richest in Germany, the putti supporting the canopies finely formed and of exuberant vitality. (5) The high altar (*Karl Stilp*, also of Waldsassen) is as rare in form as it is beautiful; the globe-shaped tabernacle (unique in Bavaria, but cf. *Gössweinstein*) is built into and framed by an Annunciation group, above it symbols of Christ crucified and risen. The whole composition has to be taken together with the picture forming the background. (The visitor should also see the interesting and beautiful *Library*.)

Kappel, 1685–9 (2½ m. N. of Waldsassen, from which bus connection or 45 mins. walk). Architect *Georg Dientzenhofer*. Pilgrimage church (pilgrimage since sixteenth century) of unusual, oriental appearance situated in somewhat commonplace open country between the Fichtelgebirge and the Böhmerwald. A wall-pillar church of trefoil, or triapsidal, ground-plan with low surrounding covered aisle or ambulatory and three slender round towers.

Noteworthy features. Exterior (plate 5): Unique and one of the strangest in the country; the rather later Dreifaltigkeitskapelle (Holy Trinity Chapel) at *Paura* near Lambach in Upper Austria (1713, by *J. M. Prunner*) shows similarities and perhaps influence. The strangeness arises from the ground-plan and the resulting elevation which can be understood only symbolically. The dedication, we recall, as also at *Paura*, is to the Holy Trinity. The basis of the ground-plan is an equilateral triangle (the usual symbol for the Trinity) within a circle (eternity). We thus get a triapsidal church with intersecting roofs over the apses and three slender, circular, minaret-like towers at the points of intersection. The appearance of the building (which is determined by the architectural lines alone) is not quite the original one as in 1881 the roof angle was altered and the towers increased in height. *Interior:* (1) The angles of the basic triangle are indicated by single, detached columns; in the apses themselves however are flat pilasters which do not impede the flow of the curves. (2) The ceiling of each apse is decorated with a fresco (repainted 1934–40 and not of great merit) devoted to one of the Persons of the Trinity. (3) Each apse reproduces in itself the triapsidal ground-plan of the whole church. (4) Though in fact the church is nothing if not a 'round church', the longitudinal axis receives emphasis by the dominant high altar and its counterpart, the organ. (5) Apart from the picturesque and happily poised organ and gallery (with very fine Madonna underneath) the furnishings are not remarkable.

Speinshart, 1691–1706 (23 m. S.E. of Bayreuth; nearest station $2\frac{1}{2}$ m., Eschenbach; bus connection from Bayreuth to Pressath). Abbey church (Premonstratensian foundation 1145). Architect *Wolfgang Dientzenhofer.* Wall-pillar church with 3-bay nave, 2-bay square-ended choir and twin towers. The solid square block of the monastery lies isolated and monumental in wide, rolling, somewhat tedious country with the characteristic conical peak of the Rauher Kulm to the N.E.

Noteworthy features. Exterior: The church is so embodied in the monastic buildings, of which it forms the N. side, that it is difficult to distinguish in itself. The most interesting feature is that it has no façade proper, the abbot's dwelling being built on in front of the towers (cf. other Premonst. abbeys, *Schussenried, Roggenburg* and *Ursberg,* where this is also the case). *Interior:* (1) Like *Waldsassen,* there are similarities with the Vorarlberg type, though the balconies are high and there is no transeptal formation. (2) The chief interest centres in the stucco-ornamentation (*Carlo Domenico Lucchese,* from Tessin) which in its enormous richness is rivalled only by *Holzen* (Bavaria) and *Garsten* and *Schlierbach* (Austria). Italianate in character and with the stiffness of the earlier period it yet repays the closest study and cannot here be described in detail. Notable are the allegorical groups on the cornices, and especially the Annunciation group around the choir arch (Angel to right, Mary to left, at apex the Holy Ghost as dove surrounded by clouds and angels in a composition in which stucco and painting pass imperceptibly into one another). (3) The stucco work is enhanced and set off by the small but brilliant frescoes (*Bartolomeo Lucchese*, a brother of Carlo Domenico).

Fulda Cathedral, 1705–12 (55 m. N. of Würzburg, 55 m. N.E. of Frankfurt; rail and bus connections from both and from many other points). Architect *Johann Dientzenhofer*. In 755 St Boniface was buried in the little church by the Fulda whose building he had supervised. On the site of the Carolingian successor of this church and over the grave of the Saint arose the Benedictine monastery which in 1752 became a Prince-Bishopric and the abbey a cathedral. The secularization in 1802 caused an interruption, but in 1829 the see was reconstituted. A basilica with 2-bay nave, slightly projecting transepts with full dome over crossing, 1-bay sanctuary with former monks' choir behind and twin-towered façade.

Noteworthy features. Exterior: (1) Like *Ottobeuren* and *Obermarchtal* the church projects at right-angles from one wing of the conventual buildings and is exposed to view on almost all sides. (2) The façade is imposing, the towers bound closely to the nave (compare *St Gallen*, *St Florian*, *Melk* and contrast *Passau Cathedral*, *Weingarten*, *Ottobeuren*, *Munich Theatinerkirche*), their shapely, tapering spires contrasting strikingly with the dome. Two points of criticism suggest themselves: (*a*) the plinth course immediately above the lower cornice is somewhat high and threatens the unity of the design; (*b*) the central window is both weak and too low and has to be 'hitched up' by the moulding and vase above it into a dominance it does not possess. (3) The dome makes a curiously double impression. In a way it harmonizes well with the whole composition, and yet it is in itself very squat and seems ready to sink into the body of the church (this insignificance is further emphasized by the lively turret over the choir). It seems to have, and yet not to have, a drum which appears only in the angles. The bulky transepts also reduce the dome's effect. *Interior:* (1) The general impression is somewhat austere, even bleak, owing to the sparseness of the decoration and the lack of colour. Particularly unsatisfactory is the treatment of the ceiling of nave and transepts; it appears as a cross-rib vault of which the ribs have not quite succeeded in meeting, an oddness emphasized by the lack of any decoration. If we stand under the dome and look back the bleakness of the nave is increased by the gaping arch under the organ gallery. (2) Unusual are the nave arcades with their intervening sections of wall, notably good the firmness and fineness of line in the aisles. (3) The narrow, pronounced but rather hard cornice exercises the usual double function of 'centralizing' and leading the eye towards the high altar. (4) The high altar is fine, its colouring in striking contrast to the surroundings, its crowning group of the Assumption of the Virgin, awaited in heaven by the Trinity, very fine, even if the almost inevitable comparison with *Rohr* is unfair. (5) Two other altars are of beauty; that in the Marienkapelle, and that of St Boniface in the crypt under the monks' choir (the reliefs—by *Johann Neudecker, c.* 1708—of the Saint's martyrdom and, in the antependium, of his resurrection, the finest works in the church). No Englishman, above all no Devonian (or Creditonian!) should omit to pay his respects at the tomb of this great Saint.

Banz, 1710–19 (18 m. N.N.E. Bamberg, 10 m. S. Coburg; rail connection to Lichtenfels—3 m.—or Staffelstein, $2\frac{1}{2}$ m., whence bus). Architect *Johann Dientzenhofer*, the architect of Fulda. Originally a Cluniac foundation (late eleventh century), 1803 secularized, 1814 ducal residence, 1920–5 Trappist, since 1933 a training college for priests working among German Catholics outside Germany. A wall-pillar church with 2-bay nave, considerably narrower and lower choir (with upper monks' choir behind), no transept, and twin-towered façade. Stands in magnificent position across the wide upper Main valley from *Vierzehnheiligen*, crowning the summit of a wooded ridge 550 ft. above the river.

Noteworthy features. Exterior: (1) In general appearance a less dramatic version of *Melk* with which it shares certain characteristics, notably a dominant and embattled aspect, as of a safe stronghold, a church founded upon a rock. (2) The façade is massive yet rhythmical, the projecting central section adding to the impression of verticality by its prominent pairs of pilasters and the raised pitch of its lower window. (3) Interesting is the manner of transition from nave to choir (seen from the terrace which, also because of its glorious view, should on no account be missed). *Interior:* Of great vitality, majesty and colourfulness. (1) Here the true rhythmical Dientzenhofer-Guarini spirit is evident on all sides. Apart from those of floor and pews there is hardly a straight line anywhere. Walls, cornices, galleries, ceilings—all have bent themselves to the shaping will of the designer (plate 33). (2) Most remarkable is the construction of the vault. The heavy transverse arches dividing the compartments of the vault take a double direction, vertically upwards and also divergently from one another, so that remarkable illusions arise as we proceed from the back of the church towards the altar and see them sometimes quite flat, sometimes deeply pointed. The reason is that we have here a nave rectangular on plan covered with a type of vault normally used for round or oval churches. (3) The three frescoes (fine works by *Melchior Steidl*) depict (from E. to W. in thematic interconnection) the Last Supper (plate 40), the Descent of the Holy Ghost, the Conversion of St Paul. (4) The high altar and that of the upper choir form a double composition to be viewed as such. (5) The visitor should not miss the fine choir stalls in the upper choir with remarkable inlaid panels (ebony, ivory, mother-of-pearl, silver) portraying scenes from the life of St Benedict.

Schöntal, 1708–36 (9 m. S.W. Bad Mergentheim, W. of road to Schwäbisch Hall; stations Mergentheim or Mockmühl, whence bus connection). Originally Cistercian abbey (since 1802 parish) church. The architect was *Johann Leonhard Dientzenhofer* who, however, died before building began. His successor who continued his plans, *Jakob Ströhlein*, also died shortly after and the building was carried to its completion by *Bernhard Schiesser*. It is included in this section for completeness and because it is of some note and interest, and not because it is in any way a characteristic Dientzenhofer church. A 'hall-church' standing on an almost unaltered medieval ground plan with 4-bay nave, 3-bay choir with narrower sanctuary, slight transeptal formation with domed crossing over and twin-towered W. façade.

Noteworthy features. Exterior: (1) The three-storey façade crowned by gable and towers is flat, simple in design, Italian in feeling, the pilaster design differing in the three storeys (Doric below, Ionic in the middle, Corinthian above, according to the accepted scheme). The towers give the impression of standing on the façade and not on the ground. It is possible to feel that the façade as a whole is not weighty enough for the length and bulk of the body of the church as a whole. (2) The gable-crowned transepts recall the Vorarlberg design, but their turrets are unusual. (3) The exterior gives no hint of the developed internal dome that we shall find over the crossing. *Interior:* (1) The soaring proportions and the lightness are impressive. Gothic feeling is strong in this hall-church with its slender pillars and absence of side galleries. (2) The stucco decoration (*Johannes Bauer*) is remarkable in more than one way, (*a*) in covering the entire pillars as well as the ceiling and other parts, (*b*) in differing notably in design as between pillars and ceiling (the more geometrical motifs on the pillars perhaps intended to give an added impression of strength). (3) The dome over the crossing is of surprising depth when we reflect that it is contained entirely within the roof. (4) The high altar (*c.* 1730, probably by *Christian Meyer*, painting of Assumption 1680 by *Oswald Onghers*) shows the thematic connection between the painting and the statuary group above (Christ looking down to welcome his Mother) that we find e.g. at *Diessen, Fürstenfeldbruck, Schäftlarn* and elsewhere.

Note on Dientzenhofer churches in Czecho-Slovakia

Czecho-Slovakia and its beautiful capital are at the moment, alas, somewhat inaccessible to the ordinary traveller from the West and, it seems, likely to remain so for the present. In the hope that conditions will become easier in time, the reader's attention is directed in this provisional manner to the chief churches built there by the Dientzenhofers.

CHRISTOPH DIENTZENHOFER

Woborischt (Obořiště) S.W. Prague (Praha). Monastery church, planned 1695, built 1702–12.

Prague-Kleinseite, St Niklas (Praha Malá Strana, Sv. Mikuláš), 1703–11. The greatest Baroque church in the city with all the characteristic rhythm in the interior, dominant dome on high drum and fine tower. Completed by *Kilian Ignaz Dientzenhofer* 1737–52.

Prague-Breunau, St Margarethen (Praha-Břevnov, Sv Markéta), 1710–15. Monastery church.

KILIAN IGNAZ DIENTZENHOFER

Prague-Alstadt (Praha Staré Město), *St Nikolaus* (Sv Mikuláš), 1732–7.

Karlsbad, St Magdalenen (Karlový Vary, Sv Majdaléna), begun 1732.

The following churches show interesting variations on the oval ground-plan:

Ruppersdorf (Ruprechtice), *Wiesen* (Všeňov), *Schonau* (Teplice-Šanov)—all near Braunau (Broumov); *Wodolka* (Odolená Voda, N. of Prague); *Gutwasser* (Dobrá Voda) near Budweis (České Budějoviče); in *Prague* itself, St Johann-am-Felsen (Sv. Jan na Skalce).

Balthasar Neumann

There can be little doubt that *Balthasar Neumann* was the greatest of the South German Baroque architects. A generation younger than Fischer von Erlach and Caspar Moosbrugger he was the contemporary of J. M. Fischer, the Zimmermanns and the Asams, but of these only Fischer von Erlach is his equal in scope and power. We have already noted the many-sidedness of his early training. He grew to be at home equally in secular, ecclesiastical and indeed military architecture, in mathematics and engineering, in casting bells and designing fountains. When we pass his works in review we find an astonishing range and mastery—the mighty Residence at Würzburg, the palaces of Brühl and Werneck, the abbey church at Neresheim, the pilgrimage church of Vierzehnheiligen, the many patrician houses (including his own in Würzburg destroyed in 1945), not to mention many other considerable and countless smaller works. He was a creator on the grand, compelling scale, who combined greatness of conception with delicacy of treatment, inventiveness with productive energy.

When considering Neumann's work there are one or two important points that we have to remember. Like J. M. Fischer, and unlike the Asams and the Zimmermanns, he was a pure architect. His primary concern was the solution of architectural, not of decorative, problems. The chief of these in connection with church architecture he, like others, saw in the blending of longitudinal axis with a central space; and each of the churches with which we shall here be concerned represents a stage towards the final solution that he reached at *Neresheim*. Neumann's, however, was a livelier, more restless and imaginative spirit than Fischer's and this difference shows itself clearly in his interiors; we need only compare *Vierzehnheiligen* with Fischer's contemporary interior at *Ottobeuren*. A second point is his good fortune in finding, as few artists have succeeded in doing, enthusiastic patronage to support him and rich opportunity for the use and development of his talents. We cannot mention his name without linking to it that of the Schönborn family, two members of which, great and knowledgeable patrons of the arts, were successively bishops of Würzburg during the greater part of his activity there and lent him, and received from him, princely support.

The secular works are not our concern here. Of the churches we shall not include *St Paulinus* in Trier, outside our area, nor such lesser works as the parish church at *Wiesentheid* (Steigerwald, N.E. of Bad Kitzingen) and the *Kreuzkapelle* at *Etwashausen* (suburb of Bad Kitzingen). The earliest of his major churches we can no longer visit (the abbey church at *Münsterschwarzach*) for it was pulled down between 1821 and 1827 in the backwash of the secularization movement. His work is represented here by the four major churches of *Gössweinstein*, *Vierzehnheiligen*, the *Würzburg Käppele* and *Neresheim*, also *Heusenstamm* and the *Hofkirche* in the *Würzburg Residenz*.

Gössweinstein, 1730–9 (15 m. S.W. of Bayreuth, 23 m. S.E. of Bamberg; from both rail and bus connections). Pilgrimage (also, since fifteenth-century parish) church; picturesquely set in a little old town of steep streets and houses clustering round the castle that perches on its crag high above the gorge of the river Wiesent and looks out over the romantic scenery of the 'Fränkische Schweiz' ('Franconian Switzerland'). A wall-pillar church with 2-bay nave, slightly projecting transepts, apsidal choir and twin-towered façade.

Noteworthy features. Exterior: Little comment is needed. The design is clear, firm and dignified; the decoration is economical and confined to the good, compact façade whose approaching steps give a welcome touch of the picturesque. *Interior:* (1) The ground-plan is an interesting, simpler anticipation of *Vierzehnheiligen* and should be compared. (2) The dominant high altar is interesting and beautiful; note here (*a*) the three approaching steps and the 3-tier construction of the altar itself (we recall that the dedication of the church is to the Holy Trinity); (*b*) the golden globe, a motif perhaps taken from the globe-shaped tabernacle at *Waldsassen* (q.v.); (*c*) the fine statuary, especially the angels; (*d*) the symbolic curtain or backcloth being drawn aside by angels and putti. (3) All the stucco ornament (*Franz Josef Vogel*) is of excellent, delicate quality. (4) The pulpit (*J. M. Küchel*) is good and richly symbolic with the four Evangelists half sitting, half hovering, writing their gospels and (above) a spring (the 'water of life') welling up from beneath the globe. (5) Looking back from the crossing we see the beautiful composition of the west end with its swinging organ gallery and elegant grouping of the pipes round the window.

Würzburg, Hofkirche, 1732–?8 (in the S.W. corner of the Residenz). A small, interesting, brilliantly rhythmical Borrominesque interior of which the straight lines of the wing of the Residenz that conceals it give no hint.

Noteworthy features. Interior: (1) The spatial character of the interior is determined by the placing of the columns in such a way that rhythm is everywhere introduced. Central on plan is a longitudinal, flat-sided oval to which is added at each end an ellipse, that at the E. being the deeper. (2) The longitudinal axis and the impression of length are strongly emphasized by the eastward thrust of the gallery in a curve above the high altar (contrast the W. gallery). This lengthways thrust, however, is in turn checked by the strongly vertical and centralizing effect of the two massive side altars. (3) The difficulties arising from the fact that the chapel is lit from two sides only are ingeniously overcome by the oblique construction of the windows. (4) The marble facings have a solemn magnificence of colour (red, purple, gold, grey, black) that recalls Viennese Baroque and it is not with surprise that we find that indeed *Lukas von Hildebrandt* co-operated in designing the interior decorations. (5) The once brilliant frescoes by *Rudolf Byss* are, as a result of war damage, considerably impaired; all the more do we appreciate the splendid side altar paintings by *Tiepolo* (1752; left, the casting out of the fallen angels, right, the Assumption). (6) The 2-storey high altar with stucco representation of the familiar composite theme of Assumption below and Holy Trinity above is a fine work deserving of attention. (7) Of the other statuary, the figures flanking the high altar should be noted, also the delightful putto atop the sounding-board of the classicistic pulpit (by *Materno Bossi*) wearing papal tiara and carrying keys.

(Though the *Residenz* itself is a secular building and though Neumann was joined by others, including Hildebrandt, in its planning, his was the chief share and no account of his work can omit reference to it. Once perhaps the greatest Baroque palace in Germany, it was burnt out on the night of 16 March 1945—the central section, mercifully enough, being saved. This the visitor is urged to see, for it contains the great staircase with *Tiepolo's* vast and wonderful fresco (Apollo, the Sun-God, and the Olympic deities surrounded by great groups representing the four continents): also the beautiful 'Gartensaal' with vivid and powerful frescoes by *Johannes Zick*.

Heusenstamm, 1739–41 (6m. S.E. Frankfurt-am-Main whence rail and bus connections). Parish church, originally built as a place of burial for a branch of the Schönborn family. It has a 2-bay nave without aisles or wall-pillars, shallow apsidal transepts, apsidal sanctuary and single built-in W. tower.

Noteworthy features. Exterior: façade and tower form together a satisfying composition, the transition from the one to the other happily effected by the flanking volutes, the whole compact and soaring with the prominent cornice and the two vases affording the requisite horizontal counter-emphasis.

Interior: (1) the four prominent columns, placed as they are, stress the effect of (a) centrality, (b) a 'crossing' (cf. on a vaster scale the four pairs of columns at *Neresheim*. (2) Decorations and furnishings are concerned with the double theme of resurrection and redemption. The three frescoes (*Thomas Scheffler* of Augsburg, colours rather smoky) show the raising of Lazarus (nave), the Resurrection (crossing) and the Adoration of the Lamb (sanctuary); the delicate and beautiful high altar (*Johann Wolfgang von der Auwera*) has the Crucifixion between glorifying angels. (3) The rhythmical, beautiful pulpit also deserves attention.

Vierzehnheiligen, 1744–72 (Main valley opposite *Banz*, q.v.). Pilgrimage church (pilgrimage since mid-fifteenth century) on site of vision of the fourteen 'Nothelfer' (='Helpers in need').[1]

[1] Technically known as 'Auxiliary Saints'.

Its building history is marred by unedifying conflicts between rival prelates, the bishop of Bamberg, and the abbot of Langheim, in respect of the choice of an architect, Neumann being the bishop's choice. The bishop won, and Neumann began work, only to find that the rivals had previously made a start with foundations so far up the hill-side that his own plan to give the scene of the vision of the fourteen saints the place of honour under the crossing was rendered impossible. Thus the present complicated ground-plan represents less Neumann's free fancifulness than a highly sophisticated attempt to rescue the situation and give the venerated spot a position of apparently central importance. The church as we have it almost defies analysis; externally a basilica with 3-bay nave, developed apsidal transepts, apsidal choir and twin-towered W. façade, its clear, almost severe exterior seems to bear little relation to the fantastic interior. It is one of the most celebrated of all these churches and in certain ways rightly so. Yet, as with *Die Wies*, I feel it has been over-praised and find myself making reservations. To me the tension between exterior and interior (always present in a Baroque church) is too little resolved; the interior, again, however technically brilliant in design, is artificial, even dislocated, in its spatial relationships compared with the unforced and fluid harmony of *Neresheim*. But these are purely personal reactions!

Noteworthy features. Exterior (plate 18): (1) Design and proportions more grandiose and festive than at *Gössweinstein;* beautiful the golden glow of the stone in an evening sun. (2) Noble though the façade is, the great number of windows is a little restless, and the upper storeys of the towers, for all their beautiful helms, perhaps slightly over-heavy. *Interior:* (1) The general effect fanciful, fairylike even, the light-effects perhaps here and there somewhat detrimental to the architectural impression. The contrast to the exterior so great that it is hard to realize that both are aspects of one and the same building. (2) The focal point of the interior is the nave altar (the so-called 'Gnadenaltar') erected over the spot where the vision was seen and, in Neumann's plan, destined to stand under the crossing, had it not been for the wicked rival. It is a work of *Jakob Michael Küchel* and one of the strangest and most brilliantly fantastic creations of late Baroque, its baldachin oddly recalling a state-coach, its statuary (by *Johann Michael Feichtmayr* and *Johann Georg Übelherr*) of the first quality. As we stand by it and look around and upwards we can see some of the devices employed by Neumann to give it an apparently central position in the church. The oval in which it stands is much larger than the others in the ground-plan and is emphasized by the manner in which the pilasters are placed, by the galleries and by the large fresco overhead. From this point, too, we can experience well the optical and rhythmical peculiarities of this fantastic interior—light playing, vistas opening, curves rocking and dancing, all in infinite flux and variation and all changing with the changing of the light. (3) Next to the nave altar the pulpit is the most remarkable object in the church, so full of wild, symbolic movement (the breath of divine inspiration, cf. *Die Wies* and others) that it seems about to fly away; note (*a*) on the sounding-board (if we can so call it) seven ray-clusters darting out of the sun representing the seven gifts of the Holy Ghost who hovers as a dove below, (*b*) the fine reliefs of the Evangelists on the side, (*c*) at the corners, the heads of putti representing the four continents. (4) The paintings are unequal and unsatisfactory: the frescoes either largely restored this century or modern (e.g. the weak one by *A. Palme*, 1867, under the organ gallery); the altar paintings largely by *Palme* and unworthy of the church.

Würzburg, Mariä Heimsuchung (commonly called '*Käppele*'), 1747–52 (across the river on the Nikolausberg). Pilgrimage church. That we can still visit this little church in its untouched beauty is a matter for gratitude. No doubt its isolated position saved it when the Allied air-raid of 16 March 1945 reduced Würzburg's ancient glory to ruins in twenty minutes. It commands a fine view and is approached by a prolonged and impressive eighteenth-century Way of the Cross with good statuary groups, up many flights of steps. The church (without the large side chapel) is of cruciform plan with three apsidal arms, domed roofs and three towers, one over the crossing and two flanking the façade.

Noteworthy features. Exterior: The comparison with *Gössweinstein* is interesting. There we have a tight compactness, a suppressed vitality, straight lines, sharp corners, little adornment, few windows. Here, freedom and graciousness, the three vivid towers beckoning an almost merry welcome; curved lines everywhere (roof, domes, towers) and bevelled corners. *Interior:* If the exterior of this church is beautiful, the interior equals it. Neumann was here supported by two great artists, *Matthäus Günther* and *Johann Michael Feichtmayr* who had once already collaborated in a single church (*Amorbach* in the Odenwald) and here produced an effect of high quality and great harmony. (1) Of *Günther's* fine frescoes (1752) that in the central saucer-dome (Glorification of the Virgin) should be specially noted. These frescoes were the first painted by him after his experience of *Tiepolo's* work in Würzburg (see p. 277). (2) The stucco work has the fanciful and feathery delicacy that is all *Feichtmayr's* own. (3) Finely rich and rhythmical are the lines of the organ gallery and organ case which together form an admirable W. end composition. (4) Not so satisfactory is their counterpart at the E. end, the late, classicistic high altar (1779) which, with its stiffly sober design and cool colouring, strikes the only alien note in the interior. (5) In the large, later side chapel ('Gnadenkapelle') by *Materno Bossi* (1778) the large late fresco (1781) by *M. Günther* should be noted.

Neresheim, 1745–92 (14 m. N.W. Dillingen whence rail, 10 m. S.W. Nördlingen whence bus). Abbey church (Augustinian foundation 1096, since 1106 Benedictine). Stands prominently above and to E. of the little town, the view of church and monastery impressive as we ascend the road. A visit here after *Vierzehnheiligen* is instructive, also poignant. Ideas traceable there are developed here with greater freedom and mastery.

On the other hand, Neumann himself died (1753) when the church was hardly above ground, and the carrying out of his designs (first by *Dominikus Wiedemann*, then and more importantly by *Johann Baptist Wiedemann*) was in some details defective. Yet from a general architectural point of view the Neresheim interior is one of the most notable achievements of late European Baroque. A type of wall-pillar church with 3-bay nave, narrower apsidal choir, transept externally prominent and square-ended, internally modified and segmental, and S.W. tower.

Noteworthy features. Exterior: There is little to detain us, the treatment in general is unimaginative. (1) The classicistic superstructure to the gable impairs an already unimpressive façade. (2) The tower (1618–20) was considered worthy of being retained from the earlier church. *Interior:* We are taken quite by surprise. The vast but heavy and featureless exterior gives hints of the plan and elevation of the interior but none of its graceful grandeur and perfection. Here the typical Baroque spatial problem finds another harmonious solution. A glance at the ground-plan will make it clear. There are in all seven ovals (with saucer domes above), two each in nave and choir, one in each transept and a larger central one forming rotunda and 'crossing'. Each is set in such a way that its axis emphasizes or retards a spatial movement. The large central oval and its transeptal ones are set longitudinally, thus stressing (individually) the length, (collectively) the breadth. The church, however, is long; the other four are therefore set transversely to retard the west–east movement and prevent the effect of the rotunda being impaired. In the church itself we see the scheme clearly only when we look up at vault sections. As a further centralizing influence may be noted the columns of the crossing, doubled, far detached from the wall, set obliquely at decisive points. Note further (1) the movement imparted by the rhythmical cornice as it swings from bay to bay (2) the splendid W. end composition of windows and organ (cf. closely *Weingarten*); (3) the wonderful frescoes (the masterpieces of *Martin*

Knoller) depicting scenes from the life of Christ showing all the loosening-up and lightening of composition characteristic of the late Baroque (e.g. in that of the risen Christ over the choir (plate 42), or that over the organ); (4) the various signs in the church that funds ran short—the almost complete lack of stucco decoration (what there is is sparse and undistinguished, 1779–92), the poverty of all the furnishings, the fact (easily detectable) that columns and saucer domes alike are of *wood* plastered over.

The Vorarlberg School

In the Austrian district of Vorarlberg, the western prolongation of Tyrol to the shore of the Lake of Constance, especially in the area of the Bregenzer Wald (Forest of Bregenz) lived five or six families who during our period produced notable and important architects. They were largely intermarried and on many occasions we find members of several families co-operating in the same building. The work of these architects shows certain fundamental similarities, and they have come to be thought of as forming a school. The chief of these families, as has already been pointed out, were those of the *Moosbruggers*, the *Beers* and the *Thumbs*; and it is with them and with their most distinguished members that we shall concern ourselves in this section. It is in a way paradoxical that their activities lay entirely outside their own home district, which in itself is poor in architecture of the period. They worked chiefly in S. Germany, but they also form an important link with the architecture of Switzerland where they built what are in fact the greatest churches of the period in that country.

It is sometimes said that the similarities in the work of these architects, which concern primarily matters of ground-plan and elevation, were due to their having been influenced less by Italian than by native tradition. This is an inexact way of putting the point, for ultimately all Baroque church architecture goes back to Italian inspiration; and indeed one design or tradition that found considerable favour in S. Germany and Austria, that of the round church, they ignore. It would be more accurate to say that there are two traditions in which they showed little or no interest, the Italian 'basilical' form (as we see it represented in the cathedral at Salzburg (plate 10) or the *Theatinerkirche* at Munich (plate 1), which in any case never found great favour in German lands at this time; and, as just mentioned, the 'round church' form (also ultimately Italian). At *Weingarten* (plate 12), where they came nearest to the basilical type, direct Italian influence (*Frisoni*) was at work on the church; and there are only two examples of a Vorarlberg church approximating to the centralized design, *St Katherinenthal* and (certainly very striking) *Bernhardszell*, both in N. Switzerland. Their own inspiration was derived rather from one Germanized form of an Italian design—that of the *Gesù* as we find it modified in the Jesuit churches on German soil (*St Michael, Munich; Dillingen*).

The characteristics of the Vorarlberg plan, though individual variations are found and hard-and-fast rules cannot be given, are broadly the following: (1) A Vorarlberg church is pronouncedly longitudinal in axis, though the question of a central space (transepts, crossing) is not ignored. (2) Internally it is a wall-pillar church, the pillars sometimes projecting deeply inwards (the exceptional character of *Birnau* will be dealt with below). (3) Its 'aisles' (in fact, however, even where the wall-pillars are pierced by openings, one can scarcely call them aisles) are all of the same height as the nave; in other words, the German tradition of the 'hall church' (Hallenkirche, the Gothic type with nave and aisles of the same height) reappears here. (4) The main arches are carried up to the height of the vault. (5) Galleries, the position and design of which varies, span across the arches at about half their height and often have an important optical function. The special cases of *Birnau* and *St Gallen* receive attention below. (6) There are slight transeptal projections, sometimes square-ended and gable-crowned, sometimes convex or of apsidal type, and the choir is slightly narrower than the nave. (7) The

119

architectural element predominates and decoration is subordinated to it (*Birnau* again an exception). (8) A twin-towered façade is usual, though by no means universal.

Of these three Vorarlberg families the most important architect members were *Caspar Moosbrugger*, lay brother of Einsiedeln abbey, and the greatest figure; *Michael Beer* and his more famous son *Franz*; *Michael Thumb* and his more famous son *Peter*. We shall now deal with their chief works on German soil, bearing in mind that we shall meet them again in Switzerland and make reference back to what has been said about them here.

Caspar Moosbrugger

Weingarten, 1714–24 (12 m. N.E. Friedrichshafen, Lake of Constance; 3 m. N.E. Ravensburg; rail connections from Friedrichshafen to Ravensburg, whence by tram). Abbey and pilgrimage church (monastic foundation 940, Benedictine 1056). Church and abbey in commanding position on rising ground overlooking the little town and the wide valley of the Schussen; the full plan for the abbey buildings which, as they stand, are incomplete on the south, was never carried out. The vast and imposing church is of wall-pillar type with 3-bay nave, shallowed apsidal transepts, 2-bay choir with apsidal sanctuary and twin-towered façade. In considering it we must bear in mind that, in addition to Moosbrugger, an Italian (*Donato Giuseppe Frisoni*) made important contributions (the upper part of the façade with towers, the dome).

Noteworthy features. Exterior (plate 12): The general effect is consolidated and majestic, self-assured and finely proportioned. (1) The façade with its low towers and its protruding convex central section has such similarities with the *Kollegienkirche* in *Salzburg* (plate 7) that the latter's influence can hardly be doubted (cf. also *Einsiedeln*, plate 13).[1] (2) The dome with its drum and lantern form a fine composition; compare and con-

---

[1] Indeed the Abbot under whom the church was built, *Sebastian Hyller* (1697–1730), had been professor at, and Rector of, Salzburg University.

trast others (e.g. *Munich Theatinerkirche*, *Salzburg Kollegien-kirche*, *Melk* (plates 1, 7, 6). (3) Considering the cruciform ground-plan and the apses so reminiscent of *Salzburg Cathedral*, the absence of any basilical character is all the more noteworthy; nave and choir walls show no suggestion of side-aisles (contrast in different ways *Ottobeuren*, *Vierzehnheiligen*, *Munich Theatinerkirche*, *St Florian*). *Interior:* The proportions are monumental and admirable. (1) Though the decoration is rich, the architecture predominates throughout. (2) The massive wall-pillars, owing to their being pierced with openings at ground and at gallery level, almost give the impression of being detached (for other aspects of this development compare the Swiss churches of *Rheinau*, *St Urban* and *St Gallen*). This impression is also increased by the concave form of the balconies which, in general, adds to the apparent width of the nave. (3) The dome rests firmly and unmistakably on its cornice and the four crossing arches (contrast *Melk*). (4) The W. end composition of organ, windows and vault is very noble (cf. *Neresheim*) and in a golden evening light of great beauty. (5) The ornamentation is concentrated in the upper regions of the church to the great emphasis of the architectural lines. (6) The fine and discreet stucco work (*Franz Xaver Schmutzer*, 1718), though contemporary, may strike us as a shade too light for the massive proportions; but we have to remember that the actual *planning* of the church began in 1684, though the building started later. (7) The frescoes are great works by *Cosmas Damian Asam* (themes: in the dome, the Church Triumphant, an endless assembly of angels and saints adoring the Trinity; over the nave, St Benedict in ecstasy surrounded by angels and saints and princes; over the choir the coming of the Holy Ghost—this one less satisfactory owing to the unconvincing heaviness of the illusory architecture). (8) The organ (*Josef Gabler*, 1737–50) is one of the greatest representatives of its period in Germany and, despite renovations and mechanical improvements, retains its Baroque quality of tone. (9) The fine choir stalls by the then 24-year-old *Josef*

Anton Feuchtmayer and the sanctuary metal screen of remarkable perspectival design (artist unknown) should be noted. (10) On the pulpit (*Fidel Sporer*, 1762–5) we find two symbolic angels, one supporting it, the other drawing aside the curtain; also the attributes of the Evangelists.

Michael Thumb

We illustrate the work of the elder Thumb by three churches, none of them of the first importance, but all beautiful and of interest as stages in, and aspects of, the work of this school.

Wettenhausen, 1670–87 (7 m. S.E. Günzburg, whence bus connection). Abbey church (Augustinian foundation eleventh century, now Dominican nuns). An interesting early example of the Vorarlberg design. The walls of the late Gothic choir and tower of the previous building were incorporated.

Noteworthy features. Exterior: Owing to the display of 'onion' domes, the church and convent buildings present a striking, almost oriental sight from the S.E. (1) The earlier choir with its external buttresses is easily recognized but harmonizes well. (2) The characteristic shallow 'transept' (cf. *Obermarchtal, Irsee, Schönenberg*, etc.) is here set unusually far W., no doubt because of the presence of the earlier tower. *Interior:* (1) Divergences from the later, fully developed Vorarlberg type are: (*a*) the lack of real wall-pillars, though the deep, dominant pilasters have an almost equivalent optical effect; (*b*) the absence of galleries. (2) The stucco ornament on the ceiling, though not so rich, compares interestingly with that at *Holzen* and *Speinshart*; the small fresco panels are characteristic for the early date.

Obermarchtal, 1686–92 (on the Danube 23 m. upstream from Ulm whence rail connection to Untermarchtal 1½ m. distant). Premonstratensian foundation 1171, since early nineteenth-century secularization parish church. Wall-pillar church with entrance bay and 3-bay nave, slightly projecting transeptal bay, 3-bay choir and sanctuary internally apsidal but externally rectangular flanked by twin towers. Prototype of

the developed Vorarlberg church scheme and as such historically important. On an imposing elevated site above the river.
Noteworthy features. Exterior: Plain, yet dignified. Note
(*a*) the transept with dwarf gable; (*b*) the unusual position of
the towers flanking the extreme E. end (as at *St Gallen*);
(*c*) the 'exposed' position of the church as a whole projecting
from (not enclosed by, or flanking) the monastic buildings
(parallels at *Ottobeuren* and *Fulda*). *Interior:* (1) The effects of
lighting and colour are uncomplicated but very fine. There are
no frescoes but the simple interplay of light and shade finds
an effective counterpart in the interplay of the two dominant
colours, the white of the walls and the brown of altars and
furnishings. (2) Two characteristic elements of the Vorarlberg
type are here conspicuously present for the first time—the
deep wall-pillars and the galleries between them. Note how
the setting back of the galleries in the central side chapels increases their transeptal character. (3) The entablature of the
pillars is treated in such a way as to suggest that they are detached from the wall (cf. *Rheinau*). (4) The altars, all but two,
are contemporary, the high altar framed in a vast niche of
symbolic shell pattern. The two later ones are by *Franz Xaver
Schmutzer* (1759). (5) The stucco ornament on the ceiling is so
designed that the absence of frescoes is hardly felt; contrast in
this respect the slightly later *Fulda Cathedral.*

Grafrath, 1686–94 (6 m. S.W. Fürstenfeldbruck, whence, as
from Munich and other points, rail and bus connections). Pilgrimage church (pilgrimage probably since fourteenth century). Wall-pillar church with 3-bay nave, narrower apsidal
choir, slight transeptal side chapels and bell turret.
Noteworthy features. Exterior: (1) The church appears to have
double transepts but the E. projections house sacristy and
another general purposes room. (2) The treatment of E. wall
('half-onion' roof abutting against a gable) is similar to that at
Donauwörth Heiligkreuz but less elaborate. (3) The turret (a
meagre reconstruction of 1817 after lightning damage) was
originally octagonal and fuller. *Interior:* A typical pilgrimage

church in which space was the first consideration; galleries would have been out of place, deep wall pillars obtrusive. (1) Frescoes are by *J. G. Bergmüller* (cf. *Diessen*), stucco ornament by *J. G. Übelherr*, *F. X.* and *J. M. Feichtmayr* (cf. again *Diessen*). (2) The four side altars are unimportant but the high altar (*Johann Baptist Straub*) is the best work in the church; the upper part, embodying in a glass coffin the bejewelled remains of St Rasso (Count Rasso = Graf Rath), shows a symbolic representation of the saint's way to heaven on the clouds.

Peter Thumb

Here we shall confine our attention to one church of the finest quality; but we shall meet the architect again at *St Gallen* and as collaborator in other great Swiss churches (e.g. *St Urban* and *Rheinau*).

Birnau, 1746–50 (N. bank of Lake Constance, on the road between Meersburg and Überlingen, from both of which frequent bus connections). Pilgrimage church and Cistercian priory in beautiful position facing out over the lake and away to the mountains, with the Säntis prominent in the middle distance and the Scesaplana farther to the E. The pilgrimage dates from the early fifteenth century but was moved to this site by the monks of Salem abbey who served the pilgrims and wished to have their church on their own land—thereby foiling the town of Überlingen that had previously drawn profit from a rowdy inn at the old site.

Noteworthy features. Exterior: Of unusual beauty and harmony, the blending of church, tower and clergy house surely happier than in the similar case of *Die Wies*. (1) In the façade, the dropping of the roof level on each side of the tower both helps the latter to soar more freely and stresses symbolically the distinction between the secular wings and the sacred body of the building. (2) The graceful tower, full of character yet unobtrusive in the landscape, is a notable achievement for an architect of a school that favoured twin towers. (3) The treatment of the body of the church is very fine and full of subtle points—the shaping of the roof, the placing of pilasters, the arching of the cornice over the windows to secure the required effect at crucial places. *Interior:* (1) In lightness and delicacy this interior recalls the Zimmermann churches, going beyond them, indeed, in its blending of architecture and decoration. (2) In a number of respects the church departs from the usual Vorarlberg scheme—in the general subordination of architecture to decoration, in the absence of wall-pillars (these being replaced by pilasters of no depth), and in the continuation of the gallery right round the church. The architect's next (and last) church (*St Gallen*) shows the exact opposite—architecture prominent, pillars also, and no gallery at all. (3) The positions, shapes and colouring of all four eastern side altars in their relations to the high altar should be carefully noted. (4) Of the fine stucco ornamentation and statuary (*Josef Anton Feuchtmayer*) the following deserve special attention: the four figures flanking the high altar (Joachim and Anna, Zacharias and Elizabeth), the two female figures showing the artist's characteristic realism at its most drastic, though it is noticeable in most of his work (plate 49); the putti everywhere, above all the deservedly celebrated figure of the 'Honigschlecker' (honeylicker) on St Bernhard's altar right of the choir arch (plate 64), and his counterpart on the left; and together with these (by the same artist) the four remaining groups of the original carved Stations of the Cross (plate 57). (5) The frescoes (*Gottfried Bernhard Götz*) are of great depth and delicacy of colouring on the favourite Baroque theme of Mary as intercessor and mediator yet, as they now are, lack the brilliance that this interior demands (and as those at Regensburg have, see p. 159); symbolically interesting are the female figures of the Virtues in the choir painting—Love (with a heart), Charity (with mirror), Faith (with cross and chalice), Hope (with anchor) and Fear (with a hare).

Michael Beer

Of the ancestor of the Beer family we shall mention one work only, and that less for its own beauty than for its importance as perhaps the earliest church in S. Germany really to reflect the Baroque spirit. It represents at the same time an interesting link between the Vorarlberg architects and those of the next group that we shall deal with.

Kempten, St Lorenz, 1652–66 (S.W. corner of Bavaria, mid-way between Memmingen and Oberstdorf, on the main Munich-Lindau line; rail and bus connections from many quarters). Until 1802 church of Benedictine Abbey (foundation 752) which became one of the most privileged in Germany; now parish church. Though the design was by *Beer* the carrying out of it was continued after 1654 by *Giovanni Serro* of Roveredo in Graubünden, Beer having for unknown reasons left Kempten. Externally the presence of the dome suggests an attempt to deal with the characteristic Baroque spatial problem. The basilical form and the general austerity of treatment suggest Italian influence. The *interior,* however, is not convincing architecturally. The domed section (choir) has not the expected centralizing function and seems even to form a separate church on its own. Either the problem has not been grasped, or if grasped not tackled. There is evidence, too, that Serro lacked Beer's generosity of treatment (e.g. dome interior). Note further: (1) the characteristically small early frescoes (*Andreas Asper* of Constance, 1660–5) and stiff but good stucco ornament. (2) The interesting scagliola (coloured polished stucco) patterns on pilasters and S. side altar in choir. (3) The attractive choir stalls (former position between choir pillars) with unusual inset landscape panels also of scagliola work. (4) The two very fine altars flanking choir arch, by *J. G. Übelherr* (*c.* 1760).

Franz Beer

The most productive and most talented member of the family. We shall come across his work again in Switzerland.

Holzen, 1696–1704 (between Augsburg and Donauwörth; from both, rail connection to Nordendorf station, thence 20 mins.

walk). Convent church (originally founded 1152 for Benedictine nuns, now in the hands of nuns of St Joseph's congregation). Wall-pillar church with high nave and lower apsidal
choir flanked by twin towers. In a prominent position overlooking the Schmutter valley.

Noteworthy features. Exterior: Only two points to remark, the
faint echo of Gothic in the design of the choir, and the position
of the towers (cf. *Zwiefalten, Benediktbeuern, Rot*). *Interior:*
(1) The eye is caught at once by the immensely rich stucco
ornament on the ceiling (Wessobrunn artist, unidentifiable
with certainty); the only parallel in S. Germany is at *Speinshart*. The artist of the characteristically small early frescoes is
also unknown (plate 38). (2) The wealth of ornament diverts
attention from the stately proportions of the building with the
deep wall-pillars and balconies characteristic of its type and
the massive cornice and entablature. The usual shallow transept, however, is lacking. (3) The rich altars have good statuary
and are iconographically interesting; the side altars with unusual carved wood antependia. (4) The pulpit has points of
interest; below, lion and lamb symbolize the qualities and task
of the preacher, while in the shell-shaped sounding-board we
see an attribute of St John the Baptist whose figure stands
above it. (5) The visitor should ask to see the organ loft and
nun's choir which together form an attractive chamber with
fine stalls. Thence also access to galleries with rewarding view
of interior as a whole and close-up view of stucco.

Irsee, 1699–1704 (S.W. Bavaria, $3\frac{1}{2}$ m. N.W. of Kaufbeuren,
20 m. N.E. of Kempten; nearest station Kaufbeuren, whence
also bus connection). Now parish church (Benedictine abbey
1183 to secularization 1803). Wall-pillar church with slightly
projecting transeptal chapels, apsidal choir and twin-towered
façade. Lies inconspicuously on the edge of the village in
wooded hill-country, the towers clearly designed as land-
marks.

Noteworthy features. Exterior: (1) A comparison alike with
Obermarchtal and with *Kempten* is of interest; the body of the

church strongly resembles the former, the façade in its simple monumentality seems to show the influence of the latter. (2) The towers are unusually slender and good for the period. *Interior:* (1) Many of the features of Obermarchtal reappear here—deep wall-pillars with heavy cornices and entablature; galleries, here too set back in the 'transepts'; stucco ornament following the architectural lines. (2) Here too we see the attempt (noticeable also in different forms at *Obermarchtal, Rheinau* and elsewhere) to give the pillars an appearance of independence from the wall; in this case the fluting and decoration sets them off against the plain wall. (3) The most interesting object in the church is the pulpit (1724–5, plate 23), modelled and rigged like a ship's bow and foremast with sail, figurehead (St Michael) and even rope-ladder up which putti are clambering, and, prominently, anchor! Other examples of this symbolic pulpit form are at *Altenerding* and *Niederding* (near Erding, N.E. of Munich, pp. 162, 167), the two latter by *Christian Jorhan* and some forty years later, and at *Traunkirchen* (Austria, W. shore of Traunsee,) 1753.

Donauwörth, Heiligkreuzkirche, 1717–22 (on the Danube, almost mid-way between Ulm and Ingolstadt; important railway junction, rail (also bus) connections from many points). Monastic and pilgrimage church (Benedictine foundation eleventh century, since 1935 served by priests of a missionary community). Stands imposingly above the river at the upper end of the town. Beer's design was actually carried out by the Wessobrunn artist-architect *Josef Schmutzer*. A fine wall-pillar church that deserves more attention than it has received.

Noteworthy features. Exterior: The treatment of the E. end is interesting; the sanctuary apse is so small that the surrounding E. wall has been embellished like a façade with gable and volutes (cf. *Grafrath*)*: Interior:* Massive, stately and admirably lit. (1) We are reminded of *Weingarten*, but on a smaller scale, both in general character and in certain details, e.g. the design of the pillars and the convex form of the galleries. (2) The altars are all distinguished and worth careful study, especially the high altar (*Franz Schmutzer*, painting by *J. G. Bergmüller*), a more important and dominant work than that at *Weingarten*. (3) The frescoes were destined for C. D. Asam but in the end carried out by a lesser talent, *Franz Karl Stauder*; that in the central saucer dome is a replacement of 1940–1 by *Franz Klemmer* of Munich.

Weissenau, 1717–24 (1½ m. S. Ravensburg; rail connections from there, Ulm and Friedrichshafen). Now parish church (originally Premonstratensian foundation 1145, dissolved 1802). The ascription to *Franz Beer* not absolutely certain, but on documentary as well as stylistic grounds probable. A large wall-pillar church with 6-bay nave, slight transeptal projection, long, narrower earlier apsidal choir (1628–31 by *Martino Barbieri*) and twin-towered façade.

Noteworthy features. Exterior: Not especially remarkable; the towers seem to have been conceived as forming a kind of link between the church and the monastic buildings in that they (like the monastic buildings, which were carried to completion only on the S. side) have no plinth whereas the central section of the façade has a high one. *Interior:* (1) The first impression is likely to be one of the lightness, spaciousness and grandeur of the nave; the second, one of a discrepancy between this and the lower, tunnel-like choir. This discrepancy is due to the excessively narrow choir arch (much narrower even than the already narrow choir), which is structurally hard to account for and undoubtedly disturbs the general effect. (2) The nave has typical Vorarlberg features, (*a*) the high arched openings through the wall-pillars forming 'aisles' at ground level (cf. the contemporary and neighbouring *Weingarten*; (*b*) the galleries, here, as also at *Rheinau*, set back from the pillar faces to increase the effect of breadth; (*c*) the slight transeptal formation with 'crossing' emphasized by the four red marble columns. (3) The excellent stucco ornament is by *Franz Schmutzer*. (4) The frescoes are not of the first quality. Those representing the Presentation in the Temple (nave, third bay) and the Annunciation (crossing) by *Karl Stauder* attempt perspectival illusion that is frustrated by the rich colouring (? over-painting). (5) The altars offer object lessons from many periods: high altar 1628 f.; Marienaltar, flanking choir arch on N., 1739 (Madonna and Child late fifteenth century from the older church); the Blutaltar, under the choir arch, 1783. (6) In the fine restrained choir stalls (1635, craftsman unknown) the spirit of the Renaissance lingers unmistakably on.

Rot-an-der-Rot, 1781–6 (7 m. W. Memmingen, whence bus connection). I conclude the chapter on the Vorarlberg School in S. Germany with this splendid church—not because its architect (a certain *Johannes Baptist Laub*, not otherwise known) was himself a member of that school but because in it the Vorarlberg scheme finds a last, late and noble expression. Indeed, one may say that the hundred years between *Obermarchtal* and *Rot* is the span of the history of Vorarlberg influence in S. Germany. Until 1803 a Premonstratensian abbey church (foundation 1126), since then parish church, though in 1947 Premonstratensian monks returned for a few years. A wall-pillar, galleried church of Vorarlberg type with 4-bay nave, broader bay of 'crossing' character containing choir, and narrower 2-bay apsidal sanctuary flanked by twin towers. Lies in a beautiful wooded valley with the Rot flowing close by.

Noteworthy features. Exterior: Of simple, noble proportions and warm ochre colouring, the gable-crowned apse and its flanking towers (for their position cf. *Zwiefalten, Irsee, Holzen*) together forming an attractive group which is further enhanced by the corner turrets to the wings of the conventual buildings. *Interior:* Its quiet beauty and majesty, as also its considerable dimensions, take one by surprise. Though late and restrained it is not cold, and it has a uniform good quality that is rare; there is hardly a blemish anywhere. (1) The squatness of the arches and the shallowness of flutings, mouldings, etc., all characteristic of the late date. (2) To retard the effect of length the attempt has been made (at the fifth bay) to introduce the impression of a 'crossing' by doubling the span of the bay and introducing massive corner piers with transverse arches enclosing circular saucer dome above (cf. *Zwiefalten*, *Diessen* and other examples). (3) The 'break-front' balustrades of the galleries introduce a welcome variation of line in place of the convex or concave curves of an earlier date. (4) The frescoes (1784, the finest works of *Januarius Zick*, son of *Johann Zick*) were painted in five months. Though full of life and colour, their quietness and subtlety are far removed from the ecstasy and turbulence of earlier decades. The characteristic Baroque sense of totality, of subordination of part to whole is gone, interest has reawakened in the individual figure, group, component part. This can be clearly felt both in the nave fresco of Christ teaching in the Temple (where the perspectival architecture above stands in no really convincing relationship to the groups below) and in the fine Assumption in the saucer dome over the choir (where the individual groups, though in varying degrees, are the centres of interest). *Zick* has here developed a clear stage beyond his frescoes at *Wiblingen* which, though only six years earlier, still retain the Baroque ardour and organic energy to a much greater degree. (5) Stucco ornament, altars and pulpit are all by *F. X. Feichtmayr the younger*; note the crescendo of the side altars in size and importance to lead the eye towards the high altar. (6) As a comparative lesson in styles the visitor should study the choir stalls and their superstructures. The stalls themselves are fine work of 1693—the organ cases above are 100 years later; yet they harmonize well. The reason is clear. Both are linked across the century by classicist feeling; in the stalls it lingers on from the Renaissance, in the organ cases (as also in that of the main organ) it has returned with classicism proper. (7) From the choir we should take a look back towards the W. and admire the fine, harmonious proportions of pier and arch and gallery.

Other interesting churches in S. Germany by Vorarlberg architects are the following: the pilgrimage church on the *Schönenberg* above Ellwangen (1682–95 by *Michael Thumb*, plate 14); the

Friedrichshafen Schlosskirche (1695–1700 by *Christian Thumb* with an excellent example of early Wessobrunn stucco ornamentation by *Johann, Franz* and *Joseph Schmutzer*); *Wald*, near Sigmaringen (1696–8 by *Joseph Beer* with brilliant later decoration 1751–65); and *St Peter* in the Black Forest, 10 m. E. Freiburg (1724–7 by *Peter Thumb* with good statuary by *Joseph Anton Feuchtmayer* and small early frescoes by *Franz Joseph Spiegler*, the master of *Zwiefalten*).

Italian and French Architects

The decisive early stimulus to the development of the architecture and art of our period alike in S. Germany, in Austria and in Switzerland came, as we have seen, from Italy. But whereas to Austria it was brought directly by Italians in the stricter sense, the bearers of it in S. Germany and Switzerland were members of the Italian population of the two southernmost Swiss cantons, Graubünden (Grisons) and Tessin (Ticino), particularly from the neighbourhood of Roveredo and San Vittore.

How far back this emigration of Italian-Swiss architects and artists into Germany and elsewhere goes is a difficult and obscure question and one that does not concern us here. The reasons were doubtless partly geographical, partly economic, partly of a more general human kind. The isolation and poverty of their home districts, we may suppose, prevented the exercise of that creative imagination which the very austerity of the scenery might have helped to develop.

In the early seventeenth century we find in S. Germany, and indeed in other parts also, members of a number of families, some with Germanized names, working and influential as architects. Two cases we have already mentioned—that of *Hans Alberthal* (in reality the Italian-Swiss *Giovanni Albertalli*) who began the *Jesuit Church* in Dillingen in 1610, and that of *Giovanni Serro* who in 1654 took over the supervision of *St Lorenz* in Kempten. In 1675 a church of a very different character was completed in Munich, the so-called *Theatinerkirche*, or *St Kajetan*. The designing and building of this church were carried out exclusively by two Italian-Swiss (*Enrico Zuccalli* and *Antonio Viscardi*), one Italian (*Agostino Barelli*) and one Frenchman (*François Cuvilliés*). It is indeed a purely Italian basilica, almost as pronouncedly so as its prototype, Solari's cathedral in Salzburg. As such it represents a quite different tradition to that of *St Michael* and the *Dillingen* church—a tradition which, as we saw when considering *Weingarten* and *Ottobeuren*, found only a modified echo here and there in South German church Baroque. Its existence, however, is significant, and we shall return to it again.

The fact seems to have been that the Thirty Years' War, though indeed it gave a stimulus to building, also impoverished Germany alike in new ideas and in native talent. The new ideas were coming from Italy and it was also Italian architects who gave them first expression in Germany, and continued to exercise important influence until well on in the eighteenth century.

The characteristic, essentially secular influence from France that led to a greater lightness, sensuousness and whimsicality above all in the decorative aspect of the Baroque, the development known as the Rococo, was not felt in S. Germany until about 1725. Here the important figure was *François Cuvilliés*, who was architectural supervisor to the electoral court from 1730 to 1753. It has more than once been pointed out that the Rococo, however greatly it flourished in the secular buildings of Europe, seems to have found the church doors in general shut against it. Not so, however, in Bavaria and in those adjoining parts of Austria and Switzerland that came under the influence of Bavarian art. By 1730 a new spirit is stirring in S. German churches, the spirit of *Steinhausen*, of *Diessen*, of *Schäftlarn*—which is also the spirit of Cuvilliés' Amalienburg (1734–9) in the gardens of Nymphenburg palace and of his exquisite little theatre in the Munich Residence (1751–3) which, though bombed and since rebuilt, displays such of the original ornament as was removed to safety.

We shall consider here the work of the Italians *Enrico Zuccalli*, *Antonio Viscardi*, *Antonio Petrini*, the *Barbieri* family and *Domenico Magzin*, and the Frenchmen *François Cuvilliés* and his son.

Enrico Zuccalli

We take two churches to illustrate his work, both essentially Italianate in character. Unlike Viscardi he seems to have maintained the Italian tradition with a certain stubbornness and to have had little interest in local spirit or native talent.

Munich, Theatinerkirche (St Kajetan), 1663–90. Built for Theatine monks by the Elector Ferdinand Maria as a thank-offering for the birth of a son and heir. As indicated above, the church was in fact the work of several hands. It was begun by *Agostino Barelli* on the model of S. Andrea della Valle in Rome, mother-church of the same order. The decisive influence, however, was that of *Zuccalli* who took over the supervision in 1667. The central section of the façade was the work of *Cuvilliés*. It is a basilica with 3-bay nave, transepts projecting in elevation but scarcely in ground-plan, full dome with drum and lantern over crossing, apsidal choir and twin-towered façade. In 1944 serious damage was done to choir, crossing and dome, and the church was not fully restored until 1956.

Noteworthy features. Exterior (plate 1): Majestic and striking. (1) The unusually expansive façade is remarkably dynamic considering that curved lines play almost no part in its structure. Compare and contrast the positions of towers to church with those of *Weingarten, Ottobeuren, Fulda, St Gallen* and the Italianate cathedral at *Passau*. Interesting and vivid are the tower-helms with their volutes (echoed in the dome lantern) and presumably influenced by S. Maria della Salute in Venice (1632–82). (2) The dome should be compared with those of *Ettal* and (possibly also the work of *Zuccalli*) *Weingarten*. *Interior:* Has suffered severely by damage and its original appearance is lost, but the fine proportions can still be appreciated. (1) The relation of arcade to clerestory shows the basilical design (contrast *Weingarten*). (2) The rich, heavy stucco ornamentation of *G. N. Perti* with its prevailing acanthus motif, but also putti and other designs, can still be studied in detail in the nave. Its strongly plastic character had important influence on the development of S. German stucco art. (3) The only considerable item of the former furnishings that survived the war is the pulpit (*Andreas Faistenberger*, 1686); high altar, choir stalls, organ and other important objects were all burnt or damaged in air-raids.

Ettal, 1710–26 (2½ m. S.E. Oberammergau; reached by bus from there, from Garmisch-Partenkirchen and from Oberau station). Abbey church (Benedictine from mid-fourteenth century to 1803 and since 1900); also pilgrimage church. We are right to consider it *Zuccalli's* work because, despite the destructive fire of 1744, the plans were his and the prominent features (façade, dome) to his design, though *Josef Schmutzer* of Wessobrunn supervised the later restoration and decoration. The ground-plan consists of two slightly intersecting circles of different diameters, the larger, retained from the (most unusual) plan of the late medieval church, forming the nave rotunda with drum-dome above it, the smaller the choir; there is also an expansive façade with low towers. The abbey lies among the mountains in the beautiful and romantic pass between the valleys of the Loisach and the Ammer.

Noteworthy features. Exterior: (1) The swinging façade, for all its character, was in fact left incomplete and received not altogether satisfactory additions during the past hundred years; of three porches planned only one was completed; the S. tower dates largely from 1906–7, the N. tower helm from 1853. (2) The relation of dome and drum to rotunda is such that it is difficult to say where the one begins and the other ends; the whole rotunda with its upper, windowed storey really forms the drum on which the dome stands. *Interior:* (1) Here we see centrality at its utmost; monks and congregation alike worship, each in a circular space. Here too the curve has absolute sway; apart from the floor and the perpendicular line of the walls there is not a straight line in the building. (2) Decoration and furnishings are of the first quality almost throughout. In the rotunda the fresco (*Johann Jakob Zeiller*, 1751–2) depicting St Benedict in a great company of his Order adoring the Holy Trinity (in all some 400 figures make up the scene) is a work full of depth and movement and showing the late tendency to a loosening of the composition that can be seen in the same artist's frescoes at Ottobeuren. In striking and interesting contrast is the later choir fresco (1769) by *Martin Knoller*. (3) The stucco work (*Josef Schmutzer* and *Johann Übelherr*) is of fine quality throughout; interesting the transition from stucco to painting round the base of the dome. (4) The side altars in the rotunda are all good works of *J. B. Straub* (1757–61), each in itself unsymmetrical, to be viewed, as is so often the case, in mutually complementary pairs belonging together as 'side-wings' to the high altar (cf. *Birnau*, and elsewhere). (5) The very fine *sacristy* should be seen.

Giovanni Antonio Viscardi

Viscardi has a special significance in the development of Bavarian church Baroque, over and above his intrinsic merits as an architect. He was the great mediator between Italian tradition and local feeling. He had the ability to attract and utilise talent where he found it, to learn as well as to teach; and his churches of importance are the products of happy collaboration with local artists. We need only think of the *Munich Dreifaltigkeitskirche* as an example of such co-operation, or compare the ground-plan of *Fürstenfeldbruck* with that of the self-consciously Italian *Theatinerkirche* in Munich. Three churches illustrate his work here.

Munich, Dreifaltigkeitskirche (Holy Trinity), Pacellistrasse, 1711–14. A small church, it had an important influence on the development of the S. German round church type and as an early object lesson in the problem of blending the longitudinal with the central. It offers an interesting comparison with an earlier work of Viscardi, the pilgrimage church of *Mariahilf* outside *Freystadt*, S.E. of Nuremberg (1700–8), a compact domed building whose plan combines in a peculiar manner cross, octagon and circle.

Noteworthy features. Exterior (plate 15): (1) Suggests a cruciform interior. (2) The vigorous façade, polygonal in form, is perhaps the earliest example in Germany of the convex Baroque façade that later found wide acceptance. *Interior:* (1) Of a cruciform character as hinted by the exterior; the effect of length is increased by the side arms being shallower, that of 'centrality' by the corners being bevelled off. (2) The architectural element is predominant despite the rich decoration (detached columns, prominent entablature). (3) The frescoes are the earliest works in Munich of *C. D. Asam* (who also painted those at *Freystadt*). (4) The stucco work (*J. G. Bader*) of unrelieved leaf-scroll pattern is somewhat monotonous. At the time of writing (1974) interior restoration is still urgently needed.

Freising-Neustift, St Peter and St Paul, 1700–15 (Viscardi † 1713) (22 m. N.E. Munich, on main line and road; frequent and regular rail and bus connections from Munich). Since 1892 parish church (originally Premonstratensian foundation 1141). 1751 a serious fire necessitated redecoration which lasted until 1756. Wall-pillar church with 3-bay nave, apsidal narrower choir, single flanking tower.

Noteworthy features. Exterior: The main interest lies in its anticipations of its great contemporary at Fürstenfeldbruck (*a*) in the treatment of the wall design, (*b*) in the shaping of the bold apse, (*c*) in the position and design of the tower. *Interior:* Of great beauty and skilful lighting and with decoration of uniformly fine quality. (1) The 3-sided piers faced with half-columns are characteristic for Viscardi (cf. *Fürstenfeldbruck*). (2) The absence of galleries across the wide arches and the longitudinal position of the side altars give a sense of compactness (contrast *Fürstenfeldbruck* in both respects), possibly increased by the fact that the half-columns are marbled horizontally only. (3) The frescoes (*J. B. Zimmermann*, 1756, after the fire) are bold and brilliant with all this painter's atmospheric quality; they depict scenes from the life of St Norbert, founder of the Premonstratensian Order. (4) The three principal altars and their statuary are by *Ignaz Günther* and show him at his best. The high altar (1756) is, together with those at *Rott-am-Inn* and *Mallersdorf* (mid-way between Regensburg and Landshut), one of his three masterpieces; interesting to note how, alongside the dramatic, rhetorical figures the classicist spirit is just making itself felt in the architectural framework.

Fürstenfeldbruck, 1701–66 (in the Amper valley 16 m. W. Munich on the main Munich–Kempten line; frequent rail and bus connection from Munich). Originally monastic church (Cistercian foundation 1263); 1803 taken over by the state, 1923–56 served by monks from Ettal, now under the parish. A wall-pillar church with 5-bay nave, long apsidal choir, no transept formation, single tower flanking choir. One of the largest and grandest of Bavarian Baroque churches, above all the interior, which, like its predecessor at *Freising-Neustift*, has hardly a weak aspect. The unity and harmony of the building are all the more remarkable in view of the facts that *Viscardi* died in 1713 and the work was carried on by other hands (*J. G. Ettenhofer*)—and indeed interrupted altogether for some years during the War of the Spanish Succession.

Noteworthy features. Exterior: In general a larger version of *Freising-Neustift* with variation in roof line and treatment of apse. The most remarkable aspect is the vast, precipitous W. façade (completed 1747), monumental but quite un-Italian in design, above all in the windows. Unusual, too, for a Baroque church, again un-Italian in character and recalling Gothic, are the buttresses to the choir apse. *Interior* (plate 29): One of the stateliest and, for all its vastness, entirely charming. A happy blend of Italian and S. German feeling, of architectural form with decorative fantasy. We shall only understand it, or indeed the church as a whole, if we keep in mind that between the laying of the foundation-stone (1701) and the completion of the decoration (1766) over sixty years went by during which important developments in style took place. (1) We find here an interior that in the most interesting manner recalls in some respects *St Michael* in Munich, in others the closely akin Vorarlberg design, in others again both these. (2) The optical effect of the galleries should be noted; the impressions of (in themselves very considerable) breadth and height are respectively increased by the main gallery being so deeply inset and by the presence of a second gallery just under the crown of the arches. The soaring movement is checked only by the cornice. (3) The impression of length is also (imperceptibly) increased by the fact that the bays of the nave become progressively wider from W. to E. (4) The motif of the plain half-column attached to the pilaster, noted at *Freising-Neustift*, repeats itself here. (5) The ceiling decoration (1730–1, except for the choir stucco ornament by *Francesco Appiani*, 1723, which offers an interesting comparison) is by the brothers *Asam*. The frescoes depict scenes from the life of St Bernard and the chief church festivals. (6) The splendid high altar (*c.* 1750, ?*E. Q. Asam*) has the spiral columns favoured by these most Italianate of German Baroque craftsmen (influence of Bernini, cf. *Weltenburg, Osterhofen*); its generous proportions fill the apse most nobly. The beauty and stateliness of this choir and sanctuary are so striking that one regrets all the more keenly the large windows that under certain conditions admit so un-Baroque a dazzle of light! (7) Equally splendid is the western counterpart to the high altar, the great organ (*J. Fuchs*, 1733) and its case (*J. G. Greiff*, 1737) with the crowds of tumbling, jubilating, music-making putti everywhere. (8) The choir stalls (*Friedrich Schwertfiehrer*, 1729) with fine inlay work should be studied. (9) The confessionals have vividly carved symbolic scenes from the Gospel story, also heads of putti representing moods of repentance (before confession) and joy (after)—one is actually wiping his tears away with his wing!

Antonio Petrini

A native of Trento, he played a pioneer role in Würzburg and the Main area comparable to those of *Zuccalli* and *Barelli* in Munich and *Solari* in Salzburg in introducing the spirit and forms of Italian church Baroque. His was the original influence that gradually transformed Würzburg itself from a medieval into a predominantly Baroque city, and the massive dome of Stift Haug still remains its visible symbol in the city skyline.

Würzburg, Stift Haug (properly: St Johannes im Haug), 1670–91. This great church is to Würzburg what the *Theatinerkirche* is to Munich and the *Cathedral* to Salzburg, the first pronouncedly Italianate church in its area. Severely damaged by fire and blast in March 1945, it was, when last visited (early 1971), after a lengthy process of restoration, now free of all scaffolding and everywhere accessible. A wall-pillar church of basilical type with 3-bay nave, apsidal choir, considerable transept span, full dome on drum over crossing and façade with projecting twin towers. The ground plan essentially that of the *Gesù* but more decidedly cruciform owing to the developed transepts.

Noteworthy features. Exterior: (1) In general massive, monumental, austere, with little ornament, making its imposing impact on the scene by its bulk and its lines alone. (2) The (now well-restored) dome is of interesting and unusual design with gallery. (3) The severe, flat façade has as its main (almost only) ornamental feature the niched statue, a motif repeated in the interior. Note, too, how the small volutes flanking the central section serve both to connect this with and to separate it from the towers. The former beautiful tapering 3-storey tower-helms (resembling those at Fulda) also now rebuilt. *Interior:* The general effect essentially an architectural one. There was no fresco decoration and little or no stucco. The dome internally octagonal on plan, not, as usual, circular. The heavy, richly moulded cornice serves to emphasize the unity of the interior. The original furnishings were contemporary (rich pulpit *c.* 1693, high altar 1694, transept altars 1692–1706, all by

Johannes Kaspar Brand, the altar paintings by *Oswald Onghers*), now almost all destroyed.

The Barbieri Family

Between 1628 and about 1760 several members of this Roveredo family were working in Southern Germany. In 1628 *Martino Barbieri* began the choir of *Weissenau* (see p. 129) which he continued until 1631 and which, when the church was rebuilt in the eighteenth century, was incorporated into the new structure. In the following year he undertook the erection of *St Walburga* in *Eichstätt*. His two sons *Pietro* and *Giulio* built the church at *Isny* thirty years later, and a great-grandson was the architect of *Bergen* in the next century. We shall deal here with these last three churches. The two latter show evident adaptation to the native form of the 'hall church'; reference was made earlier (p. 55) to the interesting rivalry traceable throughout our period in South German, in particular Swabian, churches between the indigenous and more favoured 'hall church' type of interior and the Italianate 'wall-pillar' type imported from the Roman *Gesù* via *St. Michael* in *Munich*.

Eichstätt, St Walburga, 1629–31 (on the river Altmühl, 16 m. N.W. Ingolstadt, 22 m. N.E. Donauwörth; from both places rail and bus connections). Convent church (Benedictine nuns). A wall-pillar church with 4-bay nave (westernmost occupied by balconies with nuns' choir and organ loft over), narrower square-ended sanctuary and S.W. tower.

Noteworthy features. Exterior: forms, together with the conventual buildings, a dominant and impressive architectural feature of the city. The fine steps and terrace 1682; the upper section of the tower 1746. *Interior:* (1) Frescoes and stucco decoration are of 1706; the former characteristically small, the latter stiff and geometrical in design though of delicate execution (Wessobrunn artists) and set off well by the pale pink ground. (2) Unusual the great variation in the sizes of the altars. Because of the lowness of the side galleries the first two pairs of side altars are diminutive; much larger the third pair which effect the transition to the very tall high altar that reaches to the ceiling. The high altar is of 1664, the others of 1670. (3) For the glazed W. gallery (nuns' choir) cf. the later one at Günzburg; here the design less happy, the strongly convex central part projecting almost intrusively. (4) The bulky, clumsy pulpit is no doubt the one really disturbing feature in an otherwise not unpleasing interior. (5) Behind and below the high altar is the chapel of St Walburga containing her shrine; also further good stucco work. The student of votive pictures will find rich material here; there must be hundreds, all over the walls and covering the entire back of the high altar.

Isny, St Georg, 1661–4 (13 m. W. Kempten, 20 m. N.E. Lindau; from both, as also from Memmingen, rail connettions). Architects *Giulio* and *Pietro Barbieri*. A 'hall-church' with 5-bay nave (W. bay with organ-loft), 3-bay choir square-ended and single E. tower.

Noteworthy features. Exterior: the body of the church extremely plain, the façade uninteresting. The tower attracts attention because of (*a*) its unusual position, (*b*) its richer treatment indicating later date (completed 1704). *Interior:* (1) the slenderness of the pillars, the rich and brilliant decoration and furnishings, the abundance of light all surprise us; we have to recall (*a*) that the pillars were reduced in thickness 1757–9 and (*b*) that decorations etc. are all about the same time (almost a century later than the church itself). (2) The two E. bays are slightly broader than those of the nave but this has little optical effect; the choir is marked off from the nave by the steps and communion rail and by the E. galleries. (3) The frescoes are fine works of *Hans Michael Holzhey*, 1757–8. Iconographically and theologically considered they present a development from W. to E.: the Cleansing of the Temple (under organ); David before the Ark of the Covenant; foundation of the abbey under the Rule of St Benedict who is seen in the clouds begging God's protection; the abbey receives a piece of the True Cross; the triumph of the Eucharist (over high altar). (4) The very fine and tasteful stucco decoration is by *Johann Georg Gigl* and his brother *Matthias* (1757–9). (5) The seven altars (1758–64, of wood, probably by *Jakob Ruez*) all deserve close attention; of great beauty the high altar, its mensa separate but enfolded by the concave superstructure whose columns (delicately recalling those in the church) are linked by freely swinging scrolls to the top of the picture surround. The statuary all excellent. (6) The rhythmical pulpit (probably also by *Ruez*) has fine reliefs and putti with symbolic attributes. (7) Notably pleasing is also the organ gallery with attractive putti making music (note the 'conductor' to the right!), together with its organ (1744, by *Michael Bihler*). (8) In the *Marienkapelle* (right of sanctuary) three further good altars, the original very fine choir stalls (c. 1731–5) and an interesting wooden coffered ceiling of 1680. Altogether, an interior that is worth coming far to see.

Bergen, Heiligkreuz, 1756–9 (3 m. N.W. Neuburg on the Danube, 7 m. S.S.W. Eichstätt; nearest station Hütting; bus from Eichstätt). Architect *Giovanni Barbieri*. Parish and pilgrimage church; till 1552 convent of Benedictine nuns. In its present form (a reconstruction of a former Romanesque church) consists of aisleless nave, narrow shallow transepts and 3-bay choir of 'hall' type. Of the Romanesque church have been incorporated the triple E. apse, the crypt beneath the choir, the detached bell-tower, the S. nave porch (now blocked and serving as a war memorial).

Noteworthy features. Exterior: heavy and unpromising and calls for no comment. *Interior:* as at *Isny* we are surprised at the elegance and lightness. (1) The 'hall' character of the choir increases the apparent width of the aisleless nave and offers an attractive contrast thereto. (2) The slender choir pillars bear a marked resemblance in design and proportion to those at *Isny* (which in their present form are contemporary). (3) The frescoes (by *Johann Wolfgang Baumgartner* of Augsburg) deal with the story and Veneration of the Cross and are of fine quality and great brilliance of colour, especially that over the high altar (Discovery of the Cross) which bears the artist's signature at the foot. (4) The stucco decoration (by *Josef Köpl* of Mertingen), delicate, restrained, loosely distributed, with the rocaille as basic design, is evidently intended to be of secondary importance but fulfils its function perfectly. (5) The altars and pulpit with good statuary by *Johann Michael Fischer* of Dillingen contrast well in their warmer colours with the white background. (6) The organ gallery at the W., though stately, may be felt to be a shade too high and the small organ somewhat crushed against the ceiling. Below, a wrought metal screen of fine workmanship.

Domenico Magzin

This Italian is little known, little is known about him and he built little; but he deserves mention as the architect of the larger part (nave) of a church which gave the *Asam* brothers the chance to produce one of the loveliest decorated interiors in our area. He was master-mason at the not very distant town of Landau where he had previously erected the Stadtpfarrkirche (1713).

Aldersbach, completed 1720, choir 1617 (Vils valley, 6 m. S.W. Vilshofen/Danube from which rail connection). Formerly Cistercian abbey, since 1803 parish church. Large wall-pillar 5-bay nave, deep apsidal choir and single W. tower.

Noteworthy features. Exterior: (1) The façade with its projecting tower bound in by cornice and gable is a plain but imposing work. (2) The tower (itself older, 1400) is worth attention; note the porch with flanking statuary and the fine Immaculata in niche above, also the shapely upper storey with its attractive and lively helm. *Interior:* (1) Architecturally there is no great originality; wall-pillars and cornice above are massive, there are no galleries between them, nor any attempt at a transept. The main architectural character is one of unpretentious massiveness. All the more brilliant is the effect of the decoration and furnishings which are throughout of the highest order. (2) Stucco and frescoes are by the *Asams*, magnificent in workmanship and disposition. The stucco has a noticeably Italianate character. The fresco theme is that of the Redemption of Man, the series beginning (unusually) in the W. (contrast *Einsiedeln*, where the theme is the same). Note in the great nave fresco (Nativity) Bernard, the patron saint-to-be of the Order, being summoned by an angel to contemplation and worship. (3) Here (as at *Diessen*) we have a particularly good example of side altars set transversely in a series of parallel pairs to lead the eye eastwards, the two easternmost (against choir arch) larger than the others, in preparation for the high altar itself. (4) The high altar is one of the richest and most splendid of all S. German Baroque altars (1723, by *Matthäus Götz*, the painting 1619 from the earlier altar). Note, above, the representation of the Trinity adored by angel hosts. (5) The superbly carved and inlaid choir stalls (completed 1762) are the work of a lay-brother, *Kaspar Schreiner*. (6) The richly symbolic pulpit is a beautiful work of *Josef Deutschmann* (1748, cf. his later work at *Asbach*). (7) A glance westwards at the finely rhythmical organ gallery must not be omitted; the old organ fell a victim to the secularization—the only sad gap in the uniformity of the furnishings here. (8) Note finally the dramatic symbolic putti on the confessionals.

François Cuvilliés

In choosing *Schäftlarn* abbey church to represent the work of the elder Cuvilliés we have indeed little alternative, for he built almost entirely in the secular field. Even so, a qualification or two must be added. That the plans were his there can be no doubt. But from 1740 to 1751 there was a long interruption in the process of building, due presumably to shortage of funds; and afterwards, for reasons not known, he does not appear again. The work was concluded by *Johann Baptist Gunetzrhainer*; and in the accounts a certain 'Herr Fischer' is also named and who is thought to be Johann Michael Fischer who in 1725 married a step-sister of Gunetzrhainer. Cuvilliés' plans had to be considerably modified. A shallow transept planned, and indeed begun, by him was greatly reduced and the tower of the former church, which would have been incompatible with the original design, was retained after all.

Schäftlarn, 1733–57 (Isar valley 12 m. S. Munich whence rail and bus connection). Abbey church (Benedictine foundation 760, 931 secular canons, 1140–1803 Premonstratensian, since 1866 Benedictine again). Beautifully situated at the foot of the steep, wooded left bank of the river. A wall-pillar church with 3-bay nave, 2-bay apsidal choir, slight transept formation and built-in W. tower.

Noteworthy features. Exterior: Little comment is called for, the exterior is not distinguished. The abbey makes its effect in the landscape by its complex of buildings as a whole. Indeed except for the façade and the slender tower the church is entirely enclosed by the monastic buildings. Some have seen in the façade a resemblance to that of *Rott-am-Inn* and suggested, without further means of proof, that it is the work of J. M. Fischer. In any case, it is not notable. *Interior:* One of the most beautiful of all the smaller interiors. (1) The general lightness and refinement give the church a peculiarly aristocratic atmosphere. (2) The impression of close, organic relationships between the various parts suggests the more sophisticated type of ground-plan of the middle of the century (cf. the contemporary *Berg-am-Laim*). (3) The broader 'transeptal' bay flanked by two much narrower ones, together with the great fresco over the crossing, give a certain feeling of centrality. (4) The stucco work (*Johann Baptist Zimmermann*, 1754–6) is delicate and discreet. (5) The frescoes are also by *J. B. Zimmermann* and among his best, depicting scenes from the life of St Norbert and the founding of the abbey—the subjects interesting, considering that the abbey was originally Benedictine and is so again. (6) The altars (*Johann Baptist Straub*, 1755–6) are all first-rate, especially the high altar and the four unsymmetrical altars in the narrow bays with figures—on N. St Norbert and St Joseph (plate 50), on S. St Augustine and St John Nepomuk—in ivory white in marbled niches, with the trailing clouds so characteristic of *Straub* (cf. *Berg-am-Laim*,

146

Grafrath). (7) The elegant pulpit (also *Straub*) should also be noted, with, upon its sounding board, a dramatic representation of Mother Church pronouncing excommunication against the heretic Tanchelm.

François Cuvilliés the younger

The son of the elder Cuvilliés also has a claim on our attention because, after completing his training in Paris, he returned to introduce a new spirit and a new epoch into Bavarian church architecture. In 1771 the first classicist church made its appearance in Bavaria.

Asbach, 1771–80 (Rott valley, 5 m. N.E. Pfarrkirchen, 15 m. S.W. Passau). Formerly Benedictine abbey, since 1803 parish church. A 3-bay wall-pillar church with narrower apsidal choir and a single tower flanking it on S.

Noteworthy features. Exterior: The design is very pleasing, restrained yet vigorous; the tower particularly firm and harmonious, to which the W. façade with its self-conscious rhythmical gable offers the necessary counterpoise. *Interior:* (1) We are offered an interesting, instructive and beautiful example of the transition from the late Baroque (or Rococo) to the Classicist. In the dignified poise of the design and its proportions the quieter classicist spirit already breathes, yet there is no lack of life in the lines of vault, arch and cornice. (2) In the altars, and especially in the pulpit (all by *Josef Deutschmann*), the Rococo grace and gaiety are, despite the late date 1780, still clearly felt, yet blending happily with the architecture. (3) It may well be felt that the Stations of the Cross, at least in their present position on the pilasters, somewhat mar the general harmony and impair the effect of the architecture.

Baroque reconstructions of older churches

Scattered up and down Central Europe there are many churches of older origin (Gothic or Romanesque) which in the Baroque period received interior reconstruction and redecoration. In some cases the alterations have been so extensive that we have to all intents and purposes new interiors of Baroque character. These churches cannot, of course, be considered as Baroque creations in the strict and fullest sense; but nor, clearly, can they be omitted entirely from a survey such as this. The Swiss and Austrian churches of this type will be found dealt with as they occur. In S. Germany there is a sufficient number of really notable interiors of the kind to justify a separate section devoted to them; and the more important of them are here considered in alphabetical order.

Amberg, St Georg (N. Bavaria, 25 m. N.W. Regensburg, 27 m. E. Nuremberg; from both places rail connection). Parish church. A late fourteenth-century Gothic basilica of imposing proportions with 3-aisled 6-bay nave, long, considerably narrower choir, no transepts and massive W. tower. The interior redecorated 1718–23 by Wessobrunn stucco-artists and with frescoes by pupils of C. D. Asam. One of the noblest and most successful 'Baroquizations'; the Gothic proportions and character blend admirably with the later ornamentation which has been carried out with insight and beauty. The secret lies largely, no doubt, in the fact that the Baroque work is fairly early and of sufficiently weighty calibre for the massive proportions of the church. A glance up at the elegant, much later organ case (1767) will suggest that, had the treatment been of such lightness and delicacy throughout, the general result would have been far less satisfactory. On the other hand, the high altar (1694) and pulpit (1702) have the requisite weight and suit well in their places.

Andechs (S. Bavaria, E. shore of Ammersee almost opposite *Diessen*; reached by rail from Munich to Herrsching, whence one hour's beautiful walk; motor road also with bus connection to within a few minutes' climb up stepped path.) Benedictine priory and pilgrimage church; in an unforgettably fine situation crowning a wooded hill above the lake with (from tower) superb views in all directions, on S. to the Alps and, in clear weather, to Munich away to N.E. The small church, a 4-bay 'hall-church' with apsidal choir, no transepts and single S.W. tower, has an early fifteenth-century shell extensively altered 1670–1 and redecorated in 1751–5. Despite much beauty and fine work in the interior, Gothic proportions and Baroque ornament do not here blend with entire conviction. The frescoes lie somewhat cramped and uneasy in the vault area, and the nave altars overwhelm the slender pillars.

Noteworthy features. (1) The delicate stucco scroll work by *Johann Baptist Zimmermann.* (2) The colourful frescoes (also by *Zimmermann*) depicting scenes and legends connected with the church and its pilgrimage. (3) The fine statuary: the four figures on E. pair of nave altars and two on lower high altar at sides by *Johann Baptist Straub*; those on the upper altar as well as the two vivid groups on the gallery (right, St Florian; left, St John Nepomuk) by *Franz Xaver Schmädl*; the pietà in the Schmerzhafte Kapelle (N. side of nave) by *Roman Anton Boos.* (4) The rhythmical (Baroque) gallery, which gives an effect at once enlivening and unifying (the paintings depict scenes from the legend and history of the pilgrimage). Out of this gallery, N. side, opens the Heilige Kapelle containing interesting relics and also the only still visible remains (door, vaulting) of the earlier Gothic church. (5) The Festsaal of the monastery has a fine early stucco ceiling (1670) of Wessobrunn workmanship, an interesting object-lesson in contrast to the later work in the church.

Freising Cathedral (Dom). (22 m. N. Munich on main line and road; frequent rail connections). The see first created by St Boniface in 739; the church enshrines the relics of its patron saint Korbinian († *c.* 735). An ancient and venerable building of rich architectural and artistic interest, dating mainly from twelfth century, with parts (N. tower) as old as the tenth century, and additions from many other periods. A 5-aisled basilica of 12 bays, three E. apses, raised choir projecting into nave with extensive crypt beneath, and massive twin-steepled W. façade. Rises proudly among the buildings of the little town on its hill above the Isar. In 1723–4 the *Asam* brothers decorated the interior with stucco ornament and frescoes; as was to be expected, the work was done with imagination and discretion.

Noteworthy features. (1) Despite the later decoration the original Romanesque proportions and character can be clearly felt. (2) Interesting and skilful is the placing of the heavy pilaster capitals below the crowns of the upper arcade arches; the latter are thus freed to contribute a lively undulating movement in welcome contrast to the rigid lines of frieze and cornice. (3) The stucco scroll work, beautiful as it is, may be felt to be a shade too light for the massive proportions of the church as a whole. (4) The frescoes (*C. D. Asam*) depict scenes from the life of the patron saint Korbinian together with other theological themes; characteristic for the artist is the illusory architecture in the dome fresco, also the patterned filling-in of spandrels and other background spaces (cf. *Fürstenfeldbruck*). (5) The crucifix with figure of Mary at the foot of the Cross, on the fourth pillar of the N. nave arcade, is a fine work of *E. Q. Asam*. (6) The massive and dominant but finely poised high altar is an earlier work (1624), its present painting a copy of the Rubens original removed at the secularization of church property 1803 to Munich. (7) The choir-stalls are very good late Gothic work (1483–8). (8) The octagonal Maximilianskapelle, E. of the choir, has fine earlier stucco ornament (1710) and frescoes by *Hans Georg Asam*. (The important mid-twelfth century crypt (Korbinianskrypta) beneath the choir has interesting and puzzling grotesque animal and other carvings on the pillars and should, even though not Baroque, on no account be missed. All the carvings are in an excellent state of preservation.)

Gross-Thalheim, *St Maria* (6 m. N.E. Erding, to which rail from Munich but no further regular connection). Pilgrimage church. As it stands, a church of wall-pillar type with 5-bay nave, 2-bay apsidal sanctuary and S.E. tower. Apparently an early eighteenth century adaptation of a late Gothic wall-pillar church as the

masonry of choir and E. bay of nave is fifteenth century; as
such an unusual and interesting case.

Noteworthy features. All connected with the enormously rich,
somewhat unequal but in parts excellent interior decoration
and furnishings. (1) The good frescoes (1764) are probably by
Johann Martin Heigl; the light-weight elegant tinted stucco
decoration contemporary. (2) The elaborate high altar represents various periods; structurally 1737 (by *Franz A. Mallet*),
its four figures (the Latin Fathers of the Church) of the same
date probably by *Johann Michael Hiernle*, the baldachin 1753
(statue of the Virgin *c.* 1500), the tabernacle (by *Christian
Jorhan the Elder*) 1765. (3) Also by *Jorhan*, or his school, the
fine sensitive statuary on the side chapel altars, organ and
pulpit.

Gutenzell (12 m. N.W. Memmingen, 4 m. N.E. Ochsenhausen;
rail connection from Memmingen to Kellmünz, 4 m.). Baroquized 1755–6 under the supervision of *Dominikus Zimmermann* whose daughter Maria Alexandra was a nun and from
1759 to her death abbess here (her gravestone before the communion rails, her monument on S. aisle wall close by). Originally a convent of Cistercian nuns, since 1803 parish church.
Ground-plan and elevation date in general from late fourteenth century; 10-bay basilical nave with much narrower,
short, apsidal choir, no transepts and W. bell turret. In an
idyllic and remote village.

Noteworthy features. Exterior: The bell-shaped clerestory windows are characteristic of Zimmermann's love of rhythmical
outline. *Interior:* In general, the furnishings and decoration
harmonious and of fine quality. (1) Most unusual how the
pilasters carrying the transverse arches spring from the spandrels
between the arcade arches without reaching the ground. (2) The
chief feature of the decoration: the fine, warmly-coloured (red-
browns and purple-reds prominent) and excellently preserved
frescoes by *Johann Georg Dieffenbrunner* (scenes from Old and
New Testaments and lives of saints; note the scene of the mar-
riage at Cana with its delicate lace table-cloths, recalling the

work of the nuns themselves). On the walls above the arcades paintings of the Twelve Apostles with angels in the sky bearing the respective instruments of martyrdom. (3) The stucco ornament (*Ignaz Finsterwalder*) sparse and restrained, mainly cartouche and rocaille motifs, but of good quality. (4) The pulpit (*F. X. Feichtmayer* and *I. Finsterwalder*) has a sounding-board of free and bold design modelled on that at *Ochsenhausen*, q.v. (here the figure that of St Bernhard, the founder saint of the Order, in ecstasy). (5) At W. end is the nuns' choir, unusually deep, covering the first four bays of the nave (cf. *Landshut-Seligenthal*). (6) Here and there fine metal-work (sanctuary rail, very elegant; 4-branch candlestick in N. aisle).

Indersdorf (18 m. N.W. Munich from which rail connection via Dachau). Parish church; formerly Augustinian canons. A late twelfth-century basilica with 4-bay nave, 3-bay choir added seventeenth century with lantern cupola over high altar, no transepts and twin-steepled W. façade. The rich late Baroque decoration added 1754–5, though some altars are earlier.

Noteworthy features. Interior: (1) The Baroque decoration is here noticeably constricted by the lofty, narrow quite un-Baroque proportions. (2) The fine stucco-work is by *Franz Xaver Feichtmayr* (compare his work earlier at *Diessen* and later at *Rott-am-Inn*). (3) The frescoes (*Matthäus Günther*) are among the artist's best works (theme: scenes from the life of St Augustine; other series on the same theme are found in the churches at *Rottenbuch* and *Neustift* (near Brixen), both also formerly Augustinian). They are in varying states of preservation; note especially the colouring and the depth of the great nave fresco (glorification of the Saint). (4) The fourth bay from W. shows special treatment (transverse arches, oval fresco, capitals of different design), perhaps to lend the centralizing effect of a 'crossing'. (5) The altars are of many periods: high altar, unusually pompous and towering, 1691; that in St Anne's chapel 1721 f.; those in the nave 1754–5. Some, e.g. the second pair from W. in nave, of quite unusual and exotic fancy. (6) Round the beautiful sacristy ceiling hover interesting symbolic stucco putti bearing in their hands the priestly vestments for the Mass.

Mallersdorf (18 m. S. E. Regensburg on the little R. Laber just E. Landshut–Regensburg main road). Till 1803 Benedictine abbey; 1829 church again in use, 1921 made parish church; between 1869 and 1913 conventual buildings acquired by Franciscan nuns. Church originally Romanesque (towers and W. door remain), then Gothic additions (traces in choir); after further rebuilding in seventeenth and eighteenth centuries the interior took on its present form 1747–92. As we now have it, a 4-bay wall-pillar church with 3-bay narrower apsidal choir and twin-towered W. façade.

Noteworthy features. Exterior: façade an impressive blend of Romanesque and Baroque; between the massive, rather squat Romanesque towers rises a lively Baroque gable with volutes and niched figure of St Benedict; before the façade is a two-storey apsidal entrance hall under a half dome with Romanesque door. *Interior:* (1) main (nave) fresco 1776 by *Matthäus Schiffer*, a loosely composed work of almost classicist feeling; those over choir by *J. A. Schöpf* (signed 1747). Stucco ornament in choir only. (2) The great glory of the church is the high altar by *Ignaz Günther* (1768), one of his three greatest with those at *Freising-Neustift* and *Rott-am-Inn* (both earlier). Above the painting (St John on Patmos, by *Martin Speer*), a fine statuary group of the apocalyptic scene in Revelation xii —the Virgin as the Woman in travail, the waiting Dragon and the avenging Archangel Michael. The four flanking statues are: (right) the Emperor Henry II and St Benedict, (left) St Scholastica and the Empress Kunigunda (cf. this figure with Günther's other of her at *Rott*).

Metten, 1712–29 (N. bank of Danube, 3 m. above Deggendorf from which rail and bus connections). Benedictine abbey church. Baroque reconstruction and redecoration of a late fifteenth-century church of which the choir walls and (external) buttresses remain, while in the nave the buttresses were embodied in the church as wall-pillars and the walls shifted accordingly.

Of the old church nothing is visible in the interior. As we have it now a church of wall-pillar type with 4-bay nave, narrower choir and twin-towered W. façade with apsidal central section under half-dome.

Noteworthy features. Exterior: interesting and imposing the W façade with convex central section containing entrance hall and roofed with half-dome (cf. *Mallersdorf*) and sturdy 3-storey towers topped by highly individual bulbous helms. *Interior:* while not, perhaps, of the first quality, it yet combines majesty with intimacy, variety with compactness. The proportions are generous, the atmosphere devotional. (1) The frescoes are by *Innozenz Warathi* of Sterzing in Tyrol; unusual, and especially for its date (1724), the size of the nave fresco covering the entire ceiling. (2) The very fine stucco work is also by a Tyrolese, *Franz Josef Holzinger* of Schörfling (cf. his still finer work at *Altenburg*). (3) The high altar (1720) is by *Jakob Schöpf* (cf. his still more imposing one at *Niederaltaich*), its painting (St Michael casting down Satan) by *C. D. Asam*. The view of the choir from the nave with the massive choir arch framing the high altar and flanked by equally good side altars has real nobility. (4) Very satisfying too the grouping of organ and gallery within the deep W. apse. (5) In the conventual buildings the visitor should ask to see: (*a*) the beautiful *library* which ranks with those of *Ottobeuren, Schussenried, Waldsassen* and *St Gallen* as one of the finest of the period; decoration by *F. J. Holzinger* (1706–20), the subjects of the allegorical frescoes relate to the book sections adjoining; (*b*) the *Festsaal* (1734), a noble room in the E. wing by *Benedikt Schöttl* with fine stucco work of rocaille design by *Mathias Obermayer* and a fine fresco (the Second Coming) by *Martin Speer* (1759).

Niederaltaich (N. bank of Danube in flat water meadows between Deggendorf and Vilshofen, from both of which bus connection; also by rail to Hengersberg station, 1 m.). Benedictine abbey since 731, one of the oldest foundations in Germany. Of the original Gothic 'hall-church' (1270–1306) walls and nave pillars were embodied in the Baroque reconstruction of 1724 f.

Though with the exception of *J. M. Fischer* (whose reconstruction of the choir is his earliest considerable work) no first-rank artist participated here, this interior is one of the most majestic and successful of all 'Baroquizations'. The architect was *Jakob Pawagner* of Passau.

Noteworthy features. Exterior: The façade, of quite un-Baroque proportions, was planned in early fifteenth century, though the towers were not completed until 1730–5. Gothic origins are also revealed by the external buttresses along the side walls. *Interior:* (1) The splendid proportions and the harmony between them and the decoration make their impression at once. (2) The arcades (whose pillars are actually detached) offer an interesting comparison with the pierced wall-pillar arcades of, for example, the almost contemporary *Weingarten*; the transformation of the Gothic 'hall' into the Baroque wall-pillar interior here is in appearance complete. (3) The effect of height is greatly intensified by the tall unbroken pilasters to the arcades and the high pitch of the galleries. (4) The nave side-aisle chapel ceilings are pierced to allow of vistas to frescoes at an upper level; a visit to the gallery above is much to be recommended for its fine views. (5) The restrained and tasteful stucco work is by the brothers *Allio*; the frescoes (scenes from the history of the abbey) by *Andreas Heindl*. (6) The high altar, which in the distance closes the view from the W. nobly, is a massive and distinguished work (wood) of warm colouring by *Jakob Schöpf*. (7) In the sacristy (behind high altar) is a series of very fine and rich carved cupboards (*c.* 1725) by Brother *Pirmin Tobiaschu*.

Ochsenhausen (on the Memmingen–Biberach road 12 m. N.W. Memmingen whence, as also from Biberach, bus connection). Parish church; formerly Benedictine abbey church (eleventh century foundation). Projects into and from the W. wing of the imposing block of monastic buildings. Originally a late Gothic basilica (1489–95) with 6-bay nave and 5-bay choir, no transepts and single S. tower; in 1698 the tower was baroquized and raised in height; in 1725–7 followed the Baroque refashioning of the exterior, including the rhythmical façade, and the interior redecoration (not completed until *c.* 1743). Unlike *Niederaltaich* the medieval ground-plan and elevation are here clearly recognizable.

Noteworthy features. Exterior: From E., church and monastery form an imposing group; the soaring, strongly convex W. façade of the church has nobility. *Interior:* (1) The very un-Baroque impression of great unbroken length with no centralizing features is emphasized still further by the rather hard cornice rippling uninterruptedly eastwards. (2) The stucco work (*Gaspare Mola*) is, for the date, unusually prominent in relation to the frescoes (*J. G. Bergmüller,* with biblical scenes, scenes from the history of the abbey and from the lives of various saints). (3) The high altar consists of two separate parts, the delicate mensa with superstructure in the choir (by *D. Zimmermann,* 1728) and the architectural reredos against the apse wall, the two blending into a single composition when viewed from the nave. (4) The notable pulpit (*Ägid Verhelst,* 1740–1), an early example of the loose, asymmetrical, fantastic type of late Baroque pulpit found, for example, at *Die Wies* or *Vierzehnheiligen;* the sounding-board (later directly copied at *Gutenzell*) formed of a loosely thrown tasselled canopy bearing a group of the death of St Benedict. (5) Of the side altars two offer an interesting contrast, that in the St Benedict chapel on the N. (by *Herberger,* 1741–3) and that in the St Antony chapel (1718, apparently an early work of *D. Zimmermann*). (6) The earlier choir stalls (1686, by *Ferdinand Zech*) are of good, solid, architectural design. (7) The fine organ in richly coloured case above the W. entrance is by *Joseph Gabler* (1725–30, cf. *Weingarten*).

Passau Cathedral (on the Danube at its confluence with Inn and Ilz, between Regensburg and Linz; on main line Frankfurt–Würzburg–Regensburg–Vienna). This little city of the three rivers is an undamaged gem that should be missed by no one. Its setting is unique, its beauty unforgettable. The see was created by St Boniface in 739. The previous church, a late

Gothic basilica of the fifteenth and sixteenth centuries, was largely destroyed by fire in 1662. In 1668 *Carlo Lurago* (1618–84) was commissioned to restore the choir, add a nave in contemporary style and give the interior a uniformly Baroque character throughout. Hence the church as we have it today.

Noteworthy features. Exterior: (1) In style, two clear stages are visible—the late Gothic of the richly decorated choir and central tower (except for upper section), and the Baroque of nave and W. façade. (2) Of the original windows of the choir only five remain, each now divided transversely by a strip of walling; the others were blocked up or altered. (3) The façade, of a generous breadth, is stately and reposeful, the disposition of its central section and towers recalling that of the contemporary *Munich Theatinerkirche*, also an Italianate work. (4) The Gothic central octagon over the crossing is unique of its kind, as also in that position and of that size the huge Baroque 'onion' dome that crowns it. *Interior:* (1) The existing choir and the newly constructed nave had so to be adapted one to the other that the impression of a single uniform style resulted. Thus we have an interior with the monumentality and richness of the Baroque and the soaring aspiration of the Gothic—the soaring effect being heightened by the fact that the pilasters are bare of all ornament below their capitals. (2) The stucco ornament (*Giovanni Battista Carlone*; cf. his work at *Waldsassen* and *Garsten*) is heavy but remarkably fine, especially the capitals and cornice-like imposts above with little supporting figures at the corners. (3) The main frescoes are by *Carpoforo Tencalla* (scenes from the life of St Stephen, the patron saint). (4) The body of the pulpit is by *J. G. Series*; the fine statuary is ascribed (hitherto on stylistic grounds only) to *Georg Raphael Donner*; the four Evangelist figures certainly works of a high order. (5) The high altar (symbolic group representing the stoning and vision of St Stephen) is modern (1945–53, by Professor *Josef Henselmann*, Munich), a work which seeks in modern spirit to unite Baroque drama with the element of Gothic lightness required for its position. (6) Of the side altars, the first and fourth pairs from W. merit attention as having paintings by *Johann Michael Rottmayr* (cf. *Vienna Karlskirche, Melk*). (7) The great organ (by *Steinmeyer* in Öttingen 1924–7) must not be forgotten, the largest church organ in Europe, perhaps in the world (5 manuals, some 240 stops, over 16,000 pipes), the work distributed in five sections about the church (one being above the vault) but all played from a single console (organ case by *Josef Mattäus Götz*, 1731–3).

Raitenhaslach (Austrian border, W. bank of Salzach, 2½ m. above Burghausen, 25 m. below Salzburg; rail connection to Burghausen). Parish church; formerly Cistercian abbey (founded 1146). The original 3-aisled eleventh-century basilica was converted 1694–8 into an aisleless wall-pillar church with 5-bay nave, slightly narrower choir, no transepts and single E. tower. Interior decoration was added 1737–43, a new W. façade 1751–2.

Noteworthy features. Interior: (1) The main impression is determined by the extremely rich decoration, hardly at all by the architecture. (2) Here, unlike the almost contemporary baroquization at *Ochsenhausen*, the frescoes (fine works of *Johannes Zick* depicting scenes from the life of St Bernard) have almost complete sway; the stucco ornament (*Michael Zick* and *J. B. Zimmermann*), though of fine quality, finds little room. (3) The choir-arch with its pair of colossal detached columns forms an unusual and striking frame for the high altar and also, thereby, an effective link between it and the body of the church. Above is an excellent example of a symbolic curtain drawn aside by little angels. (4) Some of the statuary is fine, e.g. the figure of St Anne on the fourth left-hand altar from W. (5) The confessionals are noteworthy.

Regensburg (Danube, between Ingolstadt and Passau), 'Alte Kapelle'. Independent collegiate foundation traceable back to the ninth century; site even older, possibly Roman. In essence the church a medieval building (nave Romanesque, choir mid-fifteenth century) baroquized in the interior 1747–65;

to a broad 5-bay nave and shallow transept is joined a long, much narrower, aisleless, apsidal choir.

Noteworthy features. Exterior: The medieval character as well as the different periods of construction clearly recognizable— the Baroque windows included; the W. tower detached. *Interior:* (1) The plain, unadorned nave pillars provide a welcome note of stability and contrast to the richness of the ornament, which increases eastwards. (2) The jubilant decoration makes this interior as rich and harmonious as the exterior is plain and divided in style. (3) The stucco ornament, by *Anton Landes* of *Wessobrunn* (nave 1750–2, choir 1761–2) is most delicate and imaginative. (4) The frescoes (by *Thomas Scheffler*, in choir by *Gottfried Bernhard Götz*) show in full, brilliant colours scenes from the history of the church and foundation. (5) The towering, majestic high altar is a work (in wood) of *G. B. Götz* with statuary by *Simon Sorg* (1762–72). (6) The organ case (with putti orchestra) is a fine later work (1791).

Rottenbuch (10 m. N.W. Oberammergau, on Schongau–Landsberg road; no rail connection; bus from Weilheim, Füssen, Schongau). Parish church; formerly Augustinian Canons. Late fifteenth century basilica (on Romanesque foundations) with 6-bay nave, apsidal choir, transept (for Bavaria) unusually developed, and single, massive tower detached from the body of the church; received 1737–47 extensive redecoration under the direction of *Josef Schmutzer* (Wessobrunn). The beauty of this interior lies in the harmony with which the decorators succeeded in blending their art with the Gothic structure with a minimum of interference with the latter. All the work is of the first quality.

Noteworthy features. (1) The important frescoes (scenes from the life of St Augustine) are early works of *Matthäus Günther* (c.f. his two other series on the same theme in the former Augustinian churches of *Neustift* near Brixen and *Indersdorf*). (2) The statuary (mostly by *Franz Xaver Schmädl*) is throughout exceedingly fine, especially the Evangelist figures on the pulpit, the figures of St Peter and St Paul flanking the high altar, and the putti everywhere, notably on the fine organ case (1747). (3) The high altar with its representation of the birth of the Virgin in statuary (in place of altar painting) is probably unique.

Tegernsee (E. shore of the lake, rail and bus communications from Munich and elsewhere). Parish (formerly Benedictine abbey) church. Benedictine foundation eighth century. Present church reconstruction 1684–8 (architect *Antonio Riva*) of fifteenth-century predecessor. Basilica with 4-bay nave (the fourth bay with very slight apsidal projection), broader but non-projecting fifth bay of transeptal character, much narrower apsidal choir and twin-towered W. façade.

Noteworthy features. Exterior: The unsatisfactory W. façade is a reconstruction by *Klenze* (1817) who reduced the height of the towers and crowned them with the present insignificant steeplets. *Interior:* Its importance lies almost solely in the fine, rich early stucco decoration (probably Italian work) and in the freshly coloured frescoes (1689–94) by *Johannes Georg Asam*, father of the brothers Asam, which have a curiously tapestry-like effect. In the large saucer-dome fresco (All Saints) note the symbolic representation of the Trinity at the summit (three seated persons within a triangle bearing the threefold 'sanctus'). The beautiful, much later St Quirinus altar (1748) in the S. nave aisle apsidal chapel has side figures possibly by *Johann Baptist Straub*. The frame-like superstructures of the high altar and the two large transeptal altars are stiff and unpleasing classicist replacements of 1820.

Waldsee (13 m. S. Biberach, 10 m. S.E. Steinhausen). Once collegiate church of Augustinian Canons, now parish church of St Peter. A fifteenth-century basilica with 6-bay nave and aisle-less apsidal choir baroquized 1712–18, the three nave aisles being covered with a single roof; the twin-towered façade added 1765–8.

Noteworthy features. Exterior: the unusual position of the towers obliquely across the corners gives an added swing to an already rhythmical façade; the tower helms finely shaped. *Interior:* (1)

26. *Steinhausen*, interior (see pp. 87–8)

27. *Ottobeuren*, interior (see pp. 81–2)

28. *Diessen*, interior (see pp. 76–8)

29. *Fürstenfeldbruck*, former abbey church, interior (see pp. 138–9)

30. *St Florian*, abbey church, interior (see pp. 234–6)

31. *St Florian*, organ (see pp. 234–6)

32. *Osterhofen*, former abbey church, interior of nave (see pp. 75–6)

33. *Banz*, a study in rhythm and perspective (see pp. 106–7)

34. *Kleinhelfendorf*, sanctuary and high altar, *c.* 1669 (see p. 165)

35. *Osterhofen*, high altar, *c.* 1732 (see pp. 75–6)

36. *Rohr*, abbey church, high altar (see pp. 94–5)

37. *Diessen*, high altar, painting and statuary above (see pp. 76–8)

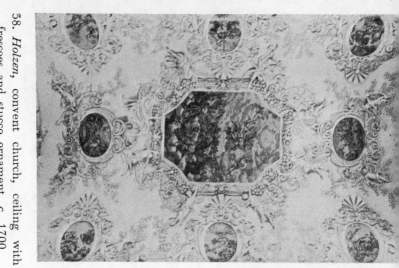

38. *Holzer*, convent church, ceiling with frescoes and stucco ornament, c. 1700 (see pp. 126–7)

39. *Steinhausen*, nave ceiling fresco, 1750–55 (see pp. 87–8)

40. *Banz*, choir ceiling frescoes, *c.* 1715 (see pp. 106–7)

41. *Volders*, nave ceiling fresco, 1766 (see pp. 251–2)

42. *Neresheim*, abbey church, choir ceiling fresco, *c.* 1773 (see pp. 116–18)

43. *St Gallen*, rotunda ceiling fresco, c. 1757 (see pp. 188–90)

Gothic traces are visible in the nave arcades, the choir windows and vault. (2) The stucco work in the nave is *c*. 1718 (in aisles *c*. 1800). (3) The vast and majestic high altar (*c*. 1714) has interesting scagliola work by *Dominikus Zimmermann* (cf. *Wemding*, Pfarrkirche, side altars).

Würzburg, Neumünster. Baroquization 1710–19. Severely damaged in March 1945 but now (July 1957) the best-restored church in the city and served as the cathedral (while the actual cathedral recovered slowly and painfully from a still worse bashing). The present dimensions and general elevation of the church date from the first half of the thirteenth century. A basilica, it had originally a 6-bay nave, E. and W. transepts, E. and W. choirs with crypts beneath and single W. tower (only one of a pair planned having been completed). The Baroque transformation left it with 4-bay nave, E. transepts and choir and, in place of the older W. transept, a domed rotunda and external façade. The original E. and W. crypts remain. *Noteworthy features. Exterior:* Attention is drawn above all to the brilliant and beautiful and fortunately undamaged façade (completed 1716, and designed by *Johann Dientzenhofer*; the statues by *Jakob Auwera*). The interplay of curve and counter-curve makes this one of the most original and dynamic of Baroque façades; its attractiveness is increased by the warm red sandstone and by the (somewhat later) approaching steps. *Interior:* (1) The earlier origin of the church is unmistakable (character of the arcades, raised choir); as is also a certain bareness that betokens the makeshift patching of damage in fact irreparable. (2) The rotunda was designed by *Joseph Greising*, its interesting (mainly undamaged and since restored) fresco 1736 by *Nikolaus Stuber*. (3) The high altar and the stucco-marble facing of the sanctuary are attributed to *Dominikus Zimmermann*; his brother *Johann Baptist* painted the original frescoes in nave and choir (since the damage of 1945 'restored' out of all recognition). (4) Of the Baroque altars and furnishings only the two elegant and attractive late side altars in the rotunda (1773) have been spared by the bombs; to which should be added the dignified later, classicist choir stalls in white and gold (1780–1, but only those on S. original, the N. row a copy replacing originals bombed).

Other Churches of Interest

Altenerding, Mariä Verkündigung (1 m. S. Erding). Parish church 1724 by *Anton Kogler* of Erding. Decorations and furnishings 1760–7. A most attractive interior. Frescoes 1767 by *Martin Heigl*. High altar, a graceful columned structure, with tabernacle and statuary by *Christian Jorhan the Elder* (cf. his work in *Niederding* and elsewhere in the district). His also the pulpit in the form of a ship with Christ and Peter, similar to the earlier work at *Niederding* (which has a merman and fishes beneath instead of water).

Amberg, (1) *Schulkirche* (*St Augustine*), 1697–1701. Formerly Salesian nuns. An aisleless building of much charm and with two fine frescoes by *G. B. Götz* (1758), that over nave unusually 'architectural' for its late date) and beautiful high altar and organ case by *Joachim Schlott* of Amberg (1758). (2) *Mariahilf* (on hill E. of town). Pilgrimage church 1697–1701 by *Georg Peimbl* and *Philipp Plankh* with stately, if somewhat squat, interior, good early stucco decoration (to the designs of *G. B. Carlone*; cf. his work at *Passau Cathedral*) and interesting early frescoes by *C. D. Asam* (1716–17, cf. his almost contemporary work at *Michelfeld* 1717–18 and slightly later work at *Aldersbach* 1720).

Au (Inn valley, below Wasserburg). Formerly Augustinian. 6-bay wall-pillar church 1708–17. Good stucco (*c.* 1715–54) and main altars (*c.* 1717); fine choir stalls (*c.* 1690). Notable also (as in *Gars*, see below) the red marble tombstones (fifteenth and sixteenth century).

Baumburg (N. of Chiemsee). Formerly Augustinian canons. 1754–7 baroquization of twelfth-century church (towers of that date); in prominent situation with extensive mountain views. Brilliant frescoes (*F. A. Scheffler*, 1756–7); fine carving on choir stalls, galleries over, and organ gallery.

Benediktbeuern (35 m. S. Munich, 7 m. N. Kochel). Formerly Benedictine (since 1930 Salesian) abbey church 1681–6. Architect unknown; similarities with *Tegernsee*, in both fine Italianate stucco, and frescoes by *H. G. Asam*. The delicate elliptical *Anastasiakapelle* (N.E. of choir) one of *J. M. Fischer's* best minor works (1750–8) with fresco (1752) by *J. J. Zeiller* and side altars by *Ignaz Günther*, or influenced by him.

Bertoldshofen (on Kempten–Schongau road, by Markt Oberdorf). Parish church 1728–31 (*Johann Georg Fischer*). An original, attractive building with beautiful interior decoration (stucco by *Ignaz Finsterwalder*, frescoes by *Matthias Wolcker*). Exquisite pulpit with figures (round the side Christ with Peter and Paul; below sounding-board the Evangelists' symbols; above, putti representing the four continents; atop of all, St Michael).

Bettbrunn (6 m. N.E. Ingolstadt). Parish and pilgrimage church. Lower stage of tower twelfth, choir fifteenth century. Nave rebuilt 1774 by *Leonhard Matthias Giessl* of Munich (influence of *J. M. Fischer* traceable, e.g. the rounding-off of the interior corners of nave produces a 'centralized' interior of octagonal feeling within rectangular outer walls). Interior brilliant with all the elegance and serenity of the latest period; especially fine the frescoes by *Christian Wink* (nave, scenes from the history of the pilgrimage 1777; choir, Transfiguration (1784). *Giessl* and *Wink* worked together at the following other churches: *Inning*, *Eching* and *Dietramszell*, *St Leonhard*.

Beyharting (N.W. Rosenheim). Formerly Augustinian canons, now parish church; 1688–70 baroquization of earlier twelfth-fifteenth century building with (1730) very fine stucco decoration by *J. B. Zimmermann* and frescoes by *Jakob Wersching*. Delicate later organ case (1790).

Buxheim (W. Memmingen). Parish church, an early work of *D. Zimmermann* (1725) with characteristic windows and good frescoes by *Georg Hermann* (1727).

Deisenhausen (near Krumbach). Parish church. A charming

building (1765–7) by *Joseph Dossenberger* (cf. *Hammerstetten* below), with excellent interior decoration (especially stucco work, frescoes by *J. B. Enderle*, and high altar).

Dietramszell (N. Bad Tölz). (1) *Maria Himmelfahrt*, 1726–41. Formerly Augustinian Canons, since 1803 Salesian nuns. Interior notable (*a*) for the fine, almost over-brilliant (yet unrestored) frescoes by *J. B. Zimmermann* (1741), that over nave showing St Augustine begging heavenly protection for his Order; (*b*) for the magnificent high altar that recalls that at *Diessen* in having a movable painting (fine Assumption by *J. B. Zimmermann*) and in the thematic connection between this, superstructure and ceiling design above (with the modification that the Holy Trinity awaiting Mary, here in ceiling fresco, and the putti holding the crown have changed places); (*c*) for the fine, vivid statuary by *Franz Xaver Schmädl* on high altar, E. side altars, pulpit and flanking the choir arch. (2) *St Leonhard*, 1769–74. Pilgrimage church by *L. M. Giessl*, just outside town in a meadow picturesquely ringed by trees, with frescoes by *Christian Wink* (1769), fine (tinted) stucco, good statuary, all classicist in feeling.

Dillingen (on Danube, between Günzburg and Donauwörth). Early Jesuit Church 1610–17 by *Hans Alberthal* with brilliant later decoration 1750–65, the frescoes the masterpieces of *Christian Thomas Scheffler*, a pupil of C. D. Asam.

Gars (Inn valley, below Wasserburg). Formerly Augustinian Canons; now Redemptorist Abbey, with seminary. Rebuilding 1661 ff. by *Gaspare* and *Domenico Zuccalli*, nephew and cousin of the more famous *Enrico* (see pp. 133–6). A rather lifeless wall-pillar church with no stucco (except in one chapel and on choir arch) and undistinguished late frescoes.

Hammerstetten (between Günzburg and Wettenhausen), St Nikolaus. A charming small church of elliptical ground-plan by *Joseph Dossenberger*, 1762, with frescoes and Stations of the Cross by *J. B. Enderle* (cf. *Deisenhausen* above) and good altars.

Herbertshofen, *St Clemens*, 1754 (on Augsburg–Donauwörth

road). Parish church by *Hans Adam Dossenberger*. Exterior compact and colourful but heavy in detail (e.g. tower cornice). Charming interior with frescoes by *Johann Baptist Enderle* (1754), that over nave with curious 'baldachin' tasselled frame-surround, optically supported by a motif of doubled pilasters flat against the ceiling. Beautiful high altar. Attractive oval Stations of the Cross, wall paintings grouped in twos or threes each within a stucco surround of scroll design.

Herrgottsruh (Friedberg, just E. Augsburg). Pilgrimage church 1751–3 with brilliant stucco by *F. X. Feichtmayr*, choir fresco by *C. D. Asam* (1738), those in nave and aisles by *Matthäus Günther*.

Höglwörth (12 m. S.E. Traunstein, 8 m. W. Salzburg). Formerly small foundation of Augustinian canons. Medieval church rebuilt *c.* 1650–89 (earlier sanctuary retained). Picturesque situation on peninsula of small lake with mountain background. Elegant and delicate later stucco ornament (*Benedikt Zöpf*, 1765). Good frescoes (*Franz Nicholas Streicher* of Trostberg, 1765), also high altar statues (Peter and Paul) and pulpit.

Ilgen (by Steingaden). Pilgrimage chapel 1670–6 with excellent harmonious stucco decoration by (?) *Johann Schmutzer*.

Inchenhofen, St Leonhard (near Aichach), in its present form 1705–6. Pilgrimage and parish church retaining its Gothic hall type. Notable especially for its immense, richly-coloured nave fresco (*Ignaz Baldauf*, 1776) spanning all five bays and showing scenes from the life of the Saint; also for the remarkably elegant and fanciful high altar.

Kleinhelfendorf (mid-way between Munich and Rosenheim). Parish church of St Emmeram by *Konstantine Pader* 1668–9 (plate 34). One of the most attractive of the smaller interiors. Important for excellent early stucco work (Miesbach school) with pale tints of rose, ochre and turquoise (plate 24). The St Emmeram chapel close by (1752) offers an interesting later contrast.

Klosterlechfeld, 1603–56 (16 m. S. Augsburg). Franciscan and pilgrimage church. The original round chapel (*Elias Holl*, 1603) now sanctuary, heightened 1656 when nave was added. Remarkable external appearance, recalling *Maria Birnbaum*. Good eighteenth century decoration and furnishing; frescoes by *Johann Georg Lederer* 1734; stucco ornament by *Johann* and *Ignaz Finsterwalder*.

Landsberg (on R. Lech, S. Augsburg). *Heiligkreuz*, formerly Jesuit, 1752–4, by *Ignatius Merani*; owing to the high position its twin-towered façade a prominent feature of the town; but its interest lies in its well-proportioned, colourful interior with good, boldly conceived frescoes by *Thomas Scheffler* (1753–5).

Landshut-Seligenthal (just outside the town on the W. bank of the Isar). Abbey of Cistercian nuns with unbroken history since 1232 (except for the years 1803–35). Present church a reconstruction of 1732–4 by *Johann Baptist Gunetzrhainer*. It is interesting principally (1) for the stucco ornament and the brilliant frescoes of *Johann Baptist Zimmermann* (2) for the admirable statuary (by *J. W. Jorhan*) on the magnificent altars and pulpit—the altars themselves being perhaps somewhat heavy for the church.

Maria Birnbaum (5 m. W. Altomünster, 12 m. E. Augsburg). Monastic and pilgrimage church 1661–5 by *Konstantine Pader*. Exterior (plate 4) with its towers and domes and curves highly remarkable, almost oriental (the earlier *Volders* in Tyrol offers the only comparison). Interior with typical restrained but admirable early stucco and no frescoes. Note in the lantern niches excellent figures of Apostles which really belong on the nave corbels in *Eresing* and are here hopelessly 'skied'.

Mindelheim (between Landsberg and Memmingen). Jesuit Church 1625–6, nave largely rebuilt 1721–2. A majestic interior with wall-pillar nave round which rhythmical galleries swing, excellent stucco (in nave later, 1722, and tinted with plastic scenes in place of frescoes), fine high altar (1737), pulpit (1722), and earlier pews (1625). Note over choir arch the symbolic (stucco) curtain drawn aside by putti, an excellent example.

Mittenwald (Austrian border, S.E. Garmisch). Parish church

1738 by *Josef Schmutzer*, apse Gothic. Exterior and interior alike highly attractive. Good stucco (*Schmutzer*); main frescoes 1740 (also high altar painting 1742) by *Matthäus Günther*. Tower painting designed by *M. Günther*.

Mödingen (N. Dillingen). Convent of Dominican nuns; church 1716–18, the earliest work of *Dominikus Zimmermann*. Stucco and frescoes by *J. B. Zimmermann*, fine pulpit *c.* 1720–30 (plate 22).

Mönchsdeggingen (between Donauwörth and Nördlingen). Former Benedictine abbey, now parish church. Baroquization 1751–2 of twelfth-fifteenth century church. Good stucco, frescoes (*V. F. Rigl*) and altars; general effect harmonious, stately and festive.

Mussenhausen (5 m. S.W. Mindelheim), pilgrimage and Franciscan monastery church, choir Gothic, nave 1755, decoration 1755–63. Chief interest the magnificent nave fresco (Assumption), 1763, by *J. B. Enderle* showing greater looseness and movement than his earlier choir fresco (1755). Fine stucco in choir and notable carved Stations of the Cross.

Niederding, St Martin, 1758–9 (2½ m. N.W. Erding). Probably by *Johann Baptist Lethner* of Erding. A very attractive interior. Three good altars with figures by *Christian Jorhan the Elder* (1761–2; cf. his work at *Altenerding*). 'Ship' pulpit also by *Jorhan*, similar in general to that at *Altenerding*.

Oberaltaich (N. bank of Danube, 6 m. below Straubing). Formerly Benedictine (since 1803 parish) church 1622–9 designed by the then abbot *Vitus Höser*. A 7-bay hall church with galleries, E. and W. apses and twin W. towers. The main interest is in the remarkable, indeed in their way unique, series of frescoes 1727–30 by *Josef Anton März* to a plan drawn up (and still extant) by Abbot *Dominikus Perger*. They depict scenes from the life of Christ and the history of the Benedictine Order, cover the ceiling space of the entire church and are executed in soft velvety colours that give them the appearance of tapestry. High altar 1693 with fine later tabernacle and statuary (1758–9).

THE CHURCHES

Oberammergau (N.W. Garmisch, near *Ettal*). Parish church 1736–42 by *Josef Schmutzer* (cf. the neighbouring *Mittenwald*). Stucco admirable (*J. Schmutzer* and his son *Franz Xaver*), frescoes important (*Matthäus Günther*), majestic high altar with fine statuary (*Franz Xaver Schmädl*, by whom also the side altars here, the high altars in *Rottenbuch* and *Schongau* and much else in Bavaria, including the altars in the attractive earlier little church, 1709, at *Unterammergau* farther down the valley.

Oberelchingen (6 m. N.E. Ulm). Formerly Benedictine, now parish church. A reconstruction (1774–85, by *Josef Dossenberger*) of a twelfth-century Romanesque cruciform basilica destroyed in a fire in 1773. Good early classicist decoration and furnishings. Colourful frescoes by *Januarius Zick*; high altar by *Thomas Schaidhauf* with painting by *Zick*.

Reisach (S. Rosenheim, near Niederaudorf). Carmelite monastic church 1737–47 by *I. A. Gunetzrhainer*. Its noble interior has a classical restraint perhaps unique for the date, its severity lightened by the rhythmical cornice. No stucco or frescoes (cf. the Carmelite church in Bamberg, 1692–1707, by *Leonhard Dientzenhofer*). Four important and beautiful side altars (and other works) in carved relief by *Johann Baptist Straub*, the reliefs (unfortunately over-painted) taking the place of altar paintings (cf. his side altars at *Schäftlarn*).

Roggenburg (S. of Günzburg). Originally Premonstratensian. Rebuilt 1752–8 by *Simpert Kramer*. Good stucco and furnishings (the frescoes 1900). High altar figures by *Anton Sturm* (cf. *Die Wies*). Superb Rococo organ case.

Scheyern (N.E. Freising, by Pfaffenhofen). Benedictine abbey church. Reconstruction 1768–9 of twelfth-century church. Good high altar with painting by *Christian Wink* and side figures by (?) *Ignaz Günther*. Sacristy with fine carving (1697).

Schongau, Mariä Himmelfahrt (On R. Lech 16 m. S. Landsberg). Reconstruction 1748–54, to a plan of *Dominikus Zimmermann*, of fifteenth-century church. Two fine frescoes by *Matthäus Günther* (over sanctuary the Holy Trinity, 1748; over the nave

Glorification of the Virgin, 1761). Boldly conceived and impressive high altar with lively statuary (1758–60 probably by *Franz Xaver Schmädl* to a plan by *Ignaz Günther*).

Starnberg, St Josef (N. end of lake). Parish church 1763–70 by *Leonhard Matthäus Giessl*. Good frescoes by *Christian Wink* (who often worked with Giessl). The high altar an excellent work of *Ignaz Günther*, 1764–5 (Holy Family between St John Nepomuk and St Francis Xavier). Fine, interesting pulpit (also probably by *Günther*) with prominent Evangelist symbols (the eagle above sounding-board).

Steingaden (close to *Die Wies*). Formerly Premonstratensian. A Romanesque church baroquized in stages: choir stucco 1663; nave stucco (*F. X. Schmutzer*) 1740–50, frescoes (*J. G. Bergmüller*, cf. *Diessen*) 1751. Interesting contrast between the earlier decoration in choir and the later in the nave; in the former the stucco predominates, in the latter the frescoes.

Tuntenhausen (N.W. Rosenheim, not to be confused with Tüntenhausen!) Parish and pilgrimage church 1627–30 (towers from earlier church 1513–33, steeples 1890). Gothic feeling lingers unmistakably on in this early Baroque reconstruction. Fine early stucco, no frescoes (though the stucco has tinted fields), contemporary good altars and richly decorated pulpit.

Vilgertshofen (S.E. Landsberg). Pilgrimage church 1686–92 by *Johann Schmutzer* with cruciform ground-plan of interesting and original design, first-rate stucco decoration (Wessobrunn school) and fresco by *J. B. Zimmermann* (1734) over high altar.

Violau (16 m. W.N.W. Augsburg, near Welden). Pilgrimage church of St Michael 1617–19 (*David* and *Georg Hobel*) with nave of hall type reconstructed in eighteenth century by *Simpert Kramer* who removed some of the pillars. Externally interesting the early windows with gabled mouldings (cf. *Elias Holl*) and the priest's house built onto the W. end. The attractive interior (nave unusually broad) has decorations etc. mainly of eighteenth century. The 12 brilliant ceiling frescoes are the masterpieces of *Johann Georg Dieffenbrunner* (1751), the fine stucco of the same date. The side altars are by *Michael Fischer* of Dillingen (cf. his work at *Welden*, *Bergen* and elsewhere). Elegant and colourful the organ gallery, case and supporting columns. High altar and pulpit 1686.

Vornbach (left bank of Inn, 7 m. S. Passau). Originally Benedictine abbey church; completed 1637 with impressive soaring façade; fine imaginative later stucco work and altar statuary by *Joseph Holzinger* (1728–33, especially the angels and putti); the contemporary frescoes (*Anton Warathy*) unfortunately over-painted since.

Weihenlinden (3 m. N.W. Bad Aibling). Servite and pilgrimage church 1653–7 by an ecclesiastical amateur, Propst *Valentine Steyr*, the older pilgrimage chapel being embodied in the present high altar. A building of robust and not unattractive uncouthness. Remarkable: (1) the twin towers rising from a common base reminiscent of the Romanesque rather than of the Baroque; (2) the un-Baroque proportions of the basilical interior, especially the squat, ugly 'triforium'; (3) the representation (upper storey niches of high altar) of the Trinity as three bearded and crowned kings of identical appearance (1698).

Welden (12 m. N.W. Augsburg). (1) *St Maria*, 1732. Parish church; reconstruction of an older building. Its main interest lies in the large oval nave fresco by *Matthäus Günther* (signed 1732 over organ), his earliest considerable work. Delicate tinted stucco ornament. (2) *St Thekla*, 1756–7, on higher ground to E. overlooking the town. A "votive" church, by *Hans Adam Dossenberger*. A very attractive building. Exterior compact, with squat W. tower and heavy cornice recalling *Maria Steinbach* on a smaller, less robust scale; the numerous windows of rhythmical 'Zimmermann' character but heavier in treatment. Interior of great interest and charm. The main fresco (of elongated quatrefoil form) by *Johann Baptiste Enderle* (1759). Admirable stucco by *Ferretti*; note especially the side altars in nave with remarkable figure groups in coloured stucco moulding. The three main altars all have elaborate painted illusory architecture, the perspectival effect helped by the curve of the walls. Note the two little pulpits (which offer good views).

Wemding (11 m. E. Nördlingen and N. Donauwörth). Pilgrimage church on hill outside town 1748–52 (*Franz Josef Roth*). Beautiful festive interior with fine stucco and painting by *J. B. Zimmermann*, his son *Michael* and his pupil *Martin Heigl* (1752–4). The high altar (1762–3) a dynamic creation of *Philipp Jakob Rämpl* with admirable statuary. Attractive choir-stalls (1759) and pulpit (1780).

Westerndorf (2 m. S.W. Rosenheim), 1668–*c*. 70. Externally circular, drum-shaped church (interior plan a Greek cross with apsidal arms); the immense 'onion' dome-roof together with the slender tower (lower part medieval) give a remarkable, oriental yet not unattractive appearance. Architect unknown but probably *Konstantin Pader* (cf. similarities with *Maria Birnbaum*). Good early stucco ornament of the *Miesbach* school (cf. the contemporary *Kleinhelfendorf* farther west).

Weyarn (just off Autobahn Munich–Salzburg at the Mangfall bridge). Formerly Augustinian canons. Rebuilt 1687–1700. Excellent stucco work and frescoes by *J. B. Zimmermann* (1729). The glory of the church lies in the statuary groups and other work of *Ignaz Günther*, especially the Annunciation and the pietà (left and right of the choir arch respectively, both 1764), the high altar tabernacle (1763) and the shrine of St Valerius (S. nave aisle, designed 1755).

Wiblingen, 1732–82 (just S. Ulm). Formerly Benedictine, now parish church. Has a complicated history. Begun 1732 by *Christian Wiedemann*, continued after 1750 by *J. M. Fischer* (apsidal transept reduced) and completed 1772–82 by *Johann Specht*. W. façade incomplete and unsatisfactory. The spacious interior combines a Baroque ground-plan with restrained general atmosphere and classicist treatment of detail and shows interesting similarities with *St Gallen* and with *Neresheim*. Frescoes by *Januarius Zick*. Beautiful *Library*.

SWITZERLAND

The historical background against which the development in Switzerland must be viewed has already been briefly outlined, and certain facts were seen to emerge which we do not need to repeat here. We have also referred to the influence of the Vorarlberg architects and of the Italian-Swiss architects on the Swiss church architecture of the period. A generalization may now be ventured to serve as a keynote for this section. It is in fact only in a very limited sense that we can speak of 'Swiss' Baroque church architecture at all in Switzerland itself. The Italian-Swiss architects, as we have seen, moved to other parts, and works of any significance at all by them on Swiss soil are few. Two may here be mentioned, both in Tessin, as showing interesting early awareness of the characteristic spatial problems—*S. Croce* in *Riva S Vitale* (1588–94, probably by *Giovanni Antonio Protta*) and the pilgrimage church at *Morbo Inferiore* (*c.* 1600, architect unknown). These, though not yet Baroque, are significant precursors of the later style. On the other hand, the Jesuits, here as elsewhere the earliest conscious bearers of the new style, were, so to speak, birds of passage, and cannot be considered as having any native cultural roots. By far the most important single influence on Swiss church Baroque was that of the Vorarlbergers and they came from outside. There remain one or two native families and a handful of isolated names; and the work of these is in many cases, as with the *Putschert* family, so late (after 1780) that it belongs to the Classicist rather than to the Baroque or Rococo and thus lies outside our field.

We shall consider here the Swiss churches under the four headings: *Jesuit churches, Vorarlberg churches*, the churches of *the Singer family*, and *miscellaneous others*.

Jesuit Churches

Four churches built under Jesuit influence may be chronologically considered and compared.

Freiburg (Fribourg), St Michael, 1604–13. Architect *Abraham Cotti.* Extensively reshaped, redecorated and refurnished 1756–71. With 4-bay basilical nave, narrower apsidal choir, without transeptal formation or galleries, the church is of interest chiefly as an example of how in their early churches (as we have seen, p. 32n.) the Jesuits adapted themselves to existing styles and forms. The proportions and spirit of late Gothic linger on here unmistakably. Frescoes by *Franz Anton Ermeltraut* (of Würzburg, 1756–7); high altar 1768–71; pulpit, organ case and confessionals all 1756–64.

Lucerne, Hofkirche St Leodegar, 1633–44. Architect *Jakob Khurer* of Ingolstadt. An interesting transitional building of basilical type with rectangular ground-plan (5-bay nave), apsidal sanctuary and late Gothic, twin-steepled W. façade (1504–15, the only part of the older building to survive the fatal fire of 1633,[1] its central part of late Renaissance character). *Interior:* Its lofty proportions come as a surprise after the squat impression made by the body of the church externally. Despite the date, proportions and elevation are not yet Baroque. Stucco ornamentation was apparently intended but never carried out (what appears to be such is only painting). The visitor should note the fine carved side altars (1640–6, by various hands) which have early Baroque character though a medieval spirit hovers about them; the splendid choir stalls (carvings by *Nikolaus Geissler,* 1639); the celebrated organ (by *Johann Geissler* of Salzburg, 1640–51, since enlarged); and the 'perspectival' metal choir-screen (*Johann Reiffel* of Constance, c. 1644).

Lucerne, St Francis Xavier, 1666–73. Architect *Christoph Vogler.* Here Gothic influence has receded and we have a convincing Baroque interior early in character with later decoration. A wall-pillar church of basilical form with apsidal choir, no transepts and twin-towered façade.

Noteworthy features. Exterior: The façade, the first of its type in Switzerland and not unattractive, is yet weak in certain

[1] Apparently caused by the shooting of crows on the roof!

details; (*a*) the cornices are too heavy and rob the pilasters of their power; (*b*) the segmental gable is insignificant and too narrow for the width it is intended to span; (*c*) the towers (added 1893), though undoubtedly picturesque, are yet not weighty enough to hold their own against the storeys below them. *Interior:* Here, on the other hand, we find nobility. (1) Spaciousness, stability, compactness, unity—these are the key-notes. Nothing impedes the view, the double pilasters give a great impression of structural firmness, the massive high altar dominates and in dominating unites, and the compactness and unity are clinched by the inexorable cornice like a hoop round the walls. (2) The colouring is distinguished, the dark, warm rose-colour of altars and pulpit is in surprisingly beautiful contrast and harmony with the whitewash. (3) The stucco ornament (as also the frescoes) in the nave is eighty years later (1749–50) and too slight for the massive proportions; compare the original work in the side chapels and on the galleries and capitals. (4) The monumental high altar and the shapely side altars and pulpit are all works of *Christoph Bruck* (high altar, however, after a plan by *Heinrich Mayer*, creator of the original stucco ornament). (5) The two-tier gallery over the entrance is typical for a Jesuit church (cf. *Solothurn* and elsewhere). (6) The ground-plan of this church should be compared with those of other great Jesuit churches, e.g. *St Michael in Munich, Dillingen, Vienna, Solothurn.*

Solothurn, 1680–8. Architects *B. Heinrich Mayer* and *P. Franz Demers,* according to the usual view; but the name of *Franz Beer* has also been suggested (*a*) because of certain Vorarlberg features of the design, (*b*) because so many of the twenty-odd churches that Beer is known to have built are unidentified, (*c*) because nothing known of the other two architects suggests that they would have been capable of the church. These are interesting reflections but we cannot follow them here. The church is a wall-pillar church with two-bay nave, slightly transeptal third bay and very much narrower single-bay apsidal choir.

Noteworthy features. Exterior: The façade alone is of interest and that because of the devices used to align it with the houses of the street. It is a clear, reposeful composition. *Interior:* Its character may perhaps be best brought out by a comparison with the Lucerne Jesuit church. It is less tight, compact, static; more manifold, more differentiated. The high altar is not over-powering; the cornice has not the relentless urge of that at Lucerne but appears only in transverse sections as it runs round the pillars. The stucco work, probably by an Italian artist, is of delicate quality.

The Vorarlberg School

The important influence of the Vorarlberg architects on Swiss Baroque has already been referred to. In fact, all the greatest churches of the period in Switzerland were built by one or other of their number. The reader who has been devoting time to the South German churches will already be familiar with the names of most of those who demand our attention here. Those who have not yet done so are referred to pages 119–20 where the origin and characteristics of this group of architects are briefly discussed.

The figures who here concern us are *Caspar Moosbrugger*, *Franz Beer* and two other members of the Beer family, *Peter Thumb* and *Johannes Rueff*. We shall deal with them and their work in that order.

Caspar Moosbrugger

Those who know Moosbrugger's work only from *Weingarten* will be surprised at what they find in his Swiss churches. In the façade of *Einsiedeln* they will no doubt readily recognize his hand; but the interior is another matter. Still less easily would they find his work in *Muri* or *Ittingen*, though if they were very observant they might, on reflection, find an echo of the *Muri* interior in the octagon at *Einsiedeln*.

Muri, 1694–8 (12 m. S.W. Zürich, 13 m. N. Lucerne; reached by rail from either). Now parish church (originally Benedictine abbey founded 1027, dissolved 1841). The problem was to re-build and extend an early Romanesque cruciform, twin-towered basilica. Moosbrugger's solution was to leave the towers and the low choir, convert the transepts into chapels flanking the latter and build out the former (basilical) nave into an octagonal rotunda with transeptal chapels and lantern windows above. The result is a plan of strange complexity, and an interior not without beauty; and Moosbrugger had a chance to try his hand at a rotunda, an attempt followed up brilliantly at *Einsiedeln*. The work was actually carried out by *Giovanni Betini*.

Noteworthy features. Exterior: The whole building presents a remarkable and disjointed appearance, with the bulky pyra-midal roof over the octagon sitting heavily on the diminutive transept, by contrast the very slender steeples, the great porch with its lean-to roof. The treatment in general is plain, even bald. *Interior:* Forms an unusually sharp contrast to the ex-terior, and contains in itself one hardly less so. (1) The rotunda is generously proportioned and full of light; the old choir, by comparison, seems low, dark and tunnel-like. (2) The stucco ornamentation on the rotunda ceiling (*Betini*) is of good quality but perhaps a trifle too light for the dimensions of the dome. (3) The frescoes (by *Antonio Francesco Giorgioli, c.* 1707–10) are original and vigorous scenes referring to the Benedictine Order. (4) The furnishings and other objects flanking the en-trance to the choir (side altars, organ galleries, pulpit and counterpart, all by *Mattäus Peusch*, 1744–5) are good in them-selves but collectively make a somewhat cluttered impression. (5) The choir is still spanned by a Gothic lierne vault to which Baroque painting has been added; the stalls (*Simon Bachmann*, 1650–1) are good work, and the century-later wrought-iron screen (*J. J. Hoffner* of Constance, 1744–6) excellent.

Disentis, 1696–1712 (Canton Graubünden/Grisons, 15 m. N.E. Andermatt, on main road and railway line Andermatt–Chur, from both of which rail connections). Benedictine abbey church (foundation date uncertain, refounded 750). The ascription to *Moosbrugger* is not indisputable as *Franz Beer* also has a claim; possibly both worked on the building. A wall-pillar church of unbrokenly rectangular ground-plan with 4-bay nave (the fourth wider), choir with narrower, square-ended sanctuary and twin-towered façade. The abbey is a ruggedly impressive block in a grand mountain setting in the upper Rhine valley.

Noteworthy features. Exterior: Calls for little comment. Unlike most Vorarlberg churches there is externally no visible transeptal formation or gables. *Interior:* (1) Here we recognize many of the Vorarlberg characteristics—the emphasis on length, the deep wall-pillars, the galleries (those in the nave set flush with the faces of the pillars, as in other early examples such as *Schönenberg, Obermarchtal, Irsee*—all in Bavaria). (2) The decorations and furnishings suffered greatly in 1799 when the village was burnt by the French and the abbey badly damaged, and again in a further fire in 1846. Original stucco work is under the galleries. Other decoration mostly 1913, frescoes 1925. Furnishings mostly later restored or replacements; high altar (1656), from a church near Deggendorf in Bavaria, replaces since 1888 the original (destroyed 1799) by *Johann Ritz* which was presumably similar in style to the existing choir arch altars which are also by him.

Ittingen, 1703 (3 m. N.W. Frauenfeld, 17 m. S.W. Constance; nearest station Frauenfeld whence bus to Warth and 20 min. walk). Formerly monastic church (Augustinian foundation, 1461 Carthusian), since dissolution (1868) in private owner-ship. The church lies in an isolated and concealed position in the Thur valley and might easily be missed. Admission is gained by ringing at the porch up the steps in the centre of the row of buildings to the right across the enclosure. Attention is directed to this church not because of its architecture, which is unimportant, but because its decorations and furnishings (added 1763–70) make it one of the most exquisite Baroque interiors in the country.

Noteworthy features. Interior: (1) The combination of colours is of rare beauty—the rose-pink and gold of the altar, the pale turquoise of the stucco, the rich deep brown of the woodwork. (2) The triple altar (*Matthias Faller*, painting by *Franz Ludwig Hermann*) is a creation of remarkably graceful and jubilant beauty. (3) The delicate stucco ornamentation (artist unknown) has preserved unrestored its original colouring. (4) The frescoes (by *F. L. Hermann* 1763–4, some of his best). (5) The fine stalls which surround that part of the church in which we stand (the former monks' choir) and separate it from the rest; together with those in *St Urban*, *St Gallen* and *Beromünster* among the best in the country. It is a strange reflection that such joyous beauty should be found in a church of the severest of all monastic orders. (The visitor should ask to see the remains of the fifteenth-century monastic buildings which form a fairly well-preserved, though partially ruinous, example of the lay-out of a small Carthusian house with its individual cells.)

Einsiedeln, 1719–35 (12 m. S.E. Zug. 8 m. N.E. Schwyz; reached by branch line from Biberbrücke on the Zürich–Arth/Goldau line). Benedictine abbey church (foundation 934). A wall-pillar church of broadly Vorarlberg type with 3-bay nave (the W. bay developed in exceptional manner into a large octagon), long narrower 4-bay double choir, no real transept formation and twin-towered façade. Except for the façade the church lies enclosed within the monastic buildings. Together with the slightly earlier *Weingarten*, Moosbrugger's second masterpiece. We must recall that here we are at the architect's spiritual home. He came from Vorarlberg, but he was a lay-brother at Einsiedeln and lies buried here. In fact, he did not live to see the church completed (†1723). The supervision passed then into the hands of *Thomas Meyer*; others who worked on the building were the brother of the architect, *Johann*, and *Johannes Rueff*, the architect of *Engelberg*.

Noteworthy features. Exterior (plate 13): (1) Impressive are the colonnaded approach; the wide, sloping square (in contrast to the steep, cramped approach to Weingarten); the grandiose

scale and the palace-like character of the pile as a whole.
(2) The façade invites close comparison with Weingarten; in
general it is less squat, there is greater vertical tendency, the
towers are more independent without competition from a
dome, the gable sharper, the cornice interrupted. (3) The
transeptal formation of the roof is misleading in as far as there
is little or no corresponding formation in the interior. *Interior:*
Not only more richly decorated but also structurally more complex than is *Weingarten*. As at *Vierzehnheiligen*, though without the unfortunate complications that arose there, the plan
was determined by a fixed object, in this case the chapel on the
site of the cell of St Meinrad as the central spot of veneration.
To give this as prominent a position as possible Moosbrugger,
applying his experience from the church at *Muri*, developed
the western bays of the nave into a great octagonal rotunda,
one side of which forms the inner curve of the façade convex.
Note especially: (1) the manner in which this chapel is structurally connected with the architecture of the octagon itself;
a pair of pillars joined by an arch combine to form at once the
back wall of the chapel, a triumphal arch above it and the central support for the arches of the octagon ceiling overhead
(the latter function somewhat similar to that of the central
column in many English Gothic cathedral chapter houses).
(2) The restrained, classicist style of the chapel itself (somewhat out of keeping with its surroundings) is due to its having
been rebuilt in 1815–17 after destruction by the French in
1798. (3) Others may agree with my own judgment that the
E. parts of the church, especially the long, narrow choir, are
architecturally weaker and less interesting than the octagon,
even beyond the diminuendo that was no doubt intended.
(4) The brilliant, possibly over-elaborate ornamentation (stucco
work and frescoes) is by the *Asam* brothers and of course of
great quality. The central theme running through it all is that
of the Redemption of sinful man for which the entire scheme
of decoration must be understood as expressing a paean of
praise in colour and figure and form. Of the frescoes, especially

notable are the large one over the choir (showing God the Son
kneeling before the Father and offering Himself as Redeemer)
and the tremendous painting in the main nave dome (the
Nativity of Christ), these two of a particularly German inner
fervour. Note too, in thematic connection with this painting,
the hilariously joyful stucco putti swinging down to earth with
long banderoles inscribed with the Good News and other re-
joicing angels precariously astride cornice angles and other
points; all this very characteristic of the Asams (cf. the almost
contemporary work at *Osterhofen*). (5) The organ galleries
flanking the choir arch are happily conceived (for the tumble
of putti about them cf. *Fürstenfeldbruck*, *Rottenbuch* and many
other cases). (6) The remarkably fanciful abbot's throne should
be noted with its charmingly irresponsible putto astride the
top. (7) The high altar is Italian work, the design by *Giovanni
Antonio Torricelli*, carried out by *Domenico Pozzi*, 1749–51.
(8) In the upper choir are good choir stalls (1675–80) originally in the lower choir, and a fine altar painting (Crucifixion,
by *Franz Kraus*, 1749).

We cannot do more here than point to a few of the main
features of this enormously rich interior. There are weak
points, of course; above all some very weak nineteenth-century
altar paintings by *Paul Deschwanden* (side altars next to those
of St Benedict and St Meinrad) who also over-painted the high
altar picture in an unfortunate manner; and the sentimental
seated figure of Christ opposite the pulpit, in very poor taste.
The visitor is advised to try to get up into the galleries from
which enchanting views down into the church and up to the
decoration can be had.

Franz Beer

This—the most brilliant—member of the Beer family will
already be known to those who have visited the South German
churches of *Irsee* or *Holzen*. His greatest work, however, was
done on Swiss soil and culminated in the church of *St Urban*. We
draw attention here to three churches of varying sizes and quality.

Rheinau, 1704–11 (on the Rhine, 5 m. below Schaffhausen, from which bus connection). Now parish church (former Benedictine abbey, first mentioned 844, finally dissolved 1862). A wall-pillar church with 4-bay nave, transeptal section, 2-bay square-ended choir and twin-towered façade. Lies very picturesquely in a loop of the river surrounded by thickly wooded hills.

Noteworthy features. Exterior: A clearly thought and clearly constructed example of its type. (1) The transept is more prominent than usual in a Vorarlberg church, both broader and higher (contrast *Obermarchtal*, *Irsee*, and even *St Urban* with its double transept formation). (2) The S.W. tower is sixteenth century (late Gothic window, also vault to ground-floor storey); the N.W. an early eighteenth-century copy of it—an interesting example, rare for the time, of deliberate imitation of older forms. *Interior:* Fine, light, generously proportioned; offers a number of points of special interest as well as one or two occasions for criticism. (1) The treatment of the pillars should be noted; we have the impression at first that they are not wall-pillars but detached. This tendency to make the pillars of a wall-pillar church appear detached we have noted at *Weingarten* and elsewhere. The effect is here achieved by a different device; the entablature projects on all sides prominently, while by contrast the wall section connecting with the outside wall is left quite blank and appears invisible (cf. *St Urban*). (2) The galleries are not, as in earlier churches (*Holzen*, *Irsee*), set flush with the pilaster faces but back a little, whereby the impression of width is increased in the nave. (3) Unfortunate is the position of the side altars—perhaps a result of the setting-back of the balconies; yet flush with the side walls they would have impeded the lighting. In any case, their size is excessive. (4) The transept, so prominent externally, seems to have disappeared here in the interior, until we discover that it is included in the choir; an unsatisfactory arrangement, for the spatial effect of a 'crossing' is quite lost. (5) Both stucco ornamentation (*Franz Xaver Schmutzer*) and frescoes (*F. A. Giorgioli*; scenes from the lives of Christ and Mary, in the main dome All Saints) are good work. (6) To be noted in the choir are the fine wrought iron screen with 'perspective' effect; the elaborate stalls (various hands, 1707–10); the unusual little choir organ, no longer playable; and the important high altar (*Judas Thadäus Sichelbein*, 1720–3) with painting of the Assumption (*Franz Karl Stauder*, 1723) and, above, the favourite motif of the crown supported by angels and putti awaiting Mary, grandly conceived and executed.

St Urban, 1711–36 (15 m. E. Solothurn, 4 m. E. Langenthal; from the latter, rail connection on the branch line to Melchnau). Now parish church (originally Augustinian foundation 1184, 1194 Cistercian until dissolution 1848). Large wall-pillar church with 2-bay nave, transeptal central section, 2-bay choir followed by second transeptal section and much narrower and lower square-ended sanctuary, and twin-towered façade.

Noteworthy features. Exterior: (1) The façade, impressive and monumental as a whole, is yet disappointing in detail, the treatment of gable, cornices and windows somewhat flat and unplastic. (2) The concave open portico in front of the entrance (and under the organ gallery) is an unusual feature. *Interior:* (1) The treatment of pillars and galleries should be compared with *Rheinau;* here the pilasters are doubled and the galleries not inset so far, but the treatment of the cornices to give the pillars greater apparent independence is similar. (2) The system of lighting is particularly skilful; from the W. not a window is seen and yet the whole long church right up to the high altar is full of light. (3) There are no frescoes but the stucco ornamentation on the ceiling is good in quality and of a design that fills the space excellently (compare closely with that in the very similar earlier case of *Obermarchtal*). (4) Here too, unfortunately, as in *Rheinau*, the altars are a source of weakness. The observer looking up the church cannot but feel that the proportions of the high altar and the main side altars in relation to one another are unsatisfactory. The side altars are too tall and flat, and the high altar, considering its importance, its distance and the light thrown upon it, too insignificant. Three really fine altars of harmonious design and the quality of the Rheinau high altar would have been the making of this in any case noble interior. (5) The W. end, on the other hand, with its composition of organ, gallery and windows is fine and in its way bears comparison with *Weingarten*. (6) The most important and celebrated feature of the furnishings is the superb choir stalls (1701–15, possibly by *Peter Fröhlicher* of Solothurn). Sold in 1853, they were bought, and brought, back from Dupplin Castle (near Perth) by the Gottfried Keller Fund in 1911.

Münsterlingen, 1709–27 (S. shore of Lake of Constance, 5 m. E. Constance; rail and bus connections from there and Romanshorn). Now parish church. Formerly convent of (twelfth century) Augustinian, then (1549) Benedictine nuns; dissolved 1848. Church of shallow wall-pillar type with 3-bay nave, transeptal section, choir with narrower apsidal sanctuary and slight W. tower. The interior is of greater interest than the very modest exterior would suggest.

Noteworthy features. Interior: (1) The plan shows a greater preoccupation with spatial problems than those of the last two churches. This becomes clear when we look at the ceiling and find the (central) transeptal section vaulted with an oval saucer dome set transversely, the choir with a circular one. (2) The decorations are good, particularly the brilliantly coloured frescoes (*Jakob Karl Stauder*). (3) The delicate iron screen is of the year 1736. (4) The outstretched hand projecting from the pulpit and holding a crucifix is found in other Swiss Baroque churches (e.g. *Fischingen*), in Bavaria at *Klosterlechfeld*.

The observation in this last church of an increased interest in the question of centrality leads us to two churches by the younger generations of the Beer family in which we see this interest expressed with still greater clearness.

Johann Michael Beer

Whether this was the son of *Franz Beer* (as is probable) or a

more distant relative of the same name and age is not certain.

St Katherinenthal, 1732–5 (on the left Rhine bank 5 m. E. Schaffhausen, near Diessenhofen; rail connection to Diessenhofen, whence 20 mins. walk). Now parish church; formerly convent of Dominican nuns (founded 1242, dissolved 1869). Towerless structure rectangular on plan with 2-bay wall-pillar nave and square-ended sanctuary. Here again the visitor should not be put off by external appearances!

Noteworthy features. Exterior: None, except an all-pervading plainness, indeed ugliness. This is perhaps an extreme case of the tendency of Vorarlberg architects to fail in their exteriors. *Interior:* Beautiful and serene with several features of interest. (1) Though on plan the two nave bays are identical in area the second appears much more spacious and indeed to constitute the body of the interior. This is due to the twofold fact that the first bay is monopolized by the wings of the organ gallery and is not marked at ceiling level by any pronounced arches; hence the second bay, which is so marked and is also unencumbered, assumes as transeptal 'crossing' the appearance and function of a central space. (2) The organ gallery with its richly carved balustrade (*Jakob Bommer* of Weingarten, 1735–6) is finely conceived and carried out, the organ itself grouping admirably with the ceiling frescoes, the gallery surging rhythmically forward to meet the counter-swing of the communion rails. (3) The church is well served by its altars (high altar painting by *J. K. Stauder*, 1738) and its stucco decoration (1733, possibly *Nikolaus Schutz*). (4) The ceiling frescoes (*J. K. Stauder*) are good but unequal; the effect of the central one, for instance, is impaired by the architectural element being too heavy and thus destroying its visionary character.

Johann Ferdinand Beer

Nephew of the *Johann Michael Beer* who co-operated at *St Gallen*.

Bernhardszell, 1776–8 (5 m. N.W. St Gallen and accessible thence by bus). Parish church. An original, compact and entirely 'centralized' design[1] in which the Vorarlberg tradition seems quite forgotten. The plan is a rotunda opening out on E., W., N. and S. into four slightly convex side arms; against the E. one the tower is built.

Noteworthy features. Interior: (1) At first sight all four projecting arms seem equally deep as well as wide. In fact this is not so; the side arms are considerably shallower. Hence, despite the uncompromising centrality of the circular rotunda, the lengthways axis receives the slightly greater stress, which is further emphasized by the high altar and the organ and the aisle between the pews (externally also, of course, by the tower). (2) The dome with its fresco seems here to grow directly out of, and to be a continuation of, the walls; there is even less cornice than at *Muri*. (3) The stucco ornament (artist unknown) is of good quality, but the vast fresco (*F. L. Hermann*, 1778) is not in general of the quality of this artist's work at *Ittingen*.

As we are dealing with this 'round church' type that is rare in Switzerland we take the opportunity to refer to another example which, though somewhat remote and unknown, is well worth a visit. Some 15 m. S.E. of Winterthur and 25 m. W. of S. Gallen, in a charming wooded valley, lies *Fischingen* with a one-time Benedictine abbey. On the N. side of the church (1684–5) was added later (1704) a chapel dedicated to St Idda (*Iddakapelle*; architect *P. Christian Huber*) in the form of a centralized, domed building. Externally its ground-plan is closely similar to that of *Bernhardszell*. The interior, however, apart from its more Italianate character, shows points of difference. The sections of wall between the side arms, at Bernhardszell merely pierced with windows, in this case open out into little niche-like chapels at the diagonal points, each with its own source of light from above.

Peter Thumb

It is usual, and almost certainly correct, to associate the great church of *St Gallen* with his name more closely than with that of

[1] Compare the little pilgrimage church of *St Ottilien* above Buttisholz.

any other Vorarlberg architect. Yet here again the picture is not quite clear. The original plan appears to derive from the Italian *Giovanni Gaspare Bagnato* (though he is otherwise known only as a secular architect), and the lay-brother *Gabriel Looser* also had a hand in it (see the wooden model of 1751 in the Stiftsarchiv); while the twin-towered façade seems to have been the work of *Johann Michael Beer*. Further, Thumb's name disappears from the building accounts after three years (1758). Yet there can be little doubt that the decisive influence in shaping existing plans to the design we see today was that of Thumb who was the first supervisor of the work.

St Gallen, 1755–86 (6 m. S. of Lake of Constance, on the main line Munich–Lindau–Zürich). Since 1824 diocesan cathedral. Originally Benedictine abbey (founded 720). The last of the great Baroque churches of Switzerland and one of the last in Europe. A wall-pillar church with large central rotunda between 3-bay E. and W. limbs of equal length, the former with twin-towered façade, the rotunda projecting considerably and covered with a squat transverse roof. The church lies in the centre of the old town.

Noteworthy features. Exterior (plate 19): (1) We can guess at certain probable characteristics of the interior—wall-pillars, a deep saucer dome in the rotunda (covered by the high roof), no galleries (incompatible with the tall windows). (2) The weak feature of the exterior is undoubtedly the long series of identically and not very imaginatively designed windows, the monotony of which the rotunda hardly breaks. (3) Even here, on the sides of the rotunda roof, the characteristic Vorarlberg miniature transept gable survives. (4) Of central importance is the beautiful E. façade with its towers. Here everything has been done to stress verticality and counteract the great length of the body of the church. The tapering of the towers, the strong upward thrust of the narrow central section whose colossal pair of columns seems to 'push up' the cornice with a vigour carried on into the steep gable and its lively turret—all this is directed to the same aim. (5) The sculpture on the E.

188

façade is a modern copy (1933) of a work by *Josef Anton Feuchtmayer* (1763–4, Coronation of the Virgin); that on W. gable is a fine Madonna (Immaculata) by *Christian Wenzinger* (1757–8). *Interior:* (1) The main features are as may be guessed from the outside. Not only, however, are there here no galleries but the wall-pillars have reached a final stage in the process of 'detachment' that in various aspects can be noticed at *Rheinau, St Urban* and *Weingarten.* (2) In general the Vorarlberg scheme as here represented has travelled far from the days of *Obermarchtal* and *Irsee.* We may suppose that the chief stimulus came from *Caspar Moosbrugger* with his bolder, more sophisticated planning and his growing interest in the rotunda as a functional section of a church (*Muri, Einsiedeln*). But some have seen other influences at work. If we compare the ground-plan of *St Gallen* with that of *Neresheim*, or visit the two churches in quick succession, we shall find it hard to deny certain quite definite similarities. Yet can we say that *Balthasar Neumann* influenced *St Gallen*? (For the possible influence of *St Gallen* on *Wiblingen*, see p. 171.) (3) The pronounced longitudinal axis is held in check by the magnificent rotunda, the dominating feature of the interior and a work not only of beauty but also (considering the diameter of the vault, 80 ft., and the unequal span of the arches) of architectural brilliance. (4) Note here the firm and varied treatment of the arches themselves (some semi-circular, some segmental, some almost horseshoe in form; those at the diagonal points narrower than those at the side and these again than those opening on to nave and choir), and the interplay of curves on various planes and at various levels (arches, saucer dome and its cornice, vaults and cornices of side-aisles, etc.). (5) The decorations show considerable inequality. In nave and rotunda frescoes and stucco ornament are of the finest quality (*Christian Wenzinger* of Freiburg-im-Breisgau, 1757–8). His fresco style is both highly individual and illustrative of the greater looseness of composition characteristic of the later Baroque; the architectural element is absent, figures hover against a background of sky and

189

clouds with plenty of space round them. In the central saucer dome (plate 43) we see the hosts of heaven in three concentric rings praising the Trinity at the centre far above. Very fine, almost classicistic in restraint, are the stucco reliefs over the aisle arches of the rotunda (scenes from the life of St Gallus, plate 58). In the choir the situation is otherwise. The stucco (*Johann Georg Gigl* and his brother *Matthias*, 1764–9), though heavier, is good. But the frescoes are a disaster; replacing paintings by *Josef Wannenmacher* (1764–6), the quality of whose work can still be seen in the Library, they were carried out 1827 by a grammar school drawing master named *Moretto*. Poor and gaudy, they ruin the effect of the choir, depriving it greatly of height when seen from the back of the nave. (6) The high altar (*Johann Simon Moosbrugger*, early nineteenth century), in itself a good classicistic work, is in design and colour quite unsuited to the church (particularly unfortunate the effect of the two angels above who seem to be straining for all they are worth to hold up the ceiling!). Contemporary with it is the organ gallery which is unobjectionable, if a little bleak. (7) Note how the choir screen (*Josef Mayer*, c. 1772) and the side altars (*Fidel Sporer*, of Constance, 1769–73), all good, take up the curve of the rotunda and at the same time direct the gaze up the choir. (8) The choir-stalls among the best in the country. (9) The confessionals (1762–3) with finely and vividly carved scenes from the Life of Christ are by *Joseph Anton Feuchtmayer* (cf. *Birnau*). (The visitor must on no account miss seeing the exquisite and deservedly celebrated Library, of 1756–9, with fine carving by *Anton Baumann*, and inlaid floor, stucco work by the *Gigl* brothers and colourful, historically interesting ceiling paintings by *Wannenmacher*. Of special charm the hilarious little coloured putti above the pilasters, representing the arts and sciences.)

Johann Peter and Gabriel Thumb

Lachen, 1707–10 (S.E. shore of Lake of Zürich, almost opposite Rapperswil; rail and bus connections from Zürich). Parish church, possibly from a design by *Caspar Moosbrugger*. Wall-pillar church with 3-bay nave, internally narrower apsidal choir (to the W.) under half-dome, and twin-towered façade.

Noteworthy features. Interior: Remarkable are the impression of length (increased by the narrower choir) and the width of the bays in relation to the shallowness of the wall-pillars. The gallery balustrade continues right round through the towers into the organ loft. Stucco work somewhat meagre (*Johann Baptist Neurone*, 1710), on the ceiling gilded and following the lines of the lunettes; painter of frescoes unknown. High altar 1738 (*Johann Kaspar*); good choir stalls 1715 (*Franz Joseph Brägger*, who also probably made the two side altars and the pulpit); organ case etc. 1806, heavy but good.

Johannes Rueff

Though in no way distinguished, he is included both as a co-operator of *Moosbrugger* at *Einsiedeln* and as designer of the large, like himself undistinguished, Benedictine abbey church at Engelberg.

Engelberg, 1730–7 (15 m. S. of Lake of Lucerne, reached by train to Stans and thence by mountain railway). Abbey church (foundation 1120). A large, barn-like building rectangular on plan without transept, apse or any variation other than an insignificant tower in the centre of the N. side. In a magnificent setting at the upper end of the valley at the foot of the snowy Titlis.

Noteworthy features. It is hard to be enthusiastic about this church. Architecturally it is equally monotonous outside and in. The *interior*, however, makes a cheerful impression and is to some extent relieved by its furnishings. (1) The architectural detail is as poor as the general design (e.g. the pilasters are nowhere continued to the ground). (2) The best things in the church are the high altar and the two main side altars (*Josef Anton Feuchtmayer*, 1733) of lively design and unusual pale colour; the high altar painting a good work by *F. J. Spiegler* (1734)—note the symbolic representation of God the Father on the clock face. (3) The other altar paintings are weak works of *Deschwanden* whose productions also meet us at *Einsiedeln*. (4) The light, good stucco work (by *Franz* and *Dietrich Wilhelm*, of Vorarlberg, 1733) does something to liven up the bald architecture.

To the above churches of the Vorarlberg group must be added the following lesser but charming parish churches:

Reckingen, 1743–5 (Rhone valley between Brig and the Grimsel Pass) by *Johann Georg Ritz*, a harmonious interior with good contemporary stucco and frescoes (*J. G. Pfefferle*), altars, pulpit and choir stalls and imposing organ and case (1746).

Mettau, 1773–6 (E. Laufenburg, N.W. Brugg). By *Johann Schnopp*. Excellent stucco work and contemporary good altars, pulpit, choir stalls and confessionals combine to form a pleasingly harmonious interior.

The Singer Family

As mentioned above, there were in the eighteenth century only two native Swiss families of architects in whose work distinct traditions developed, the *Singer* and the *Putschert* families. Of these, the activity of the latter is too late in date to concern us here. The interested reader, however, is referred for their best achievements to the churches at *Richenthal* and *Pfaffnau* (near St Urban), *Buochs* and *Beckenried* (S. shore of Lake of Lucerne, E. of Stans) and *Wohlen* (8 m. N.W. *Muri*). *Ruswil*, for special reasons, will be dealt with below.

We turn to the creations of the *Singer* family.

Sarnen, 1739–42 (in Kirchhofen just outside Sarnen at N. end of Lake; 12 m. S. Lucerne, whence rail connection). Parish church by *Franz Singer* (father of *Jakob* and *Johann Anton*, the two most prolific architects of the family). Has 3-bay nave of hall type (the third bay broader to emphasize the slight transept), apsidal choir and twin-towered W. façade.

Noteworthy features. Exterior: the (unusual) oblique position of the towers recalls the later *Waldsee* in S. Germany; but the S. tower is Romanesque up to the fifth storey (facing and cap 1784), the N. tower a copy of 1881. *Interior:* in general seems to show influence from the nearby *Sachseln*. (1) Frescoes (unusually small for the date) by *Josef Haffner* (1745). (2) Altars and stucco ornament all Vorarlberg work (*Georg Ludwig, Matthias Willenrath, Franz Moosbrugger*. (3) Above the double W. gallery is a good organ by *Joseph Balez*, 1747. (4) The carved stalls at W. end of nave were not for clergy but for town councillors ('Ratsherrenstühle').

Luthern, 1752 (17 m. N.W. of Lucerne, 2 m. N.W. of Willisau; railway station Hüswil, from which bus connection, 5 m.). Architect *Jakob Singer*. Parish church. Earliest example of a type developed by the Singers (taken over also by the *Putscherts*) and found frequently in central Switzerland; aisleless nave, narrower apsidal choir, the two linked by characteristic externally convex wall sections whose inner sides form altar niches. The church at Luthern not otherwise remarkable. Other examples of the type: two churches in the neighbourhood, *Ettiswil* (5 m. N.E. 1770–3) and *Altishofen* (5 m. N., 1771–2); farther afield, *Hochdorf* (8 m. N. of Lucerne, with later classicistic façade). The two best examples are very late in date but may be appropriately included here as representing the work of both Singers and Putscherts. The first is at *Cham* (W. shore of Lake of Zug; easily accessible from Zug by various means); parish church by *Johann* and *Jakob Singer* (1783–6) with beautiful, restrained classicistic interior, good stucco work and frescoes (the obliquely set tower late fifteenth century with steeple 1853). The second is at *Ruswil* (8 m. N.E. Luthern, on main Lucerne–Olten road with bus connection); parish church by *Nikolaus Putschert* (1783–93) with surprisingly lively interior decoration for the late date; the transitional link between nave and choir here almost of transeptal character, externally squared off and even gabled.

Schwyz, St Martin, 1769–74 (15 m. E. Lucerne whence, as from elsewhere, rail and other connections). Parish church by *Jakob* and *Johann Anton Singer*; the masterpiece of the brothers with one of the finest and most rewarding Baroque interiors in the country. It has a 2-bay nave of 'hall' type (with entrance hall), shallow and slightly apsidal transepts, narrower apsidal choir and single N.E. tower.

Noteworthy features. Exterior: (1) the gables to the transepts, rare except in Vorarlberg churches; (2) the convex W. façade containing entrance hall); (3) the finely shaped tower helm. *Interior:* very impressive alike in proportions, decoration and furnishings. (1) The effect of a transeptal 'crossing' is enhanced by the deep circular saucer dome and its prominent fresco. (2) The frescoes (1773, by *Josef Ignaz Weiss*; cf. his earlier work at *Silene*) are good compositions with warm colouring. (3) The stucco ornamentation (1772, by *Johann Georg Scharpf* and *Josef Ignaz Weiss*), though sparse, is of good quality, especially the cartouches in the spandrels of crossing and choir. (4) The seven altars all have quality (despite the weak and unpleasing nineteenth century side altar paintings, three by *Paul v. Deschwanden*). The high altar, fitting sensitively into the apse, has a painting by *J. I. Weiss* (over-painted 1874 by *Deschwanden*). Each transept has three altars (twin altars, as so often in Switzerland, against the E. walls) with good statuary by *Stefano Salterio*. (5) Fine pulpit by *Carlo Andrea Galetti* (figures by *Salterio*), the staircase attractively carried by a large volute. (6) The pleasing font is by *Galetti's* brother *Giovanni Battista*. (7) The organ gallery (double at the sides) with its fine organ case of 1780 by *Felix Schilliger* of Stans offers an imposing termination to the nave. (8) Not to be missed are the small scale but fine quality choir stalls (also by *F. Schilliger*) with excellently carved panels of scroll design. The visitor should also see the convent church (Dominican nuns) of *St Peter am Bach* (1636) with fine high altar and later statuary by *Johann Baptiste Babel* (1778–84).

Näfels, 1778–81 (30 m. S.E. Zürich, 3 m. S.W. the Wallensee; rail connection from Zürich). Parish church. Architect *Jakob*

Singer. Has certain affinities with *Schwyz*, though aisleless and far less distinguished. Here too are slightly projecting gabled transeptal arms of apsidal termination; but the 'crossing' is ignored, the barrel vault of the nave runs unbroken from end to end. Stucco ornamentation meagre, gilding later.

Other Churches

There remain for consideration a number of churches of distinction which, for one reason or another, it is difficult to group and which yet cannot be omitted and should not be missed.

Arlesheim, 1680–1 and 1760–9 (5 m. S.E. Basle, whence tram to Dornachbrugg and 15 mins. walk). Since 1812 parish church. Architect *Jakob Engel* (=Jacopo Angelini) from Graubünden; at the later date altered by *Giovanni Gaspare Bagnato*. Wall-pillar basilica with 4-bay nave, choir with apsidal sanctuary and twin-towered W. façade.

Noteworthy features. Exterior: In general a compact and pleasing design, the ground colour pale ochre, the pilasters white. The façade altered in eighteenth century when decorative details were added and the former middle pairs of windows converted into the present single tall ones—not altogether happily, as the already top-heavy upper storey receives thereby fresh emphasis. The towers seem to rise rather from cornice level than from the ground. *Interior:* Recent restoration has added greatly to its undoubted beauty. (1) The contrast between the heavy earlier architecture and the delicate later decoration is apparent at once and everywhere. (2) The flatness of the ceilings finds an echo in the squatness of the arches, both unusual. (3) There is no continuous cornice; the isolated pilaster cornices seem disproportionately prominent and heavy for their function. (4) The stucco work (1760, probably *Johann Michael Feichtmayr*), though sparse, is admirably delicate, scroll-work and putti alike. (5) Of the fine frescoes (1769 by *Joseph Appiani*) those over nave (Glorification of the Virgin) and choir (Assumption) show a great feeling of mystical light and depth. (6) The high altar is a delicate and harmonious structure of 'crown' design. Note how the curves of stucco on the wall behind appear to link the 'crown' with the fresco above (cf. the treatment where the nave fresco impinges on the side walls).

Arth, St Georg and St Zeno, 1695–6 (S. end of Lake of Zug; rail connections from Zürich, Lucerne and elsewhere to the important junction Arth-Goldau). Parish church, by *Jeremias Schmied*. 4-bay wall-pillar nave, 2-bay hall-type apsidal choir and single W. (late Gothic) tower.

Noteworthy features. Interior: (1) the design recalls in general the Vorarlberg scheme without the galleries. (2) The strongly fluted pilasters applied to three sides of the nave wall-pillars, together with the heavy entablature, give, and are evidently intended to give these optically almost the independence of detached pillars (cf. the somewhat later *Rheinau* and *St Urban* where a similar aim is attained by stressing the entablature only); the choir pillars actually are detached. (3) Characteristic for the early date is the heavy stucco ornament on arches, cornice and lunette lines; the present small frescoes apparently late nineteenth century. (4) Altars and pulpit (contemporary with the church) with their dark colouring and gilding against the white background contribute notably to the impressive effect of this interior; paintings on high altar and outer side altars 1697 by *Johann Balthasar Steiner* of *Arth*.

Beromünster, baroquized 1692–1708 and 1772–6 (12 m. N. Lucerne, on road to Aarau; bus connection from Lucerne, rail from Aarau). Augustinian collegiate foundation of tenth century. Originally (and still in essence) a Romanesque basilica of eleventh and twelfth centuries, with 8-bay nave, projecting E. transept, 3 shallow apses and N.W. tower. The earlier Baroque alterations (by *Thomas Martin*) consisted in the construction of dome and lantern, organ galleries flanking the choir, W. portico and tower gables and steeple; the later added the stucco ornamentation, frescoes and altars.

Noteworthy features. Exterior: (1) The original Romanesque plan and elevation can still be clearly seen at the E. end in the formation of transept, crossing and threefold apse. (2) The tower still has Gothic windows and, at ground level, a Gothic vault. *Interior:* (1) Here the Romanesque original reveals itself no less clearly—in the nave arcades, and in the raised choir with crypt beneath. (2) The stucco work (*Martin Frowis* of Rheinfelden, apparently his only work) is delicate without being ineffective, and nowhere interferes with the architectural lines. (3) The frescoes (*Georg Ignaz Weiss*, 1774) depict the Assumption and the Coronation of the Virgin in nave and dome respectively. (4) Altars and pulpit, all works of distinction and elegance, are by *Lorenz Schmid* (1774). (5) Most notable among the furnishings are the very much earlier, very finely carved choir stalls (1606–9) by *Melchior* and *Heinrich Fischer* with 26 reliefs showing scenes from the Life of Christ; together with those at *Rheinau, St Urban, St Gallen, Ittingen* and *Wettingen* they form one of the best sets in the country. (The visitor should also ask to see the rich *Treasury* of the church which has many magnificent ecclesiastical vessels of metal and enamel work largely of the Baroque period.)

Pfäfers, 1688–93 (in remote hill position above Bad Ragaz to which rail and road connections from Bregenz, Zürich, Chur). Originally Benedictine abbey church (foundation *c.* 740, dissolved 1838). Now parish church. Architect *Ulrich Lang*, plan possibly by *Hans Georg Kuen*. A wall-pillar church with 2-bay nave, each bay sub-divided at arcade level), choir and (behind high altar) further 2-storey bay (former monks' choir above, sacristy below), and single flanking tower.

Noteworthy features. Interior: (1) The openings through the wall-pillars are an early example (not present in the rather earlier *Lucerne Jesuitenkirche* nor in the contemporary *Obermarchtal*). (2) The stucco work is by *Giovanni Betini* and *Antonio Peri* (from Tessin); the frescoes by *Francesco Antonio Giorgioli* (1694, cf. his work in *Muri* and *Rheinau*). (3) The statue-groups on the altars mostly nineteenth century (on my last visit covered over with pictures).

Sachseln, 1672–84 (E. shore of Lake Sarnen, 15 m. S. Lucerne from which rail connection). Parish church by *Hans Winden*, apparently his only work. Has affinities with others in the district, the earlier *Stans* (which evidently influenced it) and the later *Sarnen* (which it seems to have influenced). It has a 4-bay nave of unusual hall type (the fourth bay somewhat wider and spanning the slightly projecting transept), apsidal choir and single E. tower.

Noteworthy features. Exterior: (1) The detached bell-tower adjoining the choir is Romanesque in its lower sections; the octagonal part added partly in seventeenth, partly in eighteenth century. (2) The turrets over the transepts are unusual and of doubtful significance. *Interior:* (1) The nave design is hard to classify. The ground arcades suggest a basilical form and the side-aisles have their own vaults. But above them is a second arcade storey and the upper side vaults are of equal height with the central. Apparently a hall church with a balustraded gallery running along sides and round W. end separating ground from upper arcades. (2) Between each pair of lower and upper columns flat pilaster strips are applied to the wall, seemingly to give the impression of continuity between the two arcades. (3) The general feeling is perhaps Gothic rather than Baroque, a feeling enhanced no doubt by the black (Melchthal) marble used to pick out columns, arches, pilasters and balustrade, and which, against the white ground, forms the decisive colour constrast in this interior. (4) Apart from one poor work in the choir there are no frescoes and the stucco work is meagre. (5) Altars and pulpit 1776–9 (restored 1880–9). (6) Interesting baptistery under baldachin supported by five columns.

Stans, St Peter, 1641–7 (10 m. S. Lucerne, S.W. corner of Lake, N.E. Sarnen). Parish church by *Jakob Berger* on site of Romanesque predecessor but with north–south axis. 4-bay basilical nave, narrower apsidal choir, single tower (twelfth century; steeple 1571).

Noteworthy features. Exterior: the present steps leading up to the terrace before the W. façade a nineteenth century replace-

ment of the original flight in black marble which must have
looked much finer. *Interior:* (1) The nave arcade scheme is
continued round under the W. gallery; the cornice runs right
round the church and into the choir, stopping short at the apse.
(2) This interior recalls, and perhaps influenced, *Sachseln*; here
too the colour contrast of slender dark columns against white
background. (3) There are no frescoes; and the good, if heavy,
stucco ornament was apparently added to in 1931–2. (4) The
black–white colour contrast is heightened by the dark marble
(earlier) altars which, as at *Arth,* stand out conspicuously
against the light background; as also the font. Altar figures (also
those of the Apostles on the cornice) probably by *Gregorius
Allhelg.* (5) The good organ case is of 1689–90; the pulpit 1763.

Attention is also drawn to the following lesser Baroque
churches of interest in Switzerland:

Andermatt, parish church, 1695, with good later stucco and
massive high altar (1698) by *Johann Ritz*; frescoes 1905. Together with it the rather later attractive church in the adjoining village of *Hospenthal* (1705–11). Both are works of the
same architect, *Bartholomäus Schmid*. In Andermatt the
Friedhofkapelle with pretty Rococo altar and the Mariahilf-
kapelle with stucco work c. 1740 should also be looked at.

Berne, Heiliggeistkirche, 1726–9, by *Nicholas Schildknecht*, perhaps the most elegant Protestant church in the country.

Dietwil, 1780–92 (10 m. N.E. Lucerne), with clear, compact
exterior of classicist feeling and good stucco work and frescoes.

Frick, 1716 (midway between Rheinfelden and Brugg); remarkable high altar with crown superstructure.

Horgen, 1780–1 (S. shore of Lake Zürich), by *Johannes Jakob
Haltiner*; a Protestant church with an almost Borrominesque
oval ground-plan and good stucco ornamentation by *Andreas
Moosbrugger*; spoilt by its galleries.

Laufenburg, late fifteenth-century church baroquized 1682–1702
(on Rhine, 6 m. below Säckingen). Good altars and stucco
ornament, and frescoes by *Ludwig Hermann* (1770).

Naters, 1659–70 (next to Brig) by *Peter* and *Balthasar Bodmer*. High altar 1667, side altars 1740; choir stalls and pulpit 1665.

Silenen, 1754–6 (12 m. N. Andermatt). Frescoes by *Joseph Ignaz Weiss* (cf. his later work in *Schwyz*). High altar 1715 (*Johann Ritz*); side altars and pulpit 1760.

AUSTRIA

The visitor in search of Baroque churches who passes into Austria from Bavaria will gradually become aware of certain differences in the situation that meets him there. He will find, for example, that on the whole the Austrian churches are soberer than those in S. Germany, and the more so the farther away he goes from the areas of Bavarian influence. This is due to a variety of causes, of which the chief were the persistence of Italian influences, the relatively high proportion of churches of earlier date and an unwillingness, resulting no doubt from the pervading taste of the imperial court and the higher clergy, to allow the more secular later Baroque, or Rococo, style admission to church interiors. Interiors such as those of *Wilhering* or *Wilten Pfarrkirche* (which were in fact decorated by Bavarian stucco-artists) are rare in Austria and almost all in the West. Again, he will find no such wealth of Baroque in the smaller churches of the villages and countryside. In Austria Baroque appears in the great town churches (*Vienna, Salzburg, Innsbruck, Linz*, though less in *Graz* and hardly at all in *Villach* or *Klagenfurt*), in the great monastic churches (*Melk, Göttweig, St Florian, Altenburg, Wilhering, Stams*) and in scattered pilgrimage churches (*Maria Taferl, Christkindl, Sonntagberg*). In the country it is on the whole churches of older date that he will find, though he is warned that these frequently contain important works of Baroque art. Only in the west, where Bavarian influence penetrated, and especially in Tyrol, whose people have racial affinities with the Bavarians, will he find country churches and chapels in any number. In general, though it was from Austria that the decisive early impetus to Baroque church building in the German Catholic countries came, the Baroque did not in any of its stages, especially in its Rococo stage, penetrate down among the people to the same extent as in Bavaria.

It will, for a number of reasons, be more convenient to deal with the Austrian churches by geographical areas than by architects or groups of architects. Apart from the influence of two or three great architects (*Fischer von Erlach*, *von Hildebrandt*, *Prandtauer*, *Munggenast*) the picture is too varied for individual influences to appear very clearly though we shall follow these where we can. Even in the cases of the one or two families of architects (the *Carlone* family, for instance, or in Tyrol the *Gumpp* family) who exercised widespread influence, the contributions made by the various members differed considerably in nature, quality and quantity and specific characteristics do not stand out readily.

The following division of areas will, as far as the architecture is concerned, cover the field: *Vienna and Lower Austria, Linz and Upper Austria, Salzburg and district, Innsbruck and Tyrol* (with *Vorarlberg*). Some important works of Baroque art (e.g. the statuary of *J. T. Stammel* in Styria or *G. R. Donner's* pietà in *Gurk*) lie outside these areas; they will be found dealt with in Chapter IV to which the reader is referred.

VIENNA AND LOWER AUSTRIA

Vienna

The work of two great architects, *Johann Bernhard Fischer von Erlach* and *Lukas von Hildebrandt*, meets us on all hands in our quest for Baroque in Vienna, though principally in their secular buildings. We recall that the victory over the Turks in 1683 greatly increased the prestige of the city and of the Habsburgs, and a new access of pride and self-confidence found expression in no way more clearly than in great building plans such as befitted an imperial city. At the end of the seventeenth century many parts of the city were still medieval in character; by about 1720 these had almost all been replaced by buildings in the new style. This changing of the face of Vienna was very largely the work of these two men. They were contemporaries and rivals, and alike in personality and in art they present an interesting contrast.

Fischer von Erlach (Fischer, or Fischers, as he originally was before being ennobled) was born in 1656 at St Martin near Graz and died in 1723 in Vienna. After an early training in Rome under *Bernini*, during which he also devoted particular attention to the work of *Borromini*, and a study tour in Northern Germany and Holland, he settled down early in Vienna and expended his talent principally in the service of the city. He worked chiefly for the Court, becoming in 1685 Court architect and Surveyor General of Works. And indeed, in his own restrained, intellectual nature we seem to feel something courtly, aristocratic, exclusive —qualities that find increasing expression everywhere in his work. Though he was many-sided, trained as sculptor and stucco worker and a writer on architectural history, he was primarily an architect. The architectural element is the most conspicuous in all his work, and the elements upon which he relied for his effects were line and curve, space and surface rather than colour and plastic form. His works have in consequence an austerity that is monumental and unforgettable, if at times a little bleak. It is, however, well possible that some English visitors with memories of the restraint and sobriety of Wren and his school may feel a kinship with the work of Fischer more readily than with that of his more exuberant contemporaries. Most of the actual churches that he designed are in Salzburg, but the greatest of them, the *Karlskirche*, or church of St Charles Borromeus, is in Vienna.

Lukas von Hildebrandt (born 1668 in Genoa, died 1745 in Vienna) worked chiefly for Prince Eugen and, like *Balthasar Neumann*, served early as military engineer. During his formative years he made acquaintance both with Italian and with French Baroque, and his interest and strength lay as much in decorative as in purely architectural achievement. On the whole, his buildings are lighter, livelier, homelier than those of Fischer von Erlach. With less monumental magnificence of style but greater charm, he seems to have represented rather the spirit of the people of Vienna than that of the imperial court with its dreams of power and dominion. He built not only great public buildings but many beautiful private houses, and in this way his work formed a visible link between the world of the Court and that outside it. The spirit and work of the two men can be well seen, compared and contrasted in two pairs of buildings in Vienna —two churches, the *Karlskirche* and the *Piaristenkirche*; and two secular palaces, *Schönbrunn* and the *Upper Belvedere* (both damaged by bombs, but since restored).

Karlskirche, 1716–29. Architect *J. B. Fischer von Erlach*, who, however, died while the church was building and left its completion to his son. One of the most original and remarkable churches in Europe; built as the result of a vow made by the Emperor Charles VI during the outbreak of plague in 1713. The design consists of a large, central, longitudinal oval with drum and full dome above, an externally square but internally apsidal choir and a broadly extending composite façade flanked by squat twin bell-towers and embodying other elements to which reference is made below. The building stands curiously isolated in the history of architecture; outside Fischer's own work it has no antecedents (though some have seen an influence from *Ettal*), and it has no successors anywhere. In the last war it survived seven bombs that fell around it.

Noteworthy features. Exterior (plate 11): It stands well, though no longer as well as its architect intended, and can, as few churches can, be studied to good advantage from all angles. (1) The façade is a bold and highly original composition, a multiplicity of the most diverse elements which yet are fused into an undeniable and living unity. These elements, moreover, are all symbolic in character; we cannot however here do more than point to the chief of these (for a detailed iconographical account based on the original programme by *Carl Gustav Heraeus* the reader is referred to Professor Hans Sedlmayr's *Johann Bernhard Fischer von Erlach*, p. 123 ff., see

Bibliography). We find here motifs from the ancient pagan world and from the Catholic world, from west and east, uniting in mutual supplementation and interpretation. In the columned and gabled portico we are reminded of ancient Greece; in the imitations of Trajan's column, of ancient Rome; in the dome, of papal Rome; in the design as a whole with its dome and the minaret-like columns, of Byzantine St Sophia. All these influences and memories are here taken up and blended into a symbolic whole. Again, the façade may be viewed as a triumphal celebration of the patron Saint; round the giant columns in spiral relief are wound scenes from his life and achievements; crowning the pediment is a statuary group of his apotheosis, while the flanking towers bear on their summits figures of the divine virtues of Faith and Hope. Notice, too, how the elements of the façade, as one studies them, constantly reassemble themselves to the eye in varying groups of three—the dome and the two columns, the dome and the two bell towers, the portico and the two columns. Indeed, much of the secret and mastery of this composition lies in this constant regrouping experienced as we let our eyes wander over it and view it from varying angles. This façade is certainly a crucial example of the necessity that confronts us everywhere in studying Baroque, of seeing and judging a design as a whole and not concentrating on any part in isolation. If, for example, we feel inclined to say that the portico is insignificant and spindly and crushed by the dome, we find that we have left the two great columns out of account which in some way form a link between dome and portico by conducting some of the weight of the former down to the level of the latter. These columns, perhaps, form the decisive element in the whole. However much we may at first feel them to be 'stuck on' and not in organic relation to the rest, we shall find that they cannot be ignored without the whole being disrupted. It is worth remarking that the architect has emphasized their central importance by giving them little lanterns closely similar in design to the lantern of the most central element of the entire building, the dome. (2) The dome with drum and lantern is a finely designed work, in the ribbed-dome tradition of St Peter's in Rome, oval on plan and in consequence changing its outline as one moves around it. *Interior:* Unlike most Baroque churches, less rhythmical than the exterior. Proportions clear and majestic; the general effect, though harmonious, somewhat sombre and austere, not relieved by the prevailing colours (dull gold and reddish brown) nor by the frescoes, which are not seen to good advantage. (1) We have here a good example of the use of the longitudinal oval to combine the two impressions of length and centrality. Note that there are not only twin side altars but four other smaller ones at the diagonal points, so that breadth receives extra emphasis. (2) The frescoes are by *Johann Michael Rottmayr* 1727–30 (the illusory architectural painting by *Gaetano Fanti*); especially fine that in the dome (St Charles Borromeus, with Mary as intercessor, supplicating for relief from the plague). (3) Not altogether satisfactory is the arcading of double-column-and-cornice design to the lower walls in entrance hall, rotunda and choir. Admittedly, it emphasizes the 'cruciform' impression of the interior; but this service is offset by the obvious architectural functionlessness which is made all the more paradoxical by the massiveness of the columns. (4) On the N. side altar a good painting (Assumption) by *Sebastiano Ricci*, 1734.

Peterskirche, 1702–8 (I, Petersplatz, 5 mins. N.W. of cathedral). Architect *Lukas v. Hildebrandt* working on a changed plan of *Gabriele Montani*. Collegiate and parish church on ancient site (first church possibly fourth century). Central, longitudinal oval with drum-dome above, apsidal choir and twin-towered façade, the towers set obliquely.

Noteworthy features. Exterior: Though also a 'round' church it presents a great contrast to the *Karlskirche*. The façade, in contrast to the wide span of that of the Fischer church, is tightly compressed, the angle at which the towers are set giving an extra squeeze, so tight that the cornices have got 'buckled'! The general effect, however, is rhythmical as well as compact, and the heaviness is relieved by the fine later porch (*Andrea Altomonte*, 1751). *Interior:* (1) The general impression is rich and colourful owing to the over-all dull gold and ochre tones combined with the frescoes and the altar paintings. (2) The general plan, especially the rotunda with its arrangement of side altars and lighting, similar to that of the Karlskirche, though much smaller and more tightly constructed. (3) As there, the dome fresco (of the Assumption) is by *J. M. Rottmayr* (1713) showing the glowing colours of his early work; also (as in the *Karlskirche* and at *Melk*) the complete absence of any architectural element (contrast the choir fresco with its architectural painting by *Antonio Galli-Bibiena*). (4) The remarkable group on the right of the choir arch (probably *Lorenzo Mattielli*) depicts the fall of St John Nepomuk into the Moldau from the bridge, with an angel below in the water waiting to receive his soul. (5) The rich, rather overloaded work of the organ gallery and case are later (1751).

Piaristenkirche, Maria Treu, 1716–53 (VIII, Jodok-Fink-Platz, 10 mins. W. of Rathaus). Architect *Lukas von Hildebrandt*, with later internal and external additions, some think by *Kilian Ignaz Dientzenhofer*. Monastic church of the Piarist Order (founded 1617, chiefly active in Italy, Austria, Spain; never entered England or France). A round church, the rotunda octagonal on plan, the N. and S. sides extended to form transeptal side chapels, E. apsidal limb with choir, W. limb with organ gallery and twin-towered façade. It survived a bomb on the monastery.

Noteworthy features. Exterior: The façade, as engravings show, is not in its original state, the upper sections of the towers and other details having been added in 1750. The gable wall between the towers is a trifle heavy in relation to the slenderness of the towers; yet the composition as a whole is of an attractive lightness rare in Vienna churches. *Interior:* As we have it now, the brightest and most rhythmical Baroque church interior in Vienna; *Hildebrandt* and *Borromini* combine here happily. (1) The design of the central section is unique, with the four massive piers protruding convexly inwards and housing little niched altars under round arches. (2) The absence of all decoration below the level of the pilaster capitals allows the rhythmical architecture to have its full effect; and in the decoration, the absence of gold heightens the effect of the gilded altars. (3) The frescoes are early works of that mysterious genius *Franz Anton Maulbertsch*, 1752–3, but already full of vehement movement and unearthly light. The theme of the great fresco in the central dome is the glorification of the Virgin; this, however, is not easy to see at first, for the dynamic quality of the conception has 'dislocated' the main motif (the triumph of the Cross and the Assumption into heaven) away to the left-hand side of the picture. We have here in fact a painting which is early in the development of the artist himself but late as an expression of the spirit of the time.

Franziskanerkirche, 1603–11 (I, Franziskanerplatz). Architect possibly *P. Bonaventura Daum*. Five-bay wall-pillar church with apsidal choir and single tower adjoining it. A church of no special merit but included here as an interesting early transition piece. Like the almost exactly contemporary *Jesuit Church* in *Fribourg* (Switzerland), even to some extent like the later *Hofkirche* in *Lucerne*, it shows early anticipations of Baroque still struggling with Gothic forms. The wall-pillar scheme of the interior recalls *St Michael* in *Munich* and the Vorarlberg type; in the applied stucco vault ribs Gothic influence still lingers; while the high altar in the form of a triumphal arch with illusionary painted architecture behind anticipates the full Baroque. The second right-hand nave chapel received bomb damage and the altar was destroyed.

Jesuitenkirche (or Universitätskirche) *Maria Himmelfahrt*, 1627–31 (I, Ignaz-Seipel-Platz, 7 mins. N.E. of cathedral). Architect uncertain. Considerably altered 1703–5 by *Andrea Pozzo*, from which time also the towers date. A wall-pillar church with 4-bay nave, narrower apsidal choir and twin-towered façade. Stands very hemmed in by old houses and narrow streets but its stately façade is seen to good advantage from the little square on to which it faces and with which it groups picturesquely. *Noteworthy features. Interior:* (1) Decisive for the general impression is the colouring (deep purple-red, pink, green, gold) which gives a rich but also sombre, even sultry effect. (2) The galleries within the arches were added by *Pozzo.* The resulting multiplication of columns has the effect of increasing the apparent length of the interior; but this is counterbalanced by the vast high altar which is so dominant that it seems quite near. All in all, the proportions cannot be said to show the nobility and taste of the somewhat later Jesuit church at *Lucerne.* (3) A welcome movement in an otherwise heavy, static interior is introduced by the convex form of the gallery balustrades and by the spiral columns. (4) The heavy cornice, as at *Lucerne,* runs unbrokenly round the church and is continued through that of the high altar, making the latter seem as much part of the architecture as of the furnishings. (5) The frescoes (also the high altar painting) are fine works by *Pozzo* (note the characteristic illusory dome over the nave). (6) The visitor will be charmed with the delightful pair of symbolic putti, one with horns and a tail, wrestling mildly on the underside of the pulpit.

Dominikanerkirche, 1631–4 (I, Postgasse, just round the corner from the *Jesuitenkirche*). Architects *Jakob Spatz, Cipriano Biasino, Antonio Canevale.* A wall-pillar church of basilical type with 3-bay nave, square-ended choir, flat dome, two façades (that on E. with squat twin towers).

Noteworthy features. Exterior: The fine Italianate W. façade with upper storey flanked by volutes should be compared with that of the *Alte Jesuitenkirche,* Am Hof, by *Carlo Antonio Carlone* (1662). Both breathe the spirit and influence of Italy as strongly as anything in Vienna.

Noteworthy features. Interior: (1) The wall-pillars are pierced with arches—a very early example—which, together with the basilical elevation, gives an impression of side aisles. (2) The frescoes (by various artists) have the small, medallion-like character of this early period. Some of them (that in the central saucer dome by *Nikolaus van Hoye*, second half of seventeenth century, 1836 over-painted, and those in the choir by *Carpoforo Tencalla*, same date) are interesting examples of early 'illusionary' painting.

Schottenkirche, 1638–48 (I, Freyung; a few minutes' walk from Rathaus and Votivkirche). Monastic church (Benedictine foundation 1155). Five Italian architects worked on it, including two of the *Carlone* and two of the *Allio* family. A wall-pillar church of basilical type with 3-bay nave, non-projecting transept, narrower, lower, square-ended 2-bay choir, W. façade with low twin towers and higher E. tower adjoining choir. The effect of the church considerably impaired by far-reaching late nineteenth century restoration.

Noteworthy features. Exterior: The stunted W. towers were originally planned to carry Baroque helms; the present roofs, dating from 1886, considerably detract from the appearance. *Interior:* In its present state, owing to the restoration carried out 1883–7, of no great interest or importance. The original frescoes (*Tobias Pock*), destroyed 1816, were probably good, to judge by his altar paintings (transept altars) here and others in the *Dominikanerkirche*, *Servitenkirche* and elsewhere.

Servitenkirche, 1651–77 (IX, Servitengasse). Architect *Carlo Canevale* (towers renewed 1754–6 by *Franz Sebastian Rosenstingl*). Monastic church (foundation seventeenth century). A round church with oval rotunda, short, square-ended choir and twin-towered façade. The church is of interest as being the earliest example of the 'round church' design so much favoured in Austria in the later seventeenth and early eighteenth centuries. *Noteworthy features. Exterior:* The only remarkable feature is the high, cylindrical, drum-like upper storey to the rotunda with its very un-Baroque external buttresses and its conical roof in place of a dome. Compare the external treatment of the rotunda here with that of the fifty-years-later *Peterskirche*, a church of similar dimensions. *Interior:* A composition of much beauty. (1) The basic wall colours (light ochre and grey-white) impart a lightness and serenity. (2) The lighting is effected almost entirely through the eight segmental windows of the drum (as at *Weltenburg*, which the whole construction of the rotunda recalls in more than one respect). (3) The rich, heavy stucco ornament on the flat saucer dome (*G. B. Barberini*, 1669) characteristic for the early period; note the putti drawing aside the symbolic curtains around the eight little frescoes. (4) To the right, in the later Peregrini chapel, frescoes (by *Josef Mölk*) with massive 'illusory' architecture most unusual for so late a date (1766) when the tendency was to loosen composition and concentrate on groups of figures in airy space.

Salesianerinnenkirche, 1719–30 (III, Rennweg 10; close to Belvedere entrance). Architect *Donato Felice Allio*. Convent church (foundation 1717). Round church with longitudinal oval rotunda, square-ended choir, drum dome and façade without towers.

Noteworthy features. Exterior: (1) The two-storey façade is of Italian character and, with the dome behind it, forms an admirable centre-piece for the convent wing upon which it impinges (the effect now impaired by the street wall). (2) The dome should be compared with those of the *Karlskirche* and the *Peterskirche. Interior:* Sombre and not very inspiring, the walls faced with mottled brown marbling, the light dim, the frescoes hardly recognizable. The rotunda plan differs from those of *Karlskirche* and *Servitenkirche* in having on each side two altars only (at the diagonal points).

Lower Austria

The figures of chief importance in the Baroque architecture of this area were *Jakob Prandtauer* (b. 1660 at Stanz, near Landeck in Tyrol, d. 1726 at St Pölten) and his cousin, pupil and collaborator *Joseph Munggenast* (born at Schann in Tyrol, d. 1741 at St Pölten). In looking at their work we thus do well to remember that both were Tyrolese, came, that is to say, from that part of Austria where there are racial affinities with Bavaria and Bavarian influence penetrated. Though *Prandtauer's* masterpiece at *Melk* and other important churches which he built (*Sonntagberg* near Waidhofen) or helped to build or rebuild (*Maria Taferl* pilgrimage church on the Danube and *St Pölten Cathedral*) are in Lower Austria (that is, the area below the river Enns) we also find him working in Upper Austria (at *St Florian*, near Linz and at *Christkindl* pilgrimage church just outside Steyr). He too, like *Lukas von Hildebrandt* and *Balthasar Neumann*, built town houses of charm and dignity of which there are still some good examples to be seen in St Pölten. In spirit and in his designs he was far from *Fischer von Erlach*. He well understood the secret and the effect of the swinging line and the rhythmical surface, but he made no use of the oval ground-plan. Again, he was concerned that architecture and decoration should interplay and together determine the character of an interior. Thus his work, while possessing a gravity of its own, lacks *Fischer von Erlach's* sometimes rather bleak architectural rigour. In general, *Melk* remained the decisive pattern which can be traced unmistakably in the later smaller-scale interiors of *Sonntagberg*, *Wullersdorf*, *Ravelsbach*.

In more than one case (*Sonntagberg*, less important *Wullersdorf*, probably also *Dürnstein*) a church designed by *Prandtauer* was completed by *Munggenast* so that it is not always easy to determine in detail the work of each. When, however, we consider the two major churches which may without qualification be ascribed to *Munggenast* (*Herzogenburg*, *Altenburg*) it seems justified to say that, while sharing *Prandtauer's* concern for the interplay of architecture and decoration, he also allowed his interest in the curved line to influence his ground-plans; the central, essential part of both these churches is oval in character.

Jakob Prandtauer

Maria Taferl, 1660–1710 (N. Danube bank, 8 m. above Melk. Rail connection from Linz and Vienna to Marbach, whence up the hill by bus; or better, to Krummnussbaum station opposite on the main Salzburg–Linz–Vienna line and across by ferry to Marbach.) Pilgrimage church in hill-top position comparable to *Sonntagberg* and *Andechs* with fine panorama up and down the river and to the mountains. Included here among *Prand-tauer's* works; but he was responsible only for the crossing and inner dome. Architects *Georg Gerstenbrand*, later *Carlo Lurago*. A wall-pillar church of simple but massive proportions on north-south axis with entrance bay, 2-bay nave, prominent transepts, shallow square-ended sanctuary and twin-towered façade.

Noteworthy features. Exterior: Extremely plain, ornament confined to a few façade details (porch, upper tower pilaster capitals, gable painting). (1) The transept has a spread unusual in a Baroque church, all the more so as it is square-ended (projecting transepts in Baroque churches of cruciform ground-plan usually apsidal; cf. *Salzburg Cathedral, Ottobeuren, Vierzehnheiligen*); its width is 115 ft. against a total church length of 170 ft. (the comparison with *Sonntagberg* interesting, where the measurements are 88 ft. and 195 ft. respectively). (2) To the square-ended chancel is attached the sacristy building. *Interior:* First impressions are of a harmoniousness in general proportions and colouring, and of an early date (especially noticeable in the frescoes). (1) As usually with pilgrimage churches, questions of capacity and accommodation of crowds have clearly influenced the design; hence the general spaciousness (the church is not large), the shallowness of the wall-pillars, also of the sanctuary—in the latter case to afford as close a view as possible of the object of veneration, here the little pietà above the high altar. Cf. in different ways other pilgrimage churches (e.g. *Sonntagberg, Birnau, Grafrath*). (2) The frescoes (*Antonio Beduzzi* and others 1715–17), representing scenes from the lives of Mary (crossing, transepts) and Joseph (nave), show markedly the tapestry-like appearance and the predominance of architectural motifs of early works. (3) Stucco ornament is confined to pilaster capitals and the frieze above; on the ceiling there is none. (4) Of the altars, the high altar (1736) is effective in colouring (gold on deep rose) but somewhat finicky in its design as a whole; nobler are the transept altars with fine paintings by *Johann Georg Schmidt* (Cruci-

fixion, and glorification of St Joseph). (5) The most obtrusive
object in the church is the pulpit (*Matthäus Tempe*, statuary
by *Peter Widerin*, 1727); though lauded by the guide books it
is perhaps excessively large and rich for the church and its
uniformly shining gold (though the evangelist figures round
the sides are clear and good) makes it difficult to disentangle
the symbolic statuary in the upper part.[1] (6) The organ case,
with clock perched slenderly on its arch, is a fine and elegant
work—if a little crushed in between gallery and ceiling. (7) Of
good quality also are the early confessionals in their amazing
numbers (1701), the pews (1715) and the Stations of the Cross
(*Michael Ignaz Mildorfer*, 1735).

Melk, 1702–14 (on an arm of the Danube just S. of main stream,
50 m. W. Vienna, 15 m. W. St Pölten; main line rail connection from both, also from Linz; various bus connections;
Danube ferry). Benedictine abbey church (original foundation
1111 when the Babenberg Margrave Leopold III gave the
Order his castle on the site—of which remains are still visible).
A wall-pillar church with 3-bay nave, very slightly projecting
transept with full drum-dome over crossing, 2-bay apsidal choir
and twin-towered W. façade. Church and abbey, throned two
hundred feet above the stream on a steep, narrow rock ridge
out of which they seem to grow like a living structure, present
together an unforgettable sight, surely one of the most striking
and splendid in Europe (plate 6). Majestic and dramatic from
almost any angle, the group makes undoubtedly its greatest
impression from the banks of the stream below about ten
minutes' walk westwards. The church dominates the vast pile;
but so narrow is the site, so tightly bound together are church
and abbey buildings and so organically do they cohere as a
single complex that it is hardly possible, even if it were desir-
able, to take an external view of the church by itself. The

[1] When I visited the church a stalwart Austrian with a vacuum-
cleaner strapped to his back was perched on a giddy ladder cleaning all
the symbolic and saintly figures with a homely and heartening thoroughness!

whole composition must be considered and judged in its entirety. *Noteworthy features. Exterior:* There is no access on the precipitous W. side. A motor road leads up from the little town on the E. side to the abbey entrance, to which also a steep footpath leads up on the S. side. We approach the church from the E. through the two great courtyards of the abbey. (1) The façade (accessible only on a conducted tour lasting about 45 minutes) is rhythmical and beautiful. The firm upward thrust of the clustered pilasters in three diminishing heights and breadths is countered and balanced by the cross-ripples of the richly moulded cornices. The tower superstructures (rebuilt by *Munggenast* after a fire in 1738) are intricate, lively and beautiful and recall in certain details the tower at *Dürnstein*. Though the best view of the façade itself is naturally from the terrace in front of it, this is yet only a partial aspect. The façade as a whole really combines church façade, the flanking and incurving wings of the monastic buildings and the semi-circular terrace that links these; and this complete view can be seen only from below, and at a distance. (2) The very fine dome of bell form is quite unlike those of Vienna churches and more akin to some in Salzburg (e.g. the *Erhartkirche* there); characteristic, however, and indeed unique, is the stepped or storeyed outline which gives the dome horizontal bands instead of the vertical ribs in the tradition of St Peter's at Rome. *Interior:* Always solemn, on dull days even sombre, yet of great richness, splendour and harmony. (1) The visitor is perhaps struck first by the colouring in its mingled warmth and brilliance, predominantly old gold and reddish ochre, with white appearing only in the ceiling frescoes above; the colour scheme in general not dissimilar to that in *St Pölten* cathedral. (2) From the colour the eye passes to the fine proportions and the rich and imaginative treatment of the walls. The sense of height is almost Gothic, and indeed, in relation to the breadth, it is great —a result, no doubt, of the nature of the site. Just as on the façade, so here, the walls and cornices have taken on a light, lively rippling movement. It will also be noted that there is little actual wall surface not in some way faced or decorated. The fluted pilasters and the delicately designed galleries play their special parts in lifting and lightening. (3) The bold treatment of the crossing should be noticed, also here a further device to reduce the impression of mass; there are no prominent transverse arches or cornices to the crossing, so that one feels that the dome is 'hovering' rather than resting on any material support (contrast the crossing at *Weingarten* where the dome sits firmly on its clearly marked crossing arches). (4) The frescoes (begun 1716) are fine, vivid works by *Johann Michael Rottmayr*; the later tendency towards greater looseness of composition makes itself felt already here in the nave frescoes where the painter has let the subject of one picture flow over into the next across the transverse arch. The architectural motifs (as in the Marmorsaal of the abbey) are by an Italian, *Gaetano Fanti* (cf. the contribution of another Italian to the frescoes at *Herzogenburg*, and similar cases elsewhere). (5) Of the furnishings, the high altar (*Antonio Beduzzi*, completed 1732) is a notable work with first-rate statuary, especially the centre group (*Peter Widerin*, 1727) that takes the place of the usual painting: Peter and Paul taking leave of one another; above them, supported by angels, the symbolic crown motif of the promised reward of victory and beneath it the words '*non coronabitur nisi legitime certaverit*' ('he shall not be crowned except he have fought the good fight'), while far in the height God Father sits upon a globe. The nave side altars were begun in 1732. (6) Remarkable also are the pulpit (*P. Widerin*), alike for its own quality and in the unobtrusive manner in which, in this none too broad church, it nestles away against its crossing pier without impeding the view; and the fine, rich organ case (1733).

Sonntagberg, 1706–17 (3 m. N. Waidhofen, to which railway connection from Amstetten and Steyr; thence, in summer, bus, otherwise car or 2 hours' walk). Pilgrimage and parish church in a hill-top position (2,200 ft.) of great magnificence, grander than *Maria Taferl* and rivalling *Andechs*, with a vast

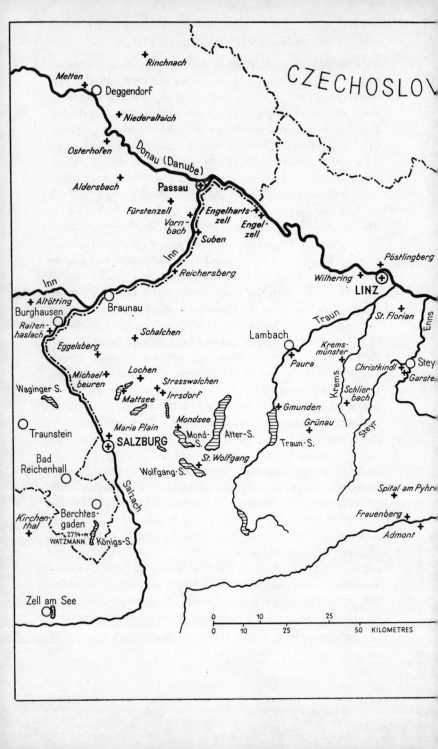

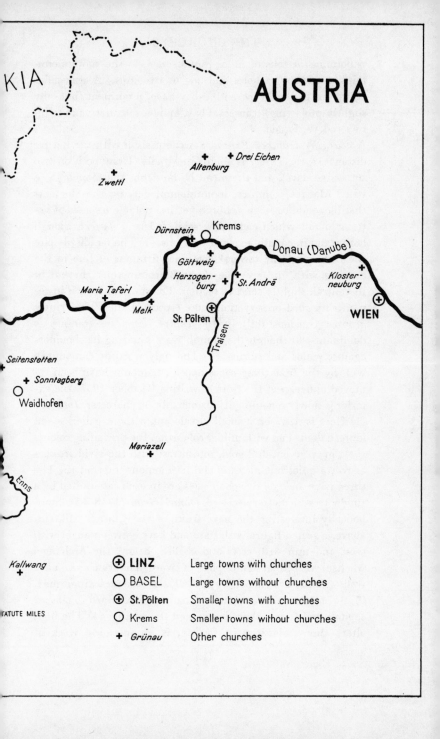

KIA

AUSTRIA

+
+ Drei Eichen
Altenburg

+
Zwettl

Dürnstein ○ Krems

Donau (Danube)

+
Göttweig
Herzogen-
burg +
St. Andrä
Kloster-
neuburg +

Maria Taferl +
Melk

⊕ St. Pölten

⊕ WIEN

Traisen

Seitenstetten
+
+ Sonntagberg
○ Waidhofen

Mariazell
+

Enns

Kallwang
+

STATUTE MILES

⊕ **LINZ**   Large towns with churches
○ BASEL   Large towns without churches
⊕ St. Pölten   Smaller towns with churches
○ Krems   Smaller towns without churches
+ *Grünau*   Other churches

panorama for tens of miles round, on S. to the snow mountains. (Close by, a hotel and one or two inns.) A wall-pillar church of basilical type with 3-bay nave, prominent (but only slightly projecting) transeptal bay, apsidal sanctuary and twin-towered W. façade.

Noteworthy features. Exterior: A comparison with the not far distant *Maria Taferl* is almost inevitable (I saw both on two successive days), and there can be no doubt that *Sonntagberg* wins. Massive, compact, monumental, defying the elements that blow and rage, this church yet has notable fineness of exterior detail which cannot be said of *Maria Taferl*, though both stand in equally exposed positions. (1) The façade (despite the rather stumpy towers) combines firmness of line in the cornices with an agreeable slight Borrominesque rhythm in its central, slightly concave section. The statuary here is in remarkably good preservation; note especially the Holy Trinity group ('Gnadenstuhl') in the centre. (2) The transept is dominant—as though the church were squaring its shoulders against winds and storms. (3) The ugly wartime camouflage will, by the time these pages appear, no doubt have been removed entirely; at the time of writing (October 1957) the exterior is slowly regaining its former shining character. *Interior:* (1) Here is *Melk* on a smaller scale but without galleries and lantern dome and with milder colouring; the prevailing colours grey, grey-green, dull gold, in contrast with the vivid frescoes above; a quiet but majestic and harmonious interior. (2) The three nave and the two choir bays are in each case united by a single fresco, masterpieces of *Daniel Gran* (1738–43). Symbolically interesting the nave fresco of the Church Militant: above, a seated figure with tiara and keys between angel with cross and nun with cross and chalice; below, the Archangel Michael with papal staff in place of sword. The frescoes on nave walls and in nave chapels by *F. J. Wiedon* are undistinguished. (3) As at *Maria Taferl*, stucco ornament is confined to pilaster capitals and frieze; there is none on the ceiling. (4) The high altar, almost classicist in feeling, is an imposing work of

Melchior Hefele (1755–6). The transept altars have good statuary groups by *Johann Georg Dorfmeister* (1768). (5) Of good quality are also the pulpit (*Hefele*, 1757) with seated figures of the Old and the New Covenant, and the organ (1776) with its gallery 'supported' by a pair of angels. (6) There is unfortunately also a certain amount of very weak (? nineteenth or twentieth century) statuary (some nave side altars, S. transept altar). In general, this interior, when I saw it, did not give me the impression of being as well cared for as *Maria Taferl* with its vacuum cleaner, and clearly needed a bit of furbishing up here and there.

St Pölten Cathedral, baroquized 1722–50 (on main line Salzburg–Linz–Vienna; various bus connections). The church consists structurally of a mid-thirteenth century nave and choir and a W. façade (only the S. tower completed) of a century earlier. The 6-bay nave basilical, choir narrower and sanctuary apsidal. *Noteworthy features. Exterior:* In general, extremely plain, especially the façade. Baroque additions noticeable in the slight façade ornamentation (statues, etc.), the fine tower helm and the six lanterns broken through, and built above, the aisle roofs. *Interior:* Few baroquized churches offer a greater surprise than this in the contrast between exterior and interior. The astonishing richness inside produces a combined impression of brilliance (the unusually lavish gold on pulpit, organ, choir stalls, altars and elsewhere—every statue is gilded) and warmth (the reddish stucco-marble facings, the deep brown of the woodwork of pulpit and choir-stalls, organ and confessionals). In general, this interior has a warmly devotional atmosphere. (1) The character of the earlier structure, almost submerged, betrays itself only in the arcades and in the barrel vault. (2) The quality of the decoration and furnishings, of frescoes, statuary and woodwork alike, is fine throughout and gives, for all its elaboration and richness, an impression of massive harmony in tones both brilliant and deep. (3) The long vault is decorated from end to end by a series of frescoes uninterrupted by stucco; that of the Last Judgment is ascribed to *Bartolomeo Altomonte*, the others to *Daniel Gran* (all after 1739). Of the fine paintings above the arcades (scenes from the life of Christ) the two easternmost are by *Daniel Gran*, the others by *Thomas Friedrich Gedon* (1743). (4) The high altar structure (except for the undistinguished nineteenth-century mensa and tabernacle which stand free) is architecturally linked with the wall and consists of the two E. choir pilasters united by a cross-arch and a painting replacing the central apse window—a composition which to me is the weak point of the interior and no match for the rich and massive organ at the W. end. (5) The elaborate, shining pulpit is highly symbolical; around the body are putti with symbols of the Cardinal Virtues and in front a most unusual single relief in which all four Evangelists are present with their symbols; on the sounding board above, an angel supports the crucified Christ and a putto points at the scene.

Other, lesser churches wholly or partly by Prandtauer

Christkindl, 1708–9 (2 m. E. Steyr). Just into Upper Austria, but included here because of the *Prandtauer* association. Small pilgrimage church consisting of rotunda with E., N. and S. (half-height) apses, dome on drum above and twin-towered façade. Planned and begun by *Carlo Antonio Carlone*, finished by *Prandtauer*.

Noteworthy features. Exterior: Of great shapeliness and charm the miniature façade, with its interesting tower-helms and the little gable with niched statue of the 'Christkindl'. *Interior:* (1) The delicate fresco is by *Karl Reselfeld*. (2) The little high altar (symbolic representation of the Trinity who appear—God Father, Dove, Child—with little cherubs in a swirl of golden clouds) is a delightful Rococo composition with rare globe-formed tabernacle (cf. *Dürnstein*, *Waldsassen* in Bavaria). The N. side altar appears to have suffered some damage. The pulpit contemporary with the church.

Ravelsbach, 1721–5 (11 m. W.S.W. Hollabrunn). Parish church.

A miniature version of *Melk*; basilical wall-pillar church with 3-bay nave, developed transept, apsidal sanctuary. Furnishings (5 altars, pulpit, organ) all good, *c.* 1730.

St Pölten, Karmeliterinnenkirche, 1712. Noteworthy the fine façade with concave central section and niched statuary (some figures lost).

Wullersdorf, 1725–33 (5 m. N.N.E. Hollabrunn). Parish church, completed after *Prandtauer*'s death by *J. Munggenast.* Plan similar to *Ravelsbach* but transept here non-projecting. Original W. tower replaced 1822 by the present towers. Altars, pulpit and organ contemporary with the church (high altar painting 1828).

Josef Munggenast

Dürnstein, 1721–5 (N. bank of Danube, 5 m. upstream from Krems, between Melk and Vienna; rail connection from Vienna, Linz, St Pölten; bus from St Pölten, Melk, Krems). Formerly Augustinian canons, founded 1410, dissolved 1776; now parish church. *Jakob Prandtauer,* as well as *Matthias Steinl,* probably co-operated in the design. A wall-pillar church with 3-bay nave, narrower apsidal choir and single tower. In a highly picturesque situation on a bend of the river, just above water level, backed by the steep, high, craggy hill with ruins of the castle where Richard Lion-Heart was held prisoner (1192–3).

Noteworthy features. Exterior: Two features call for attention. (1) The fine porch giving access from the main courtyard is by *Matthias Steinl;* in design it resembles an altar (perhaps intentionally) with its flanking columns, its superstructure, its statues of the four Latin Fathers of the Church, its figure of the risen Christ with Cross in the arch. (2) The tower (plate 21), the most beautiful Baroque tower in Austria, perhaps anywhere, seems to grow organically out of the terrace on which it stands, the great corner buttresses giving its lower part something of the appearance of a tree trunk. Above the vigorous main cornice rises the shapely and imaginative upper storey, the obelisk motifs applied to the angles at half height greatly enhancing the firmness and verticality of the lines as they sweep upwards from the base. The superstructure reappears in essence later on the towers of *Melk* (q.v.). The statues on the corners recall the *Salzburg Kollegienkirche*. This splendid tower repays careful study. *Interior:* (1) The chief point of architectural (and optical) interest lies in the treatment of the nave galleries with their convex-concave swinging movement and the effect of this on the appearance of the nave arches. (2) To the visitor coming from *St Pölten*, *Melk* or *Altenburg* the lack of colour in this interior may strike something of a chill, a fact which he might bear in mind in arranging his order of visits. Even the stucco ornament (by *Santino Bussi*), though of fine quality, seems slight under the circumstances and is confined to the ceiling. (3) In the choir should be noted the high altar tabernacle with its rare globe form (cf. *Christkindl*, *Waldsassen* in Bavaria) and the fine choir stalls with gilded reliefs illustrating the *Te Deum*; also the pulpit flanking the choir arch with, amongst much else, reliefs depicting scenes of preaching and inspiration—Paul preaching, John the Baptist preaching, Christ in the Temple and the miracle of Whit Sunday.

Altenburg, 1730–3 (18 m. N. Krems; rail connection from Krems to Horn, thence 15 min. by bus). Benedictine abbey church (foundation 1144). This abbey is of an architectural and artistic importance comparable to *Melk* and *St Florian*. Entirely and admirably restored after long and damaging military occupation, the buildings, with their fresh pale ochre, cream and white colours and pleasantly laid-out courtyards, now present a charming as well as a noble sight. The church itself stands curiously at an angle across the inner court, the façade just clear of its W. wing, the choir protruding through its E. wing. It consists of a central, longitudinally oval, internally domed rotunda (appearing externally only in the form of a massive transept) to which are added an unusually deep apsidal choir and a single W. bay and lofty tower.

Noteworthy features. Exterior: (1) The visitor should go first to the W. side of the 'Prälatenhof' and study the (clearly intended) combined façade effect offered by the central section of the E. wing of this court together with the (white) tower rising immediately behind it. (2) The chief interest lies in the tower itself which forms an interesting contrast with that at *Dürnstein* and an equally interesting comparison with that at *Zwettl*, these two being of a not much earlier date. The energy and grandiose beauty of *Dürnstein* have here given place to a static, almost classicist repose and a tendency to aim at effect by detail (the statues and the small sculptured group, the little columns and pilasters on the upper storey, the urns and vases). The *Zwettl* tower, dating between the two others, seems to reflect elements of both of these. (3) For the manner in which an external transept formation camouflages an internal rotunda compare the (almost contemporary) case of *Steinhausen* in Bavaria, though there we find more hints of the internal design than here. *Interior:* (1) The first impression is likely to be made by the colouring, which is remarkable alike for its rich variety and for the resulting harmony. We have pilasters and cornices brownish red; side altars greyish rose; high altar and small niche altar columns light grey, the former on yellow-ochre bases; organ, pulpit, altar tabernacles and picture frames in black and gold; stucco ornament white and gold on pale turquoise grounds; and over all, the great frescoes with their brilliant riot of colours. Yet it all blends harmoniously. (2) The rotunda has, as frequently, in addition to side altars proper also altars at the diagonal points which have an important optical effect. (3) The greatest things in the church, which in themselves amply repay a visit, are the brilliant and dynamic frescoes by *Paul Troger* and his pupil *J. J. Zeiller* (1732–4). They should be studied in detail, with the aid of a glass if possible. Their subjects are: over the sanctuary, the Church as source of salvation; over the choir, the Heavenly Jerusalem with apostles, martyrs and virgins worshipping the Lamb; over the organ, David with the Ark of the Covenant; over the rotunda, greatest of all, an apocalyptic representation of Revelation chapters xii and xiii (which the visitor would in any case do well to read, for they form the source of themes frequently repeated in Baroque church art). The vision is that of a Woman in heaven with a crown of stars and the moon under her feet, in travail, and caught up to God out of reach of a dragon that is waiting for the birth of the child. The central scene is shown in the E. part of the great fresco: we see God the Father sitting in incredible majesty upon a cloud-throne up-borne by angels in dazzling light, and below, the Woman, her left hand raised in horror at the many-headed dragon which the Archangel Michael is attacking as he plunges headlong down with flaming sword. Other demonic creatures are being buffeted to blazes by splendidly muscular angels! This fresco is of a wild, unearthly movement and power and of a visionary light and depth that are unsurpassed. (4) Magnificently deli-cate and sensitive are the stucco ornament and the statuary by *Franz Josef Holzinger* (1734–5); attention is called especi-ally to the groups of music-making putti fronting the organ gallery, the ornament and relief of St Cecilia beneath the gal-lery and the putti over the altars in the niches. (5) The high altar (structurally incorporated with the wall, as at *St Pölten* and elsewhere in this district) shows the frequent thematic connection between painting (Assumption) and statuary above (Holy Trinity, putti with crown). (6) Other furnishings are both fine in themselves and offer interesting comparisons in style: confessionals (*c.* 1690), choir stalls (1733), pulpit (1740), organ (1773). It is only a pity that the pews, old though they are, are so commonplace in quality.

(The visitor should also see the abbey rooms on view, at least the library. This, together with those at *St Gallen, Schussen-ried, Ottobeuren, Wiblingen* and perhaps *Waldsassen*, is one of the great abbey library rooms of the Baroque period; it has further frescoes by *Troger* which, later in date and quieter in conception, form an interesting comparison with those in the church. He is, however, warned that a graded scale of fees is

charged for the visit, the highest being for a 'group under ten'
—a single person being counted as a group under ten!)

Herzogenburg, 1745–67 (7 m. N.N.W. St Pölten, from which
rail and bus connection). Augustinian abbey church. Wall-
pillar church of roughly symmetrical ground-plan with W.
bay, 3-bay nave (the central bay wider and deeper and appearing externally as a transept, 2-bay apsidal choir and W.
tower. Externally massive but of no great distinction, it has
one of the noblest interiors known to me.

Noteworthy features. Exterior: The unusual height of the
tower (230 ft.) is due apparently to the fact that the earlier
(Gothic) tower was largely retained and then built upon. The
increasing lightness of treatment upwards is effective. The
upper storey of tabernacle form surmounted by superstructure
of volutes bearing steeplet and cross is elegant but seems somewhat small in scale and consequently 'skied'. *Interior:* Of a
magnificent and stately harmony and repose alike in proportions and in colouring. (1) The effect (though this is not really
apparent in the ground-plan, still less externally) is that of a
central, longitudinal, flat-sided oval with E. and W. arms
added. Transverse and lengthways axes here fuse perfectly,
each with due emphasis, the latter receiving the requisite extra
stress from the cornice line and the magnificent procession of
the transverse arches overhead. (2) The colouring is subdued
and unusual yet serene and attractive (in general, greyish-
green in varying shadings; lilac-rose on the cornices; and on
altars and pilaster capitals a striking combination of dull gold
on a copper background). (3) The brilliant frescoes are by
Bartolomeo Altomonte and show a greater freedom of treatment than his somewhat earlier ones in *Wilhering*; especially
fine that in the central saucer dome (St Augustine and saints in
glory, 1755). (4) Stucco ornament is found only on pilaster
capitals and frieze (cf. *Sonntagberg, Maria Taferl, St Pölten*).
What appear as such, and replace it, on walls and ceilings are
painted architectural and scroll designs (by *Domenico Francia*,
1751–6) of remarkable illusory plasticity and great technical

virtuosity (note especially the pendentives of the central dome and the corbel-table 'supporting' its base). (5) The marble high altar is an imposing classicist work of *Jakob Mösl* (1770) with painting by *Daniel Gran* (1746) and statuary by *Joseph Rössler*, its upper storey faced with burnished copper leaf. The side altars (also marble) are fine, restrained structures with paintings by *Altomonte* (1760–3). (6) Of similar good quality are pulpit and choir-stalls (*c.* 1750). (7) The finest object in the church, alike in itself and in its setting, is the exquisitely designed and poised organ (*Joseph Henke*, 1749–52). I have seen nothing better. This W. end composition of organ and gallery as a whole is in its way as notable as those of *St Florian* or *Weingarten*. The niched figure of King David visible through the arch of the organ, it should be realized, is—not a statue in a real niche—but *Francia's* most surprising piece of illusory painting in the church!

Other churches of interest in Lower Austria

Dreieichen, 1744–50 (3 m. S.E. Horn from which bus connection). Pilgrimage church on hill-side. Architect probably *Leopold Wissgrill* of Horn. A wall-pillar church with central oval rotunda (appearing externally as transept), apsidal sanctuary, W. bay and twin-towered W. façade. Built under the auspices of the then Abbot of *Altenburg*, its plan recalls that of the abbey church.

Noteworthy features. Exterior: (1) The shapely gabled transept gives no hint of the oval interior (cf. *Altenburg*, *Herzogenburg*). (2) The upper storeys and helms of the towers built 1814–19. *Interior:* (1) The influence of *Altenburg* seems clear (oval rotunda, niche chapels, lighting). (2) The most important feature is the central dome fresco by *Paul Troger* (1752) showing the glorification of the Trinity by Mary and groups of saints; one of his latest works, to be compared with the earlier ones in Altenburg. (3) Altars are all good; the attractive 'transept' altars (*c.* 1730) installed 1952 to replace unsuitable nineteenth-century works.

Göttweig, baroquized *c.* 1625–*c.* 1660 and after 1750 (12 m. N.
St Pölten, 5 m. S. Krems; rail connection from St Pölten and
Krems to Furth-Göttweig whence bus, or 45 min. walk;
direct bus connection from Krems). Benedictine abbey church
(foundation from *Passau* 1073). This church is included here
not because it is in itself of any striking interest (it is an incomplete and rather garish patchwork, no part of which is of
the first quality) but because to make the visit is to see what
survives of a complex of buildings which, had it ever come to
completion, would have been one of the grandest of Baroque
creations and whose situation alone still offers an imposing experience and, in clear weather, a fine view. The abbey be-
strides the top of a high wooded hill a few miles to the south
of the Danube and as one approaches it from the north presents
a majestic sight, especially when lit by the rays of an evening
sun. Alike in conception and in situation it embodies, as only
Melk and perhaps *Weingarten* do, the power and confidence of
its age. But when we reach the hill top we soon realize that
what we find is only a torso. Signs of incompleteness meet us
first perhaps in the towers of the church, but are present on all
hands. The architectural history centres round a few dates. A
serious fire in 1580, followed by another in 1608, made necessary the replacement of the late medieval buildings, which
proceeded from about 1620 to about 1660 under the direction
of *Cipriano Biasino*, a native of Como, and included the present
nave of the church. A further disastrous fire in 1718 (in which
the church escaped) necessitated another large-scale reconstruction (plans by *Lukas von Hildebrandt*) which, however,
turned out to be too ambitious, costly and lengthy and was
broken off incomplete in 1783. The most notable part of the
whole complex is not in the church—the grandiose abbey
staircase (*Kaiserstiege*) with a vast fresco by *Paul Troger*
(1739).

Noteworthy features. Exterior: The façade, classicistic in feeling, with its uncompleted towers, was added in the second
period of reconstruction (after 1750). *Interior:* The first general

impression is unfortunately one of garishness, largely because of the ugly nineteenth-century colouring of walls and ceiling. (1) We find a 4-bay basilical nave joined by a dominant and richly decorated choir arch to a narrow, slightly higher, apsidal Gothic choir raised on steps with crypt beneath. (2) There is characteristic early stucco ornamentation (1668) of good quality in the nave side chapels. (3) Contemporary with the nave are also the high altar (1639; fine painting of the Assumption by *Andreas Wolf*, 1694) and the pulpit (1642), both by *Hermann Schmidt* of Essen. (4) The nave side altars and paintings date from 1768–83. (5) The tripartite, screen-like organ (1704) is very heavy and unattractive; the visitor who has just seen the lovely *Herzogenburg* organ a few miles away inevitably (however unfairly) compares the two.

(By the time these pages appear it is to be hoped that the restoration of the façade will have been taken in hand of which, when I visited the church some years ago, there seemed to be considerable need. I could not help comparing its shabby and crumbling appearance with the recently restored *Altenburg* buildings.)

Krems, Pfarrkirche St Veit, 1616–30 (left bank of Danube between Melk and Vienna; rail and bus connections with Vienna, Melk, St Pölten). Architect *Cipriano Biasino* of Como, who undertook the first reconstruction of *Göttweig*. A basilical wall-pillar church with 4-bay nave (fourth bay projecting), narrower apsidal choir and single tower. Interesting as one of the earliest Baroque churches, but with an interior which, through later decoration, has completely lost its early character.

Noteworthy features. Exterior: Of chief interest is the large, most unusual porch like a miniature twin-towered and helmed façade. *Interior:* Stately and harmonious, with admirable lighting of the choir. (1) To enter the church is to leap a hundred years; all decoration and furnishings are at least a century later than the church itself. (2) The frescoes (*Johann Martin Schmidt*) replace the original stucco ornament that would have been characteristic for that early date. (3) The high altar (*Josef*

Mattäus Götz, 1733–5) is horseshoe-shaped on plan and of an unusual depth. (4) On the pulpit (*Götz*) are four interesting putti wearing the Evangelists' symbols on their breasts—a manner of representation I do not remember having seen elsewhere. (5) Also by *Götz* are the choir stalls with vivid carved reliefs of martyrdom scenes.

St Andrä-an-der-Traisen, 1725–9 (8 m. N.E. St Pölten from which rail or bus to Herzogenburg, thence just over 1 m.). Formerly Augustinian canons (foundation *c.* 1160), now parish church. Wall-pillar basilica with 3-bay nave and narrower, apsidal choir; the squat tower twelfth century in lower, thirteenth century in upper part, the cap an ugly nineteenth-century reconstruction after fire damage.

Noteworthy features. Exterior: Only the façade calls for comment; this is a shapely, elegant though small-scale composition with decoration of niched statuary, flanking volutes with sitting figures, good porch and (in gable) a relief of St Andrew on the way to crucifixion. *Interior:* The proportions are good, the stucco ornament delicate. The chief interest lies in the small, brilliant frescoes by *Paul Troger* (from W. to E.: King David, St Augustine, the Assumption, Christ with Peter and Andrew, the Resurrection, Whit Sunday), by whom also the high altar painting (crucifixion of St Andrew). Furnishings in general contemporary with the church and harmonious but, except for the pulpit, undistinguished. The visitor should see the *sacristy* (on the N. side) with fine later stucco and two good frescoes.

Seitenstetten, baroquized 1630–90 (1 m. S.E. St Peter-in-der-Au station on main Salzburg–Linz–Vienna line; bus connection from Amstetten also on main line 15 m. farther E.). Benedictine abbey church (foundation 1112) built 1254–*c.* 1300 with 6-bay nave, narrower apsidal choir and W. tower.

Noteworthy features. Exterior: Stands entirely enclosed by the conventual buildings except for the W. façade. This (ascribed by some to *Prandtauer*), which forms the central section of the E. wing of the very dignified and reposeful main court, is of slightly concave line and has a good marble main door with statuary (1711) by *Hans Schwäbl* of Salzburg; the figures of Peter and Paul on the steps are by *Josef Anton Pfaffinger*, also of Salzburg. *Interior:* A curious case of Gothic and Baroque meeting without blending; the Gothic architecture everywhere apparent (arcades, vault), the early baroquization purely ornamental and additional, and, it must be added, the general effect not very satisfactory. (1) The fluted strip pilasters are very meagre and join most awkwardly with the large corbels from which the vault springs. (2) The characteristic rich, heavy, early stucco ornament (*Stephan Ober*, of Seitenstetten; best that in the choir side apses, by *Johann Spaz* of Linz, *c*. 1690), though in itself good, does not harmonize with the architecture, despite the cartouche designs so carefully fitted into the nave vault partitions. (3) High altar and pulpit (1703) have good statuary by *Franz Joseph Feichtmayr* of Linz; the six nave side altars (by *Jakob Pokorny* of Garsten, 1697) show elaborate, wind-blown scroll and foliage designs that recall on a small scale the side altars at *Garsten*.

LINZ AND UPPER AUSTRIA

Linz

Although Linz is a good centre from which several abbey churches of interest may conveniently be reached, the town itself has no churches of the period that need detain us long.

The largest is the twin-towered so-called *Alter Dom*, the old cathedral and formerly Jesuit church (1669–78), a wall-pillar building of moderate size and quality, a year or two later than that at *Lucerne* but not nearly so distinguished; good choir-stalls (*Michael Obermüller*). Farther up the Landstrasse is the *Ursulinenkirche* (*Michael Krinner*, 1732–72), also twin-towered, with perhaps the best façade in the town, the towers with lively helms. It, too, is a wall-pillar church, the nave with the unusual arrangement of two bays separated by a niche-like half-bay. In the Klosterstrasse by the Landhaus is the *Minoritenkirche* (*Johann Matthäus Krinner*, 1752–8) with good stucco ornament, high altar with painting by *Bartolomeo Altomonte* and, on the first and third side altars on each side, good paintings by *J. M. Schmidt* (Krems). Perhaps the most worthwhile church is the little *Seminarkirche* (Harrachstrasse) by *Lukas von Hildebrandt*, 1725, with high altar by *B. Altomonte* and side altar paintings by *J. G. Schmidt*. On the opposite bank of the river is the *Pöstlingberg* (electric railway; extensive view) crowned by a pilgrimage church (1738–48) with good furnishings and interesting late frescoes (*Andreas Groll*, 1899).

Upper Austria

From Linz may be conveniently reached the following abbey churches of interest: *St. Florian, Wilhering, Kremsmünster, Schlierbach*; to which may be added *Garsten*, though this actually lies outside the town of Steyr.

Kremsmünster, baroquized between *c.* 1615 and 1712 (20 m. S.W. Linz from which rail connection either direct to Kremsmünster-Markt whence 20 min. walk, or with change at Rohr to Kremsmünster-Stift and then 5 min. walk). Benedictine abbey church (foundation 777) built 1232–42; baroquization from *c.* 1670 under the direction of *Carlo Antonio Carlone*; many still later additions. A basilica with 5-bay nave, triapsidal E. end and twin-towered W. façade.

Noteworthy features. Exterior: The towers (mid-fourteenth century) have received. Baroque ornamentation and helms, and a baroque façade and porch have been added below (not altogether convincingly). *Interior:* (1) A number of signs reveal that the body of the church is of late Romanesque date—the character of the arcades, the raised choir, the three apses. (2) The rich, heavy, Italianate stucco (on the ceiling apparently following the rib-lines of a former vault) and the small, brilliant, medallion-like frescoes (scenes from Old and New Testaments) are both characteristic for their early date. (3) Of the other decorations the most important are the series of angel figures flanking the side altars, quite outstanding in force of expression those kneeling on the St Agapitus altar (S.E. apse) and the St Candida altar (N.E. apse); all are works of *Michael Zürn the younger* (1685). (4) The altars are otherwise not distinguished, though the high altar has a good painting (Transfiguration) by *Johann Andreas Wolf*. (5) The design of the organ gallery is not altogether happy; the volute-like corbels are far too many and heavy for the support of an obviously light structure. (6) When I visited the church the pillars had sixteenth-century Gobelins wrapped round them, an embellishment odd in effect and of questionable taste but done (according to the guide) only on great festivals.

The visitor should be sure of seeing the remarkable fish-ponds (*Carlone* and *Prandtauer*) with their colonnades and their statuary, and should also ask to see the magnificent *Kaisersaal* (1696, huge fresco by *Melchior Steidl*), the fine library room with valuable MSS including an eighth-century copy of the Gospels and the *Treasury* (with 'Tassilokelch' of *c.* 780). He may also wonder what the strange, skyscraper-like building E. of the abbey is. It is in fact an eighteenth-century observatory (1748–59), is 150 ft. in height, now contains extensive natural history collections which can be inspected and offers a good view from the top.

Schlierbach, 1680–1713 (10 m. S. Kremsmünster; rail and bus connection from Kremsmünster-Markt; 15 min. walk from station and bus stop). Cistercian abbey church (founded 1355 for Cistercian nuns, since 1671 occupied by monks). Architect *Pietro Francesco Carlone*. Little known, but rewarding. The church (which needs a sunny day!) is a wall-pillar building with 3-bay nave, narrower 2-bay square-ended choir, no transept and single E. tower.

Noteworthy features. Exterior: (1) The church forms one side of a picturesque little courtyard with fountain, its warm ochre

and brick-red colours contributing greatly to the effect.
(2) The elaborate and elegant tower helm should be noted.
Interior: (1) The main first impression is one of immensely
rich early decoration, the wealth of stucco ornament paralleled
in Austria at this date only by *Garsten;* note that the choir
frescoes are set lengthways, those in the nave transversely
(cf. *Waldsassen*). (2) The colour contrast is striking; below
gallery level all dark colours (brown, black) and gold; above,
white, brilliant colours and no gold. (3) Most unusual the
carved and gilded wood appliqué on pilasters and walls, in
some cases framing flower medallions in underglass painting.
(4) The three-tiered high altar (with good figures of the Latin
Fathers of the Church and unusually early spiral columns)
dominates the whole church and foreshortens it. (5) Interesting the various designs of the side altars and the fact that
they, though the wall-pillars are deep, are put lengthways
(perhaps to increase the impression of length?). The visitor
should also see the *Library* (fresco with interesting early
perspectival illusion) and the *Bernhardisaal* (both 1712).

Garsten, 1677–93 (just S. Steyr, from which rail and bus connections). Formerly Benedictine abbey church (foundation
twelfth century), since 1787 parish church. Architect *Pietro
Francesco Carlone*, succeeded by his son *Carlo Antonio* (1679).
A wall-pillar church with 3-bay galleried nave, slightly narrower 2-bay square-ended choir, and twin-towered W. façade.
As the former abbey buildings are now a prison, and unmistakably so, the place as a whole has lost somewhat in attractiveness.

Noteworthy features. Exterior: Of chief interest is the flat,
rectilinear façade. This, consisting of two main storeys, has
the peculiarity of appearing also to divide into two and to consist of a twin-towered church façade superimposed on that of
an Italian *palazzo*. The impression of disunity is heightened by
the uncompromising cornice and by the repetition of the high
plinth-course at ground level and again just above the cornice;
as a result, the towers appear to rise from the cornice and not

from the ground. *Interior:* (1) Owing partly to the dominance of the high altar, partly to the almost oppressive wealth of decoration, the church appears unduly short (its actual length is 150 ft.)—and that despite the series of transverse arches and the lengthways position of the choir frescoes, both features that in themselves tend to increase the impression of length. (2) The immensely rich stucco ornamentation (on my visit shockingly dusty) can be paralleled only at *Schlierbach* in Austria and at *Speinshart* and *Holzen* in Bavaria; as usual in early work, leaf and fruit motifs are plentiful, but the figures and statuary, despite their massiveness, are of fine quality and deserve close attention (*Giovanni Battista Carlone*; cf. his earlier work in *Passau Cathedral*). (3) The characteristically small frescoes are good works of *Michael Christoph Grabenberger*. (4) The high altar has (like that at *Schlierbach*) unusually early spiral columns, and two thematically connected paintings, the Assumption and the Coronation of the Virgin, by *Frans de Neve* of Antwerp, 1683. (5) The tapestries hung across the pilaster bases and in the choir I could wish away; they add further richness to an almost indigestibly rich interior and detract attention from the architecture.

(The visitor should also see the *Losensteinerkapelle* and the *Sacristy*.)

St Florian, 1686–1715 (8 m. S.E. Linz; reached by tramline E from Linz to Ebelsberg, thence by light railway; bus connection also from Steyr). Abbey church (foundation 555 on the site of the grave of St Florian, 1071 Augustinian Canons). Architects *Carlo Carlone*, after 1708 *Jakob Prandtauer*. A wall-pillar church of basilical type with 4-bay nave, non-projecting transeptal bay, single-bay apsidal choir and twin-towered W. façade. The church, which forms part of the N. wing of the abbey buildings, stands on the foundations of a Gothic predecessor the walls of which were partly used in the reconstruction.

Noteworthy features. Exterior: (1) The façade is of noble proportions, strongly rectilinear. Note how the middle section, from the segmental gable downwards, spreads increasingly across the tower walls; this doubtless emphasizes the organic connection of towers with nave but seems also to weaken somewhat the firmness with which the towers stand. (2) The basilical form of the nave can be clearly seen from the N. side; the N. exterior of the slightly later (Vorarlberg) *Weingarten* nave forms an interesting contrast. *Interior* (plates 30–1): The visitor coming from *Prandtauer*'s great church at *Melk* will feel himself in a different world. Certain similarities of proportion may suggest themselves, but the wall surface here is white, there is little gilding and the church is full of light though its situation is low. (1) The impression of height is both accentuated (by the gigantic half-columns) and retarded (by the galleries impinging heavily on them and also resting on a lower row of arches of their own). The fine, rich, heavy cornice exercises a strongly unifying effect on the interior as a whole and also forms a line of demarcation between the world of reality below and the 'supernatural' world of the frescoes. (2) The frescoes (*Georg Anton Gumpp* and *Melchior Michel Steidl*, 1690–5) are of interest in a number of ways. They represent the earliest departure in an Austrian church from the usual early 'medallion' type embedded in a mass of stucco ornament; each covers an entire vaulting bay. In other words, we see here the fresco painter beginning to win in the competition with the stucco artist as a decorator. Again, the device of illusory perspective is freely used and takes various forms—and with varying success. Where architectural motifs are employed (as in frescoes of earlier date and under Italian influence was almost inevitable) the treatment is perhaps too heavy and we are not altogether convinced. In this respect, let the visitor compare the fresco in the main saucer dome with that over the organ at the W. end. (3) It is possible to feel that there is a certain lack of colour harmony in this interior, that the pervading yellows in the frescoes do not blend altogether happily with the white, the grey-brown and the black-and-gold elsewhere. The general absence of gilding (except on the prominent pulpit and on the organ case) is remarkable. (4) None of the altars is distinguished; the high altar indeed has some difficulty in holding its own in its important position in this spacious interior. There is only one notable altar painting, that of the third side altar on the S. (*Rottmayr*); many of the others are weak nineteenth-century works. (5) The carved choir stalls, on the other hand, and the galleries above them are contemporary and magnificent (*Adam Franz* of Linz, Plate 56) with their white putti playing about in the carving above, making music, and, with extraordinary effect, standing in pairs, caryatid-like, supporting the reading desks below. (6) From the choir a glance must be cast back and upwards at the splendid W. end composition of organ gallery, organ case, monumental flanking half-columns bearing the massive, rich cornice and entablature and dominant arch with its vista through to the visionary fresco—a truly grand prospect (plate 31).

(The visitor should not miss seeing those portions of the abbey buildings accessible, particularly the fine *porch* in the centre of the W. wing, the double open *staircase* (*Stiegenhaus*), the *Kaisersaal* and the *Library*, all of great quality. The music-lover is reminded that the composer *Anton Bruckner* was a chorister and later organist here and lies buried in the crypt.)

Wilhering, 1734–50 (S. Danube bank 5 m. above Linz from which regular bus service). Architects *Johann Haslinger* (of Linz) and (tower) *Mattäus Götz* (of Passau). Interior decoration planned and carried out by *Martino* and (his son) *Bartolomeo Altomonte*. Cistercian abbey church (foundation 1146) replacing a previous twelfth-century building which, together with the entire abbey, was destroyed by fire in 1733. It has taken over the cruciform plan of its predecessor, has a 3-bay wall-pillar nave, apsidal transepts, slightly narrower apsidal choir and W. tower. The interior of the church is a jewel of late Baroque art and has very few parallels in Austria. *Noteworthy features. Exterior:* (1) The composition of W. end is such that tower and façade merge; the impression is of a massive tower of which the lower storey broadens out into narrow wings. This is due to the unifying effect of the double pilasters in all the three storeys, the tall central window and the interrupted cornices. (2) The porch is twelfth century, together with a portion of the cloisters the only survival of the previous buildings. *Interior:* (1) The chief characteristics are richness and delicacy, also lightness; this is in one way remarkable because the white of the walls, almost entirely covered (in Italian fashion) with pilasters and decoration, is visible only in strips. (2) The conspicuous reddish cornice runs right round the church, lending at once a unifying and a rhythmical note. In the choir it is perhaps a shade too heavy. (3) The brilliant frescoes (*Bartolomeo Altomonte*) are thematically connected round the person and significance of the Virgin. The theme begins in the high altar painting (Assumption of the Virgin), passes thence to the fresco above (choirs of angels receiving her with jubilation) to the fresco over the crossing (allegorical representation of various aspects of Mary as Virgin and Mother) and finally to the nave fresco (glorification of Mary in heaven). (4) The high altar and the fresco above it are thus connected in theme. The altar painting shows the Assumption into heaven, the statuary above shows the Holy Trinity awaiting her with a crown supported by angels; the fresco on the ceiling shows angels in choirs, and indeed with full orchestra (violins, double basses, flutes, oboes, bassoons, trumpets and drums can all be seen!) celebrating her arrival. Similar thematic connection between altar and decoration above is found in the high altar compositions at *Diessen*, *Schäftlarn* and *Fürstenfeldbruck* in Bavaria. (5) Stucco ornament and statuary (*Johann Georg Übelherr* and *Johann Michael Feichtmayr*) are, as might be expected, of a very high order; note especially the Trinity group over the high altar, the group over the W. crossing arch and the characteristically lively and charming putti on pulpit, choir organ and main organ. (6) Two exquisite compositions are the pulpit and its remarkable counterpart the choir organ (both by *Nikolaus Rummel* of Rothenburg-on-the-Tauber, 1746, the organ with the original console still in use). (7) The beautiful and skilful lighting effects are due mainly to the important W. window, the (doubled) N. transept window and the side windows to the high altar.

(The visitor should ask to be shown the fine abbey guest rooms with rich ceiling decoration, good eighteenth-century furniture and tiled stoves.)

Other churches of interest in Upper Austria

Engelszell, 1754–63 (S. Danube bank, just downstream from Engelhartszell) with good statuary by *J. G. Übelherr* (pulpit notably fine), and seven altar paintings by *B. Altomonte*.

Paura, 1714–22 (near Lambach). Architect *Johann Michael Prunner*. A pilgrimage church dedicated to the Holy Trinity and with symbolic ground-plan and elevation that recall *Kappel* in N.E. Bavaria (see p. 103) though the architecture here is finer. The ground-plan is triapsidal with three towers standing, not as at *Kappel* between the apses, but on their peripheries and forming rectangular extensions to them. The equilateral triangle thus formed is bisected in each of its sides by another smaller one whose points are the three porches and which in the elevation passes over into the upper rotunda and dome that bind the building together. As at *Kappel* the fundamental motif is the equilateral triangle within, and itself containing, a circle.

Noteworthy features. Exterior: (1) Though there are only three towers and three porches the church yet contrives to present from each of its three sides a 'twin-towered façade'. (2) The convex appearance of the central section of each of these façades is determined by the upper rotunda and not, as might at first be thought, by the apses, which appear only in the interior and on the ground-plan and are not seen from the outside. (3) The design is finely rhythmical, the concave tower sides acting as counter-curves to the rotunda; the firmly moulded cornice at half height rippling round the body of the church and the towers alike with sinuous binding force and in lively contrast to the abstract circle of the dome cornice above. *Interior:* The apse altars frame windows through which pictures are visible painted on the inner tower walls behind and lit by side windows.

Reichersberg, 1629–44 (Inn valley, 20 m. upstream from Passau). Good late frescoes by *Christian Wink*, 1778–9.

Spital-am-Pyhrn, 1714–36 (Pyhrn pass, between Windischgarsten and Liezen). Architect, as at *Paura*, *J. M. Prunner*. A fire in 1742 severely damaged nave and façade (the latter, owing to the fall of the towers, completely, and not very imaginatively, rebuilt). The fine, colourful frescoes of *B. Altomonte* preserved only in the impressive choir. The nave whitewashed, but the lines of the arches, galleries and cornice interesting. In its original state this must have been a sumptuous interior.

SALZBURG AND DISTRICT

Salzburg, after Vienna, was the second great centre of architectural development in Austria during the Baroque period. Here too, as in Vienna, court patronage was the decisive impulse, but it was the patronage not of the imperial court but of the independent prince-archbishops who were at once ecclesiastical and secular rulers. Here too, as everywhere, the early influences were Italian. Archbishop *Wolf Dietrich* (1587–1612) can be considered the planner and originator of Baroque Salzburg. His designs were carried on by his successors *Marcus Sitticus* (1612–19) and *Graf von Lodron* (1619–53), who between them introduced the Italian manner. Characteristic of the energy and thoroughness, indeed ruthlessness, with which the work was undertaken was the complete demolition of the medieval cathedral which, though the building had suffered damage from fire on more than one occasion, was deplored even by contemporaries. As in Vienna, the influence of *Fischer von Erlach* went far towards giving the city its new character; but whereas in Vienna he built only one church, in Salzburg his main contribution lay in the field of church architecture.

Cathedral (Dom), 1614–28. Architect *Santino Solari* of Como.

The first building on the site was consecrated in 774. Holds a place in Salzburg similar to that of *St Michael* in *Munich*; the two together form the two epoch-making designs in the early history of Central European church Baroque. But there is, as we have mentioned earlier, a difference. *St Michael*, though also ultimately Italian in design, is strongly modified by local taste. Salzburg Cathedral was the first avowedly Italian church north of the Alps; it reproduces with self-conscious fidelity the Italian basilical model. It is a cruciform basilica with aisled nave of four bays, projecting apsidal transepts and choir of identical plan and form and twin-towered façade. On 16 October 1944, during the first air-raid on the city, a bomb fell on one of the crossing arches with the result that the dome had to be rebuilt.

Noteworthy features. Exterior (plate 10): (1) The clearness and austerity of the design are remarkable, especially in the body of the church whose unadorned smoothness is uncompromising. (2) The marble façade, though richer (towers completed 1655), shows as yet none of the rhythmical movement that later became a widespread feature of façades (*Munich Theatinerkirche*, but above all the *Salzburg Kollegienkirche* and the churches that it influenced). *Interior:* The design is clear, the proportions noble. (1) It is instructive to compare a bay of the nave of this church (relatively low arch between massive pillars, gallery filling the entire space between it and the cornice) with later developments in wall-pillar churches of basilical type (*Munich Theatinerkirche, St Florian, Weingarten*). (2) The double pilasters (carried on by the double transverse arches across the vault) together with the colossal crossing piers combine to give an effect of great structural power and solidity. (3) The lighting is of interest—the nave relatively dim and (as it was before damage and doubtless will be again after repair) the choir flooded with light. (4) The decoration, though not superlative, is good: stucco ornament by *Josef Bassanio* (*c.* 1630); small ceiling frescoes (over-painted in oil after a fire in 1859) by *Arsenio Mascagni, Ignazio Solari*; wall paintings by *Mascagni* and *Solari*.

44. *Diessen*, high altar statuary (see pp. 76–8)

45. *Rohr*, detail of high altar statuary (see pp. 94 5)

46. *Osterhofen*, high altar statuary group (see pp. 75–6)

47. *Steinhausen*, high altar; St Paul (see pp. 87–8)

48. *Die Wies*, nave; St Jerome (see pp. 89–91)

49. *Birnau*, pilgrimage church, nave; St Thomas (see pp. 124–5)

50. *Schäftlarn*, abbey church, side altar; St Joseph and Child (see pp. 145–7)

51. *Rott-am-Inn*, parish church, nave side altar; Cardinal Peter
Damian (see pp. 82–4)

52. *Hopfgarten*, choir arch altar; St Francis Xavier (see pp. 257–8)

53. *St Wolfgang*, parish church, statue of Christ in nave (see p. 266)

54. *Michaelbeuren*, abbey church, high altar; St Ulrich (see p. 266)

55. *St Wolfgang*, nave altar (see p. 265)

56. *St Florian*, choir stalls; St Jerome (see pp. 234–6)

57. *Birnau*, Stations of the Cross (see pp. 124–5)

58. *St Gallen*, stucco relief over rotunda arch (see pp. 188–90)

59. *Steinhausen*, nave window (see pp. 87–8)

60. *Dischingen*, parish church, window glass design (see p. 261)

61. *Diessen*, head of processional staff (see pp. 76–8)

62. *Fiecht*, abbey church, pew in nave (see pp. 253–4)

63. *Osterhofen*, South nave altar, putto (see pp. 75–6)

64. *Birnau*, St Bernard altar, putto (see pp. 124–5)

65. *Fiecht*, putto on confessional (see pp. 253–4)

66. *Osterhofen*, St John Nepomuk altar, putto group (see pp. 75–6)

The churches of J. B. Fischer von Erlach

Dreifaltigkeitskirche, 1694–1702 (on E. bank of river). Not his
earliest church but his earliest in Salzburg. A kind of prelude
to the Vienna *Karlskirche*, its ground-plan essentially the same
though on a smaller scale and less extreme. Central to the design is the oval rotunda with square-ended transeptal chapels
and full drum-dome over, to which are added an apsidal choir
and a broad twin-towered façade.

Noteworthy features. Exterior: (1) The unusual concave
façade (found again in *St Jakobi* at *Innsbruck*) is usually said to
be an echo of Borromini's S Agnese (Piazza Navona) in Rome;
and the influence is no doubt there, though the façade of
S Agnese is flatter and less rhythmical at a distance of some
fifty years. Here the concave form of the façade seems to move
the dome forward (unlike *St Jakobi* where the dome is over the
choir and the church much longer). (2) Even the casual observer will perhaps feel the proportions of the towers and their
resulting relationship to the dome to be unsatisfactory. In fact,
until a fire in 1818 they had flat-topped upper storeys of stone
with oval windows (simpler versions of those of the *Kollegienkirche* but without balustrading and statuary); the later height-
ening and alteration have impaired the effect and robbed the
dome of its full significance. *Interior:* (1) The dome fresco is by
J. M. Rottmayr (1700). (2) The high altar, originally designed
by *Fischer*, was altered and spoilt in 1843. (3) Good statuary
on side altars by *B. Mandl* (1702), much later putti by *S.
Stumpfegger* (1748).

Kollegienkirche, 1694–1707. Built as the university church. One
of the most remarkable and influential of all the churches.
As with the Vienna *Karlskirche*, whether we consider it
beautiful or not we cannot deny it genius and bold originality.
The design consists of a Greek cross with E. and W. limbs extended each by one bay, full dome over the transeptal section,
apsidal sanctuary and twin-towered façade.

Noteworthy features. Exterior (plate 7): The highly interesting and remarkable façade claims our chief attention. The

energetic convex central section, the direct opposite of that of the *Dreifaltigkeitskirche*, is the forerunner of many others (*Weingarten* and *Einsiedeln* in particular, but also *Berg-am-Laim*, *Ottobeuren*, *St Gallen* and others; see plates 12, 13, 16, 17, 19). It is a fine, strong composition, the upper storey with its powerful gable taking up with manifold emphasis the upward thrust of the great pilasters below. The coupling of the two lower storeys by this row of massive pilasters gives an effect of great stability. Note how, in the crowns of the towers, the movement of the supporting volutes is continued in the upward curve of the cornices and balustrades and results in a pleasing harmony based on rhythmical tension. The statuary on the tower parapets no doubt influenced *Munggenast's* design for his tower at *Dürnstein*. *Interior:* Despite its lightness, austere and static to an extent even greater than the Vienna *Karlskirche*. With sparse stucco and no painting (except the pale tinting on pilasters, cornice and transverse arches) it makes its appeal by its naked architecture and its lighting alone. Longitudinal and transverse axes blend well; unusual is the height in proportion to the width. (1) Note how the two gigantic columns, attached above to the cornice, form a huge choir arch, or rather a triumphal arch to the sanctuary. (2) The high altar itself is insignificant. But the remarkable stucco composition rising behind and above it as a sort of reredos deserves close attention; two cloud columns, symbolic clouds of incense, as it were, rise from off the altar on each side of the window to meet in the ceiling, with putti and angels hovering in and about them, and above the altar the Virgin against an aureole of sun rays. (3) The only splashes of colour are contributed by the transeptal altars and their paintings and these are not seen on entering.

Johannisspitalkirche, 1699–1704. This little church is chiefly of interest for those studying the development of *Fischer's* work, but in itself not striking. The side altars have good paintings by *J. M. Rottmayr*, 1709.

Ursulinenkirche, 1699–1705. Stands on a difficult, wedge-shaped site (hence the shallowness of the towers clamped against the sides). The façade recalls faintly the *Kollegienkirche* in the strongly projecting (though here not convex) central section and in the coupling of the lower storeys by massive pilasters. The interior well-proportioned and attractive; good altars and pulpit (probably all by *Fischer*) and later frescoes by *Christof Anton Mayr*, 1756 (that above the organ not, as is usual, painted to face the worshipper leaving the church); finely rhythmical organ gallery.

The churches of Giovanni Gaspare Zuccalli

G. G. Zuccalli, nephew of *Enrico Zuccalli* (the architect of the *Munich Theatinerkirche*), was almost the only Italian-Swiss architect who worked in Austria during the Baroque period.

St Erhard, 1685–9. In itself of no great importance this little church offers an interesting comparison both with *Zuccalli's* other Salzburg church *St Kajetan* and with *Fischer's* rather later *Dreifaltigkeitskirche* (as the forerunner of the Vienna *Karlskirche*) which it must have influenced.

Noteworthy features. Exterior: The façade has a certain similarity with that of the *Dreifaltigkeitskirche*, but the classicist portico recalls rather the *Karlskirche*; the steps and the balustrading however strike an individual note. Unusual and new is the bell-shaped dome (a later variation we find at *Melk*) without ribs and with turned-up 'lip'. *Interior:* The breadth of the church appears in proportion to the length much greater than it is because on entering we stand immediately under the dome. Note how the altar stucco figures mingle above with the ceiling stucco.

St Kajetan, 1685–1700. The façade with its side wings is a very pleasing composition. In comparison with *St Erhard* the dome here gains prominence externally through the absence of towers. The interior impression of breadth is given entirely by the transversely-set oval rotunda; there are slight adjoining transeptal sections but these are very shallow. The W. limb is covered by the organ gallery and the E. limb (monks' choir) closed off. There is a fine fresco by *Paul Troger* (1728).

(Other churches in the neighbourhood by *G. G. Zuccalli* are the parish church in *Hallwang*, 4 m. N.E. Salzburg, and the oval St Anthony's chapel in *Sollheim*, 3 m. N.E. Salzburg.)

Stiftskirche St Peter. A church or chapel stood on this site in the ninth century. The present building dates in essence from 1127–43 but was extensively altered in the seventeenth and eighteenth centuries. It is in fact Salzburg's only Romanesque church. We include it here (*a*) because of its good late Baroque tower helm (1756) and interior furnishings, (*b*) to direct the visitor to one of the most picturesque places in the city—the church with its dreamy churchyard right under the castle rock that is hollowed out with early catacombs (entrance to the latter from the churchyard). In the attractive interior; (*a*) the later but good frescoes (*Franz Xaver König*, 1757); (*b*) the even later high altar with one of the finest paintings of *J. M. Schmidt* (Krems), 1775; (*c*) the sixteen other late Baroque (side) altars.

Other churches in Salzburg District

Maria-Plain, 1671–4 (3 m. N. of Salzburg; tram to Bergheim, thence 20 min. walk). Pilgrimage church. Architect *Giovanni Antonio Dario*. Wall-pillar church with 4-bay nave, two rows of galleries, narrow apsidal choir and twin-towered façade. In interior, good altar paintings by *J. M. Schmidt* (Krems).

Kirchenthal, 1694–1701, 2½ m. S. Lofer, in high remote situation reached from the road Bad Reichenhall–Saalfelden–Zell am See). Architect *J. B. Fischer von Erlach*, and his simplest church. The ground-plan has similarities with the later *Kollegienkirche* in Salzburg. Here, too, as with the Salzburg *Johannisspitalkirche* and *Ursulinenkirche* no interest is shown in the oval form. The three-storeyed façade recalls that of Salzburg cathedral.

INNSBRUCK AND TYROL
Innsbruck

Tyrol, of all Austrian lands, is that which has not only the longest contiguous frontier but also the closest racial similarities with Bavaria. Thus we may there expect to find, and do find, deeper Bavarian influence upon the art and architecture than upon those of any other part of Austria. The Italian influence recedes; the work of *Carlone* on the *Servitenkirche* at *Rattenberg* and *Guarinoni's* church at *Volders* are the only two important examples. The chief talent was that of the Innsbruck family of *Gumpp*, three members of which produced work that will meet us at various places. We also find that in Tyrol the Baroque spread down among the people to an extent not found elsewhere in Austria. There are scarcely any great monasteries—*Stams* is the only one—but we find a considerable number of village churches and chapels built during the period.

After Vienna and Salzburg, Innsbruck was the third important centre of Baroque among Austrian cities; together with the city itself we must take its outlying, but actually older, suburb of *Wilten*.

Jesuitenkirche, 1627–40. Architect, the Jesuit *Karl Fontaner*. Already mentioned as one of the earliest Jesuit churches N. of the Alps. Very seriously damaged by bombs in 1943–4 which greatly impaired its original character and destroyed all the furnishings. A wall-pillar church with 2-bay nave, non-projecting transeptal section, apsidal choir and twin-towered façade. The plan is clearly reminiscent of the *Gesù* and the elevation much more so than the Jesuit churches in *Dillingen*, *Lucerne*, *Vienna* and elsewhere. The façade was not completed until 1900–1. The *interior* of this church, with its wall-pillars, transeptal section and galleries (in the transept set back for appearance of extra breadth) shows as clearly as any the meeting point between the Vorarlberg design and that of the Roman *Gesù*.

Mariahilfkirche, 1647–89. Architect *Christoph Gumpp*. A round church with central rotunda bearing dome with lantern but no drum, apsidal sanctuary and 2-storey porch.

Noteworthy features. Exterior: (1) The unsuitable bell-cote dates from nineteenth century. (2) The bell-shaped dome recalls that of *St Erhard* in *Salzburg. Interior:* (1) The dome, a beautiful composition, rests on six arches of equal height and breadth; the 'pillars' between these are really sections of the wall. Note how the double pilasters are continued upwards into the tapering ribs of the dome. (2) The frescoes are by *Kaspar Waldmann* (1689), the lantern painting a modern replacement of older bomb-damaged work. (3) The good wrought-iron screen at the entrance is of 1731; the altars are classicistic.

St Jakobi (Stadtpfarrkirche; parish church), 1717–24. Architects *Johann Jakob Herkommer* (of Füssen in Bavaria) and after his death *Johann Georg Fischer*. The most important church in the city and the first fully developed Baroque church in Tyrol. Considerably damaged 1944. A large wall-pillar church with 2-bay nave, projecting apsidal transeptal chapels, 2-bay square-ended choir (corners externally bevelled off) with drum-dome above and twin-towered façade.

Noteworthy features. Exterior (plate 8): (1) The façade has a concave central section (cf. *Salzburg Dreifaltigkeitskirche*); its design and window arrangement somewhat monotonous, its strong horizontal tendency largely the result of the cornices being so heavy and the pilasters so weak. (2) The position of the dome (over the choir instead of the 'crossing'), intended no doubt to give extra light to the high altar, is in a church of this length not happy in its effect; its relation to the towers is lost and too heavy a weight is thrown on one end of the building for the effect to be aesthetically satisfying. *Interior:* Finely proportioned, colourful, harmonious; the restorations of war damage very skilfully done. (1) The very shallow wall-pillars necessitate the side-altars being placed lengthways. (2) The unusual position of the dome, while it does indeed give great added light to the sanctuary, here in interior also gives a certain feeling of having been displaced from its central position. (3) The upright oval side windows, appearing, as they do, to 'push up' the cornice over them and 'balance' the window above, add both rhythm and a vertical movement. (4) The rich and colourful decoration is the work of the *Asam* brothers and offers an interesting comparison with their later work. The stucco, compared with that at the slightly later *Einsiedeln* or *Osterhofen*, is still somewhat stiff and heavy. The frescoes are unequal; in many the architectural element is unconvincingly heavy, whereas in that over the organ the 'illusion' succeeds (cf. a similar case at *St Florian*). (5) The W. end composition of organ gallery, organ case (excellent, *P. Trolf*, 1725) and windows, bears comparison in its way with the best (such as *St Florian* or *Weingarten*). (6) The pulpit (*Nikolaus Moll* of Innsbruck, 1724) is a lively and beautiful, if somewhat restless, work supported by angels and with putti drawing back the symbolic curtain above.

St Johann am Innrain, 1729–35. Architect *Georg Anton Gumpp*. One of the smaller but perhaps all in all, despite considerable superficial bomb damage, still architecturally the most satisfying Baroque church in the city. A wall-pillar church with 3-bay nave, apsidal choir with surrounding chapels, twin-towered façade and large portico. When I last saw the church it was still in urgent need of external restoration.

Noteworthy features. Exterior: (1) The towers with their lively interplay of curves, arched cornices, volutes and helms are of great charm and elegance, the happiest in the city. (2) The same cannot be said of the heavy portico (added 1750) which strikes a discordant note. (3) Though there is no suggestion of a transept, even here the transverse axis is duly marked at each side by a composition of rounded half-columns, entablature, volutes and little gable. *Interior:* Of equal elegance. (1) The liberal use of half-columns combines with the heavy, rhythmical entablature to increase the impression of length. (2) The high altar appears incorporated into the architecture in that its flanking detached columns are but the termination of the arcading that runs round the church. (3) The stucco work has a classicist restraint and elegance; the very late but brilliant fresco (1794) is by *Josef Schopf.*

Wilten, Stiftskirche, 1651–67, decoration 1702–7 (tram connection from city centre in 15 mins.). Architect *Christoph Gumpp.* Monastic church (foundation 870, Premonstratensian since 1138). Damage done 1944 by four direct hits on W. part of nave and façade now restored. An extended wall-pillar church with 3-bay nave, 2-bay choir and façade with single flanking tower.

Noteworthy features. Exterior: (1) The impressive (later) façade with its deeply concave, niche-like central section under gable roof, in itself a fine and original work, loses a little by the tower; whether it would have gained or lost more had the second tower been completed must remain a debatable point. (2) The tower shows perhaps the first example of a feature peculiar to Tyrolean towers of the period—the marking of the transition from the lower square to the upper octagonal section by means of broken gables (cf. *Wilten Pfarrkirche, Kematen, Jesuit Church* in *Solbad-Hall* and many other cases). *Interior:* Characteristic heavy early Baroque. (1) Despite the deep wall-pillars there are no galleries in the nave (though in the choir they are present). (2) The altars are massive but uniform, contemporary and good of their kind. The high altar (1665, by *Paul Huber,* painting by *Ägid Schor*) has in its upper part a remarkable adaptation of the Throne of Solomon—Christ seated on a throne at the end of a perspectively depicted stepped hall flanked by lions and columns. The pulpit, though of the same date and scale as the altars, seems somewhat out of scale with them. (3) Of the frescoes (*Kaspar Waldmann,* 1707, compare his earlier work in the *Mariahilfkirche* at *Innsbruck* and his later in the *Damenstift* at *Solbad-Hall*) two larger and four smaller medallions at the W. end are new, replacing originals bombed.

Wilten, Stadtpfarrkirche, 1751–5. Architect *Franz Xaver Penz,* a secular priest of great artistic imagination and gifts and widespread influence on Tyrol Baroque church architecture. We shall meet him again at *Neustift* in the Stubai valley (cf. also his other works at *Fulpmes, Gossensass* and *Amras*). A wall-pillar church with 2-bay nave, narrower, lower, apsidal choir and twin-towered W. façade. A church to be numbered among the most beautiful not only in Austria but the whole of our area, a peer of Die Wies and Steinhausen, Birnau and Wilhering.

Noteworthy features. Exterior: (1) The ugly wartime dirty-grey-green camouflage was removed only in 1956 when the original colouring was restored as at present. (2) The design is compact and elegant with one or two features to note: (*a*) the curious broken-gable decoration so characteristic for Tyrolean church towers as marking the transition to their (usually octagonal) upper storeys appears here too in its usual place but is also repeated at the base of the façade gable (for a variation cf. the façade of *Götzens*); (*b*) the upper nave windows of the tripartite type found elsewhere in Innsbruck, but finer here. *Interior:* Of great harmony and delicate distinction and deserving of detailed attention. (1) The colouring is everywhere of the softest and most delicate, the impression festive and most refined: white walls; white stucco touched with gold on backgrounds of pale rose, gold or ivory; frescoes with blue, grey-blue, red-brown and ivory predominate. (2) The wall-pillars are shallow yet deep enough to take slender transverse side altars; there are no galleries and there is no transept. (3) The variation in the designs and the grading of the colouring of the side altars from W. to E. should be noted—the first pair darker and more static, the second lighter and more rhythmical, in deliberate approximation to the fanciful and exquisite baldachin of the high altar. (4) The stucco ornament and statuary (*Franz Xaver Feichtmayr*) is of the finest and most delicate (especially in the spandrels of the arches and over the side wall paintings); also his statuary on the altars. (5) *Matthäus Günther* has given us nothing finer than the frescoes in this church. Their theme is the favourite Baroque one of Mary as intercessor, which is here treated in relation to the deeds of Esther and other of her Old Testament prototypes. In certain details and in colouring they recall his rather earlier works in the *Käppele* at Würzburg, with which they should be compared. Yet in the nave painting (Judith with the head of Holofernes) he goes beyond *Käppele* in dramatic grouping and movement, and in the power of the threatening, thunderous, unearthly atmosphere in which he symbolically envelops the whole scene.

Tyrol (with Vorarlberg)

In, or just aside from, the Inn valley and easily reached from *Innsbruck* by rail or bus are the following churches:

Solbad-Hall (8 m. E. Innsbruck, rail and bus connections). There are three churches of some interest in this little town, two of them early forerunners of later developments. The *Damenstiftkirche* (architect unknown) was built as early as 1567 and in 1629–30 baroquized. Of chief interest is the rich early stucco ornament which reflects the Renaissance as much as it anticipates the Baroque. The lantern over the sanctuary is a feature that was later repeated more than once in Tyrol (in *St Jakobi* at *Innsbruck* it has developed into a full dome). The church was robbed of its furnishings at the time of the secularization; the present ones date from after 1912 and are unworthy of the church. The *Jesuitenkirche*, on the E. side of the same little square (architect *B. Stefan Huber*, 1608–10), in itself undistinguished, is interesting as one of the first Jesuit churches N. of the Alps and a very early copy, though small and inferior, of *St Michael* in *Munich*; by contrast, the *Innsbruck Jesuit church* goes back more directly to the *Gesù*. The later tower (with characteristic broken-gable transition from square to octagonal section) and the attractive, Italianate gabled façade should be noted. The interior elevation with its three orders is very squat and cramped. The *Pfarrkirche St Nikolaus* is a strange example of a replanned and later baroquized Gothic church. Early in the fourteenth century the present choir was added to the then existing nave, the latter in turn in the fifteenth century widened by the addition of a N. aisle and for the sake of supposed symmetry divided down the middle by an arcade—with the resulting dislocation of axis that we now see. In 1752 came the baroquizing of the interior, its most remarkable feature being the removal of the Gothic vaulting ribs to give the appearance of a Baroque vault which was then duly ornamented with stucco work and frescoes (*Josef Adam Mölk*). The result, though strange and colourful, cannot be called satisfactory. Note, too, the attempts to give 'capitals' to the pillars which, as frequently in German Gothic churches, previously had none.

Volders, *St Karl Borromäus*, 1620–4 (S. bank of Inn, 9 m. E. of Innsbruck whence rail and bus connections). Servite monastery church. Architect the talented amateur *Dr Hippolyt Guarinoni*. Many later additions and alterations were made. The tower was not completed until 1735 and then not as the architect had planned. During the restoration of 1765–6 the dome was crowned with a lantern and all the original stucco decoration in the interior was replaced. The church is a remarkable example of a symbolic ground-plan and elevation. The core of the building is a domed rotunda surrounded on E., S. and N. by three semicircular domed sections intersecting with it and with each other and housing choir and transeptal chapels; to this are added, on W. a rectangular bay with entrance hall, and on E. (adjoining choir) a tower. From a sketch of the church by *Guarinoni* we find that the three smaller domed sections are to be understood symbolically as the three saints of the Catholic revival in contemplation around the light-bringing mystery of the Immaculate Conception (the central rotunda with its lantern).

Noteworthy features. Exterior: Remarkable in every way, comparable only to the Bavarian pilgrimage church of *Maria Birnbaum* (1661–5, see p. 166). (1) Most unusual the design of the domes and the manner of their intersection; also the surface moulding on walls and tower. (2) The unique tower (plate 20) shows all that remains of the original intention whereby it should reproduce in miniature the ground-plan of the church and culminate in three small domed turrets around a larger one (its upper storey is now octagonal). *Interior:* (1) Here further architectural complications reveal themselves (though their presence can be guessed externally) in the form of four niche chapels at the diagonal opposites of the rotunda. (2) The stucco work (except for original fragments hidden behind the main side altars) is all later, in W. side chapels *c.* 1710, in the main church 1765–6 by *Georg Gigl*. (3) The central fresco (plate 41) is a fine work of *Martin Knoller* (1766) full of cloudy space, energetic movement, light in all variations; the theme is the glorification of the patron Saint (note the tempestuous group showing the Archangel Michael driving fallen angels over the edge—down into the church!).

Stams, baroquized 1729–34 (22 m. up the Inn valley from Innsbruck, on Innsbruck–Landeck–Bregenz line with regular rail services). Priory church (Cistercian foundation 1273).The original church, completed 1284, forms the core of the present one. *Noteworthy features. Exterior:* (1) The long, narrow appearance of the church is due to the fact that what we have is really only the central aisle of the old church, all that is left of the side aisles being the projecting chapels. This is seen more clearly from the interior. (2) The façade taken together with the domed Heiligblutkapelle forms a picturesque group impaired only by the too conspicuous pent-roofs covering the earlier portico. *Interior:* (1) We see at once that the proportions are not Baroque (dimensions: length 260 ft.; breadth only 36 ft., with chapels 75 ft.; height 49 ft.). The general effect colourful if somewhat unbalanced. The large Crucifixion group above the crypt does something to reduce the effect of length. (2) The most remarkable object in the church, which strikes and puzzles the visitor at once on entering, is the high altar (*Bartholemäus Steinle* and *Wolfgang Kirchmayr*, 1643) which from a distance looks like a dustsheet hung up to conceal repair work. It represents in fact a highly ramified and heavily laden Tree of Life carved in wood, springing from Adam and Eve and bearing as its noblest fruits figures of saints and, crowning all, Mary and the Child, the whole supported by an architectural framework. To this was added in the eighteenth century a very heavy stucco curtain backing, drawn aside in the usual manner by putti, which may well be thought to be in questionable taste. (3) The other decorations are good—delicate stucco ornament (*F. X. Feichtmayr*); brilliantly coloured frescoes showing scenes from the life of the Virgin (*J. G. Wolker*, 1754; those in apsidal choir chapels 1696 by *Ägid Schor*); good choir-stalls and confessionals with symbolic scenes in pewter inlay (*Georg Zoller*).

More harmonious and in some ways more rewarding than the abbey church itself are two other much smaller buildings which must on no account be omitted. To the right of the abbey church and reached from its entrance hall is the already mentioned *Heiligblutkapelle* rebuilt in its present form by *Johann Martin Gumpp*, a small work of unusual harmony and beauty. A few steps up the hill is the parish church of *St Johann* (fifteenth century, baroquized 1755) revealing a Gothic interior that has been baroquized in the later period with rare skill, taste and success. All the decoration is work of the finest quality: stucco ornament, frescoes (*F. A. Zeiler*, especially good the central one depicting the Sermon on the Mount) and altars (*Reindl*, 1764).

Fiecht, 1740–4 (17 m. E. of Innsbruck; rail connection from there, or Kufstein, to Schwaz, then 15 min. walk). Benedictine abbey church (foundation tenth century at St Georgenberg, moved to Fiecht 1706). A fire in 1868, the last of several, destroyed all the old furnishings. Damage done by occupation during and after the last war now skilfully restored. A wall-pillar church with 4-bay nave, slight transeptal projection apsidal in form, apsidal choir and single tower at corner of nave.

Noteworthy features. Exterior: Of a smooth and unadorned austerity. The tower, Italianate in character, added late eighteenth century. *Interior:* Of great and delicate beauty and adorned by the same two great artists who worked together in the *Wilten Stadtpfarrkirche*; the two interiors should be closely compared. (1) The basic colours are pale green and pale rose on which the pale ivory bands and stucco work rest, all leading up to the warmly colourful frescoes. (2) The stucco work is by *F. X. Feichtmayr* and of the first quality (note especially the pilaster capitals). (3) The frescoes (scenes from the life of the Virgin), by *Matthaus Günther*, show the artist beginning to show a preference not only for greater looseness but also for a certain asymmetrical quality in his composition (seen more clearly still in the considerably later work at *Götzens*). (4) The confessionals are good, in particular the symbolic putti (one, most remarkable, with a death's-head (plate 65), another in the sackcloth of the penitent, another—representing sin—with black wings and a snake round his shoulders!). Whether the figures of saints are in their original positions here could not be verified and seems unlikely. (5) Of fine quality too are the pews with their carved reliefs and scroll pattern (plate 62).

Neustift, St Georg, 1768–74 (half-way up the Stubai valley, 15 m. from Innsbruck; reached by mountain railway—Stubaitalbahn —to Fulpmes, thence in 20 min. by bus). Architect *Franz Penz* (of the *Wilten Pfarrkirche*), the last of his churches and not a distinguished work. Parish church; a broad, rectangular 3-bay building, the centre bay projecting slightly, and single tower.

Noteworthy features. Such as they are, all in the *interior*. (1) The four transverse arches of the central bay seem to be an attempt to impart 'centrality' to the shapeless, barn-like interior. (2) The frescoes are good, by various hands: centre (Pentecost) by *Josef Anton Zoller*; over choir (Last Supper) by the same; the other two (assembly of saints and, over organ, angels making music) by *Franz Keller*. The furnishings are in various styles: pulpit late Baroque, high altar with sculptured reliefs classicistic in feeling, E. windows unusually ugly twentieth-century glass.

Götzens, 1772–5 (5 m. S.W. Innsbruck, bus connection). Architect *Franz Singer*. An elegant parish church which surprises the visitor with an even more beautiful interior, one of the best in Tyrol. A wall-pillar church with 2-bay nave linked by a concave transition wall to an apsidal choir, and single tower. The manner of transition from nave to choir recalls the churches of the Singer family in Switzerland (see p. 192ff.) who originally came from Tyrol.

Noteworthy features. Exterior: (1) A good example of colourful painted decoration (pilasters, capitals and bands) doing duty for these actual architectural features. (2) The broken gable on the façade has already been mentioned in connection with the *Wilten Pfarrkirche* where it recurs in a similar position. *Interior:* Design, colouring, decoration and furnishings all combine to make this a really notable interior. (1) The absence of hard lines and sharp edges (e.g. the cornice ripples, corners are bevelled off, etc.) give this interior a structurally soft and mild effect. (2) The great glory of the church the brilliant frescoes (his last important works) by *Matthäus Günther*. That over the choir depicts the twelve apostles in heaven, that over the nave Peter and Paul driving away demons. Note particularly the latter with its richness of colouring, its remarkable perspectival depth and its asymmetrical design (a characteristic already noted at *Fiecht* and widely traceable in his later work). (3) The only disturbing element in the interior is the modern window glass; destroyed in the last war, it has unfortunately been replaced.

Zell am Ziller, 1772–82 (13 m. up the Zillertal; reached by rail to Jenbach and then narrow-gauge Zillertal line, or by bus from Innsbruck). Architect *Andreas Huber*. Parish church. A wall-pillar round church with shallow square-ended transeptal chapels, apsidal choir, W. limb and tower.

Noteworthy features. Exterior: tower and steeple are the only survivals from the earlier Gothic church. *Interior:* (1) The rotunda shows the design (a favourite one of the Bavarian *J. M. Fischer*) of an octagon below and a circular dome above with side and diagonal chapels. The contrast between the octagonal and the circular elements here is stressed by the treatment of the cornice which is not carried back to and round the walls. (2) The fine, characteristically airy late fresco (showing representatives of Old and New Testament adoring the Trinity) is by *F. A. Zeiler*. (3) Altars and other furnishings contemporary but strongly classicist in feeling.

Ranggen, 1775 (5 m. W. Götzens, 10 m. W. Innsbruck; bus connection). Architect *Franz Singer*. Parish church. Begun in the year in which *Götzens* was completed, within walking distance of it and yet offering a striking contrast to it. A wall-pillar church with 2-bay nave, niche-like transition-sections (as at *Götzens*) to apsidal sanctuary and single flanking tower.

Noteworthy features. Exterior: Here, too, as at *Götzens*, the tower survives from an earlier Gothic building. *Interior:* The life and movement of the *Götzens* interior has here given place to a sober classicism, a quiet serenity, alike in the architecture and in the furnishings. A comparison between two features alone in the two interiors is significant—the pulpits and the cornices. A variation on the *Götzens* plan lies in the fact that here the concave transition from nave to choir is carried up into the ceiling (cf. *Ebbs*). The high altar has dignity, but its columns are perhaps a shade too massive. It is suggested to those who think of visiting *Götzens* and *Ranggen* in succession that they go first to *Ranggen*, so that this quiet but beautiful church may make its full effect.

The following churches may be conveniently reached from *Kufstein:*

Rattenberg (S. bank of Inn, almost mid-way between Innsbruck and Kufstein; rail and bus connection from both). *Servitenkirche, St Augustin*, 1707–9. Architect *Diego Francesco Carlone*. Rebuilding of a fifteenth-century church of which the present nave is a relic. The interest for us lies in the *interior* and in the choir. We have a feeling of being in a theatre with the sanctuary as stage and the nave as auditorium; this is due partly to the narrow choir arch with its side altars which together give the impression of stage-wings, and partly to the lightness of the sanctuary compared with the nave. Note (1) the general structure of the choir, especially the manner in which the bevelling of the crossing pillars prepares the way for the pendentives of the dome; (2) the curiously emphatic base-ring of the dome; (3) the fine fresco of St Augustine in glory (*Johann Josef Waldmann*) which nevertheless shows much of the stiffness of the early period and appears overcrowded and 'bunched' —as though the artist were above all concerned to fill the space with figures, their grouping and their movement being secondary; (4) the altars, all good, 'especially the high altar. The hideous painting of the nave dates from 1893. *Pfarrkirche, St Vigil*, baroquized 1728–32. Like that in Solbad-Hall, a very obvious baroquization of a Gothic interior. Note *(a)* the treatment of the columns to which composite capitals with high imposts and entablature have been added; *(b)* the vault, whose ribs, as at Hall, were removed to give the required field for stucco ornament and frescoes. The nave frescoes early works of *Matthäus Günther* (1737).

Hopfgarten, 1715–64 (10 m. S. Kufstein, on line and road Wörgl–Kitzbühl–St Johann–Zell am See; from all these places rail connections). Architects *Kassian Singer* and *Andreas Huber*. Wall-pillar church with 2-bay nave, slightly projecting transeptal section, 1-bay apsidal choir and twin-towered W. façade. *Noteworthy features*. The originality of the church lies in its very shapely exterior, particularly in the façade (plate 9), which is an unusually attractive composition. The up-thrust of the central section (lower window group, cornice, gable) taken up in miniature in the upper tower cornices to find its outlet in the gay steeples is a happy, almost jaunty conception. The lively lower trio of windows recall the style of *Dominikus Zimmermann*. Had the architect been a Vorarlberger he would probably have crowned the little transepts with diminutive gables. The *interior* is pleasing and stately, the furnishings contemporary, uniform and good, especially the two side altars and their statuary (St Francis Xavier with negro putto on right, plate 52).

Ebbs, 1748–56 (5 m. N.E. Kufstein, off main road to Rosenheim–Munich; bus connection). Architect *Abraham Millauer*. Parish church, with 2-bay nave, narrower and lower choir with apsidal sanctuary and single N. tower.

Noteworthy features. Exterior: A certain austere harmony and compactness of proportion give the church, though it is not large, an imposing massiveness. The plain, firm, lofty pilasters bind the building well together. It may perhaps be felt that the segmental section above the façade cornice is a trifle heavy and weakens the effect of the gable above. *Interior:* (1) Here again, as at *Götzens* and *Ranggen*, though the exterior gives no hint of it, the link between nave and choir takes the form of concave wall sections projecting deeply into the church and containing niched altars. (2) The niched altar motif is continued round the nave, the side walls of which have in fact the general design of a niched altar set between windows. Note how the wall-sections containing these altars give the impression of broad, massive pilasters with bevelled edges, an effect increased by the facts that their entablature is interrupted by the flanking windows and that they are connected across the ceiling by a transverse arch. (3) Decorations and furnishings are contemporary and harmonious without being of the first quality. Closer inspection of the ceiling explains the curious impression it makes at first glance; the decoration is entirely fresco (by *Josef Adam Mölk*); there is no plastic stucco work at all (what appears as such is painted imitation). The only (very slight) real stucco in the church is on the pilaster capitals and the wall between them. Particularly shapely and attractive is the pulpit with its four putti symbolizing the cardinal virtues.

Vorarlberg

Interesting in other respects, this western tip of the Tyrol, though the home of some of the most important Baroque architects, has itself little to detain those in search of Baroque churches. There is, of course, a considerable amount of Baroque art scattered up and down the area, but little of more than local interest and moderate quality. The following churches may be mentioned: the baroquized interiors of the *Bregenz Pfarrkirche* (1738, by *Anton Beer*) and of that at *Braz* near Bludenz, and the attractive parish and pilgrimage churches of *Bildstein* above Bregenz (1663–92, fine monstrance 1683) and *Bartholomäberg* near Schruns (1729–43, good altars; crowning high altar tabernacle a noteworthy earlier carved representation of the Last Supper in a columned hall, by *Michael Lechleitner*, 1635).

4. Stucco-ornament and Statuary

Stucco-ornament

The use of plaster for architectural and decorative purposes is ancient. Ornament of this material was applied to Greek temples in the fifth century B.C. It was in the fourteenth century, and in Italy, that stucco art, as we know it later, began to flourish when (as also in England in Tudor times) it was applied to decorate ceilings and the upper parts of walls. At first it was not associated with fresco-painting at all.

In the Baroque we can trace both a development in the style of stucco ornamentation and a diminishing in its importance as a decorative element. In the earlier phase (up to *c*. 1710) either it holds the field alone without frescoes (*Obermarchtal; Kleinhelfendorf*, plate 24) or it preponderates decisively over them (e.g. *Holzen*, plate 38; *Garsten; Rheinau*). Rich, even exuberant, it yet has a stiff, 'clotted' character and tends to follow architectural lines or fill ceiling or wall sections. The motifs are mainly leaves and fruit, though volutes are found on capitals, and figures (angels, etc.) at prominent points. Gradually, however, changes appear. The architectural element disappears; stiff, symmetrical designs and realistic leaf and fruit motifs give place to scroll-work of increasingly abstract, unsymmetrical and feathery nature (e.g. *Einsiedeln; Diessen*, plate 25; *Wilten Pfarrkirche*). One particular abstract form came, after about 1720, to exercise a decisive influence in the adornment of wall and ceiling surfaces, notably in certain positions such as spandrels and crowns of arches. This was the French *rocaille*, a graceful design of delicate scroll and counter-scroll outline, varying in form yet maintaining everywhere its characteristic asymmetrical harmony (plates 25, 41, 43, 57, 60). Another development, referred to elsewhere, must also be noted here. This was the technique, introduced by the brothers *Asam*, of blending stucco elements with fresco painting to facilitate the transition from the three-dimensional sphere to the two-dimensional and enhance the general illusory effect. Thus we find, for example, that figures or objects round the base of a ceiling fresco, where the painted, visionary scene with its ecstasy and illusion passes over into our real world, are sometimes partly painted and partly of stucco, thus sharing both in the real and in the visionary world (plate 41).

The earliest influence in the field of stucco work came, of course, from Italian artists, and it is to this that the heavy, formal characteristics of early stucco ornament throughout the area are primarily due. As examples of Italian work may be mentioned that of *Carlo Antonio Carlone* (the chief member of an extensive family of architects, stucco-artists and painters) at *Garsten* (1685), *St Florian* (1687), *Kremsmünster* (1690) and *Passau Cathedral* (completed 1703); that of *Giovanni Battista Carlone* at *Waldsassen* (1695 f.), also at *Passau*; that of *Carlo Domenico Lucchese* at *Speinshart* (1696 f.); that of *Giovanni Niccolo Perti* in the *Munich Theatinerkirche*; and (later) that of *Alberto Camesina* at *Vienna* (*Karlskirche* 1725 f., *Petrikirche* 1730 f.). Italian influence (if not workmanship) can be seen in other early S. German stucco ornament, such as that at *Tegernsee* (1684 f.) and *Holzen* (*c.* 1707 f., plate 38).

After the end of the seventeenth century, however, by far the most important and widespread influence came from the school that developed at *Wessobrunn* (S. Bavaria, 6 m. S.W. *Diessen*). Of the once extensive buildings of the monastery here less than a quarter remain, and those of no architectural importance, though a visit is recommended on account of the fine examples to be seen there of the school's earlier work (Fürstentrakt and Gästetrakt and adjoining rooms and staircase, partly in colour). But Wessobrunn craftsmen worked far and wide over the whole of our area and beyond it, from the Rhineland to Bohemia and from northern Bavaria down into Switzerland. As chief representatives of the school (together with their main works) may be mentioned:

Johann Schmutzer (1642–1701); Obermarchtal (1689).

Franz Schmutzer (1676–1741): Rheinau (1708 f.), Weissenau (1711), Weingarten (1718).

Josef Schmutzer (1683–1741), son of Johann: Wessobrunn (1707 f.), Rottenbuch (1737 f.), Oberammergau Pfarrkirche (1737 f.). Often worked with the painter Mattäus Günther.

Johann Georg Übelherr (or Übelhör, 1700–63): Diessen (1763–8), Wilhering (1744–6), Ettal (1748–52), Maria Steinbach (1756 f.). Worked in association with J. M. Feichtmayr. Concentrated more on actual figures than on scroll-work.

Franz Xaver Feichtmayr[1] (1705–64): Diessen, with his brother, Stams (1742 f.), Wilten Pfarrkirche (1754–5), Indersdorf (1754–5), Rott-am-Inn (1760).

Johann Michael Feichtmayr[1] (1709–72): Diessen, Zwiefalten (1747), Ottobeuren (after 1754), Vierzehnheiligen (1764). Probably also Arlesheim (1760). The work of both brothers of striking delicacy.

Statuary

This may, of course, be of many materials. In S. Germany and Switzerland there is a great deal of stucco statuary, in Austria relatively little. Stucco, though in itself synthetic, has the advantage of combining the visual appearance of stone or marble with a lightness in weight that made possible such boldly imaginative work as that of the Asams on the high altars of Rohr or Osterhofen.

South Germany. The following sculptors are of chief importance:

Egid Quirin Asam (1692–1750). Principal works at Rohr (1717–19), Weltenburg (1717–21), Einsiedeln (1724–6), Innsbruck St Jakob (1722–3), Osterhofen (1726 f.), Munich

---

[1] The reader is warned that the spelling of these names is variable. Sometimes we find Feucht-, sometimes Feicht-, sometimes -mayr, sometimes -mayer. The spellings given are the usual ones.

STUCCO-ORNAMENT AND STATUARY

St Johann Nepomuk (1733 f.), *Aldersbach* (1745 f.). The most
versatile of the S. German Baroque sculptors and probably
the greatest. The *Asams*' aim of blending realistic and
visionary elements achieved with notable power in some of
his statuary. His greatest work the Assumption group at
Rohr (see p. 94 ff.) but very fine also the St George group at
Weltenburg, the Holy Trinity group above the high altar at
Munich, the altars at *Osterhofen* (plates 35, 36, 45, 46, 63, 66).

Joseph Anton Feuchtmayer[1] (1696–1770). Member of a Wessobrunn family. Worked chiefly in the Lake of Constance area:
Weingarten (1720), *Birnau* (1747–50), *St Gallen* (1760–70).
His talent many-sided, ranging from an almost drastic
realism (*Birnau* high altar, figures of Anne and Elizabeth) to
ecstasy (*Nenzingen*, Martinskapelle, hovering putto) and intimate devotion (*Mimmenhausen*, Pfarrkirche, font group).
Notable for his insight into child nature; his putti of unusual
fascination (e.g. *Birnau*, the celebrated 'Honigschlecker', but
also his counterpart across the aisle). Characteristic for many
of his figures a certain ruggedness of line and an almost
abrupt turning movement of the body that emphasizes
curiously its physical presence (plates 49, 57, 64).

Johann Baptist Straub (1704–84). Worked only in wood, his
figures often whitened, with some gilding. Principal works:
Diessen (pulpit, 1739–41), *Berg-am-Laim* (1743 and 1758–9),
Andechs (nave-altars, eastern pair, 1751–5), *Schäftlarn*
(altars and pulpit, 1755–6), *Ettal* (side altars and pulpit,
1757–62), *Altomünster* (nave altars, 1765 f.). His work in
great contrast alike to that of *Feuchtmayer* and to that of
his pupil *Ignaz Günther*. His figures quiet, of a restrained,
almost courtly gravity and of a more spiritualized, less physical, presence (plate 50).

Ignaz Günther (1725–75). Pupil of *Straub*. Principal works:
Altenhohenau, right bank of Inn 3 m. below Rott (altars,
1761 f.); *Rott-am-Inn* (altars, 1762); *Weyarn* just off autobahn Munich–Salzburg, 20 m. S.E. Munich (pietà, Annun-

[1] See footnote on previous page.

ciation group, Valerius shrine, high altar tabernacle; 1763 f.);
Freising-Neustift (high altar, 1765); *Mallersdorf* (high
altar, 1768–70); *Nenningen; Würtemberg*, 30 m. E. of
Stuttgart, 10 m. E. of Göppingen (pietà in cemetery chapel,
1774). His work brilliant and penetrating but with the
characteristics of a later date, combining elegance with a
certain languid, even chilly, sophistication. Typical the
drooping eyelids and mannered gestures alike in queen
(Kunigunde, right of high altar at *Rott*), priest (Cardinal
Peter Damian, left side altar of nave at *Rott*, plate 51);
and angel (Annunciation group, *Weyarn*). His art is seen at
its deepest and most perfect in his last work, the wonderful
pietà at *Nenningen*.

Other important groups of statuary will be found referred to
in their contexts, e.g. the two great groups of the four Latin
Fathers of the Church, one, probably by *Joachim Dietrich*, in
the sanctuary at *Diessen* (plate 44); the other, by *Anton Sturm*,
in the nave at *Die Wies* (plate 48).

Austria. From the point of view of the visitor in search of
Baroque who may be using this book it is unfortunate that in
Austria important Baroque statuary is so often to be found in
Romanesque or Gothic churches which, as such, are not included
here. Attention must, however, be directed to the work of the
following major artists, wherever it may be found, in buildings
of the period, or not:

Thomas Schwanthaler (1634–1705). The ancestor, and the
most distinguished member, of a family of carvers and
sculptors, a late descendant of which was the Ludwig
Schwanthaler whom we find working for Ludwig I of
Bavaria well on into the nineteenth century. Of Suebian
extraction, he was born and lived in Ried and worked chiefly
in N.W. Austria and the Salzkammergut. Principal works:
Ried (22 m. E. Braunau, 25 m. S. Passau), high altar (1665)
and side altars (1669); *Schalchen* (12 m. S.E. Braunau, on
Salzburg road), high altar 1672; *St Wolfgang*, double altar in
nave 1676, his chief masterpiece (plate 55); *Gmunden* (N. end

of Traunsee), high altar of parish church, 1678; *Mehrnbach* (3 m. W. of Ried), high altar, 1697. His work looks backward and forward. Gothic influence seems here and there unmistakable (in his treatment of drapery, e.g. the flanking figures of the *St Wolfgang* altar). Yet his way of placing his figures standing free without background (*Schalchen*, *Gmunden*) was an innovation. His figures are noble, intense yet serene. But the flowing lines seem sometimes to conceal a latent energy which, when the chance comes (*St Wolfgang*, the group of St Michael casting down Satan, crowning the altar), bursts out with great dramatic power.

Michael Zürn the younger (1636–?92). Nephew of the sculptor-brothers Martin and Michael Zürn of Wasserburg-am-Inn who have also left some fine works (*Wasserburg*, *St Jakob*, pulpit; *Eggelsberg*, 12 m. S. Braunau, crucifix). His principal works date between 1682 and 1690 and are at: *Kremsmünster* q.v., angels, especially on E. side-apse altars (kneeling), others in nave, 1682–3 (standing); *Mattsee* (12 m. N.E. Salzburg), figures of Sebastian and Rochus from a former altar, 1685; *Frauenberg* (upper Enns valley near Admont), high altar, 1685–8; *Grünau* (8 m. E. of Traunsee), figure of St Catherine on side altar, 1690; *Gmunden*, figures of Zachariah and Elizabeth in the parish church, after 1691. An artist of many moods suggesting a deeper inner restlessness and tension. He ranges from the quiet beauty of the *Grünau* St Catherine to the tormented and mannered (yet almost contemporary) figures at *Gmunden*, and from the nobility of the *Frauenberg* St Catherine to the passionate defiance of the *Mattsee* St Rochus. The *Kremsmünster* angels in themselves offer interesting contrasts from a dynamic Bernini spirit to an almost classicist poise. He has nothing of the serenity of *Schwanthaler* or *Guggenbichler*.

Meinrad Guggenbichler (1649–1723). A native of *Einsiedeln*. Possibly a pupil of *Schwanthaler*. Principal works (chiefly in the Salzburg district, the Inn area and Upper Austria): *Strasswalchen* (15 m. N.E. Salzburg), high altar 1675, his

STUCCO-ORNAMENT AND STATUARY

first work; *Mondsee* (N. end of lake), five side altars and
pulpit and other figures, 1681–4; *Irrsdorf* (2 m. S.E.
Strasswalchen), three side altars, 1684; *Michaelbeuren*
(15 m. N. Salzburg), high altar in abbey church (plate 54),
1691; *St Wolfgang*, three side altars, pulpit, Ecce Homo
statue, 1706 (plate 53); *Lochen* (5 m. N.W. Strasswalchen),
high altar, pulpit, 1709; *Oberhofen* (3 m. S.E. Strasswalchen), all altars, pulpit, 1712. To me, at least, the greatest
of the Austrian sculptors in wood. From the earlier works
at *Mondsee* to the rare and majestic beauty of *Michaelbeuren*, the deeply moving Ecce Homo at *St Wolfgang* and
the quiet beauty of the *Lochen* Mary at the Cross his figures
combine a profound and yet intimate humanity, a depth of
feeling transfigured by restraint and a grace of poise and
movement that put them among the noblest creations of
Austrian and German Baroque art. The wonderful *Michaelbeuern* altar has the further importance of containing the
earliest examples north of the Alps of what are called in
German 'Schwebefiguren'; the two saints are seen to be, not
standing on the earth or on pedestals of earthly firmness, but
'hovering' on clouds borne up by angels (plate 54, cf. *St Wolfgang* pulpit; the idea copied frequently later).

Georg Raphael Donner (1693–1741). Worked first in Salzburg,
later in Pressburg (Bratislava) and finally in Vienna. Many
secular works, of which some are here mentioned. He
favoured lead as a material. Principal works: *Salzburg
Schloss Mirabell*, staircase putti, 1726; *Vienna, Baroque
Museum* (many works, especially the original figures from
the *Mehlmarktbrunnen*, c. 1738), *Altes Rathaus* (*Andro-
medabrunnen*, 1741); *Gurk Cathedral* (pietà 1740–1, his
masterpiece); *Klagenfurt*, diocesan museum (Ascension
figure, c. 1741); perhaps also *Vienna Piaristenkirche* (figures
on high altar), *Klosterneuburg* (cemetery gate) and *Passau
Cathedral* (pulpit statuary). His art, with its restrained and
reposeful dignity, seems like a remarkably early herald of
the classicism of the end of the century. It is certainly free of

tension and extravagance; form and spirit find mutual accord. Yet, though we feel an unmistakable breath of things to be, there is none of the later formalism and tendency to shallowness. The great pietà at *Gurk* combines a harmony of form which the classicists seldom attained with a profundity of feeling which they perhaps never felt.

Johann Thaddäus Stammel (1695–1765). A native of Graz where he studied under *J. J. Schoy*; 1720 in Italy, from 1726 working in *Admont* in the upper Enns valley. Worked entirely in his Styrian homeland (which in fact is outside the area otherwise covered by the section of this book on Austria). Principal works (all in wood): *Frauenberg* (near Admont), high altar, 1736; *Strassgang* (3 m. S.W. Graz), high altar of St Martin's church, 1738–40, perhaps his masterpiece; *Kallwang* (Liesingtal, 18 m. S.E. Admont); Nativity scene, 1751; *Admont*, Stiftskirche, Nativity scene 1753–6 and representations of the Four Last Things, in the Library 1760. In the work of this important, powerful and in many ways attractive artist two tendencies seem to mingle, indeed to conflict. There is, on the one hand, the true Baroque sense of indwelling form relating the parts and details organically and significantly to one another and to the whole. But it has a struggle to maintain itself against the artist's own vigorous realism and intense interest in detail. This struggle is observable in the altar at *Strassgang*; it is very clear in the Nativity scene at *Kallwang*. In his figures, too, more than one aspect is traceable. There is something of the mellow inwardness of *Guggenbichler*, but more often a stark, drastic energy and sense of drama (*Admont*, group of Hell and the Damned Soul, in Library). It may be suggested that, if *Donner* anticipates the coming classicism in his serenity of form, *Stammel* does so in his preoccupation with detail. But in fact, his art looks back as much as it looks forward. It is in any case an art close to life and nature and home tradition; and in it, for all its Baroque dress, the spirit of the late Middle Ages lingers unmistakably on.

5. Fresco-painting

It may perhaps be useful, before we pass to consider the painters and their work, to draw attention to one or two characteristics of the art itself which distinguish it from other forms of painting and should always be borne in mind by anyone studying frescoes.

(1) Unlike the painting on canvas or wood, the fresco is fixed in its position and indeed depends for its effect largely upon its special relation to the space that it occupies. The fresco-painter must endeavour to utilize all the possibilities of the ceiling (or wall) area at his disposal with an eye to producing the greatest effects of colour and perspective. Two considerations are here of particular importance—the distance of the painting from the beholder, and the movements he makes in viewing it. A large-scale ceiling fresco, for example, can be seen only from a considerable distance; further, we build up our idea of it from the varying aspects that it presents to us as we move from place to place. Both these facts have to be taken into account by the artist; and it will be clear that where the fresco has to cover a domed surface the problems of perspective are greatly complicated.

(2) The technical difficulties of the art are formidable. As the colours have to be applied to a lime base not yet dry, the work must be done quickly and, as corrections are hardly possible, with great sureness of touch. The speed, indeed, with which some of the greatest of these series of frescoes have been accomplished is astounding. Again, the chemical interaction between base and colours has to be carefully judged, and only a relatively limited number of colours is in fact at the painter's disposal in this respect.[1]

[1] Discussions of all these problems will be found in Mrs Merrifield's useful little book (see Bibliography).

(3) It will be clear that, the position and size of a fresco being what they are, only certain types of theme are suitable for portrayal. The intimate is, of course, quite out of place. Themes must be epic, dramatic, eventful; the treatment broad, monumental. A fresco will fail if the conception lacks scale or the treatment is niggling or fussy.

The opportunity may here be taken to add a few further words on the general subjects of the themes, arrangements and positions of Baroque church frescoes.

Themes. In the case of a large-scale series of paintings for an important church the theme was normally set by the clergy of the church in question. Some of these 'programmes' are still in existence in writing (e.g. *Oberaltaich, Melk, St Florian*). In the majority of cases we find some well-known theological theme with, perhaps, adaptation to local conditions and history. Among the most frequent are the following:

(1) The Redemption of Man through the mercy of God in sending His Son.
(2) The Glorification of the Holy Trinity.
(3) The life of Christ or of Mary, culminating in the Resurrection and Ascension of the former and the Assumption and Coronation of the latter.
(4) Mary as Intercessor, portrayed with her Old Testament prototypes.
(5) The life of some Saint (usually the patron Saint or the founder of the Order) culminating in his glorification.
(6) The story of the pilgrimage (in a setting partly historical, partly legendary, partly theological) of which the church is the home and centre.

Single paintings in lesser churches are usually devoted to some theological theme or some scene from the Old or New Testament or from the life of the patron (or some other) Saint.

Arrangement and position. The central theme of a major series of paintings will be found developed in the main frescoes of choir, crossing or dome (if this exists) and nave. Aisles, side chapels and transepts are reserved for subsidiary scenes. Representations of the Last Supper or of the Sacrifice of Christ in some aspect will find a natural place above the sanctuary or high altar. The Ascension, the Assumption, the Adoration of the Trinity and the glorification of the patron or founder Saint will be found depicted in a position of especial prominence such as the saucer dome over the crossing or the main fresco of the nave. We recall here again that ceiling frescoes stand in thematic connection with other representations in the church below. Thus the fresco above an altar will often be found to continue and complete the theme of the altar painting below it. Thus, again, we find above the organ over the main entrance to the church (and, unlike the other frescoes, *facing* us as we leave) a painting of angels singing or playing on instruments, often flanked by the patrons of music, David with his harp and Cecilia with her organ. Certain parts of a church offer special possibilities for introducing particular symbolic groups in smaller paintings (or, indeed, in statuary). A frequent and favourite example is the crossing with its four arches and four corner spandrels; here we often find the four Evangelists or the four Fathers of the Western Church with their symbols, or the four continents to which the Gospel is to be preached.

The art of the fresco has, of course, a long history. It was widely practised in the early Roman Empire (House of Livia on the Palatine in Rome; Pompeii[1]). The basic problems of perspective, however, which underlie the great illusory effects later achieved by Baroque painters were only gradually understood. Early forerunners in the field of perspectival experiment were *Paolo Uccello* (1397–1414), *Tommaso Masaccio* (1401–28) and *Piero della Francesca* (1418–92). But the first decisive figure was *Andrea Mantegna* (1431–1506). His frescoes in the chapel of S. Cristoforo in the church of the Eremitani at *Padua* (1454–5) mark the first serious revolt against the tyranny of the flat wall surface by treating it as if, so to speak, it were not there. Though inside a building we seem to look through the wall to the outer world beyond. In similar fashion, his ceiling of the Camera degli Sposi in the Castello at *Mantua* (1468–74) disregards the roof and

[1] See the wonderful frescoes in the National Museum in Naples.

leads the gaze upward into the 'open sky' through a circular opening with a balustrade over which all kinds of fascinating beings, human and other, peer down at us from a convincing yet non-existent dimension. Fifty years later at *Parma* (S. Giovanni 1520–4, the Duomo 1526–30) *Correggio* covered in each case an entire inner cupola, treated as an undivided whole, with a single great visionary fresco, and in doing so opened a new epoch in the art of fresco painting. The significance, the possibilities and the method of this treatment of ceiling spaces were made clear. From the Parma frescoes the way leads direct to the work of *Andrea Pozzo* (1642–1709) whose frescoes in *S. Ignazio* in *Rome* and whose treatise on perspective (see bibliography) represent, alike at the practical and at the theoretical level, the first attainment of mastery over the problems involved and were of far-reaching influence on the later development of the art. Italian fresco painting reached its greatest brilliance in the work of the Venetian *Giovanni Battista Tiepolo* (1696–1770) whose great fresco in the Würzburg Residenz influenced the later German masters.

A general survey of church fresco painting in the area we are here considering will show that it passes through certain broad phases similar to those exhibited in the stucco art. In the earlier period in which, as we have seen, it plays a subordinate part in relation to stucco, the treatment tends to be stiff and formal, though the colours are often brilliant; the effect of these small early frescoes resembles that of enamel plaques or medallions. Then comes a time when the fresco begins to increase in independence and size, the scenes depicted become more complex, dynamic and visionary, the treatment gains in freedom and dramatic power. Later we find a relaxation of tension, a quietening of tone, a clearing of the air which lead, not at first, but towards the end of the eighteenth century, to a loss of power and depth. With these three broadly outlined periods in mind we pass to consider the more important artists and their work.

Early Period (up to *c.* 1710)

In S. Germany good examples of early fresco work are offered by the two series by *Johannes Georg Asam*, the father of the more famous brothers, at *Benediktbeuern* (1682–90) and *Tegernsee* (1689–94) which lie some 28 m. S. of Munich and 15 m. apart. They form an interesting comparative study. For though in both we note a certain stiffness of treatment and similar brilliant colouring, the slightly later paintings at *Tegernsee* have gained in size in relation to the stucco ornament. Other characteristic examples of the small early fresco are at *Speinshart* (1696 f., by *Bartolomeo Lucchese*, the brother of the architect of the church) and at *Holzen* (*c.* 1708, artist unknown; plate 38). In Austria, the early phase may be illustrated by the frescoes of *Matthias Rauchmiller* in the *Vienna Dominikanerkirche* (*c.* 1670), and, in the west, by the work of two Tyrol families, those of *Schor* (*Stams* choir chapels 1696, by *Ägid Schor*) and *Waldmann* (*Wilten Stiftskirche* frescoes by *Kaspar Waldmann*, 1707; the *Rattenberg Augustinerkirche* dome fresco by his nephew *Johann Josef*, 1708, is interesting as being large and ambitious and yet static). In Switzerland the frescoes of *Francesco Antonio Giorgioli* at *Muri* and *Rheinau* (both 1707 f.) represent the early period.

It should be emphasized that the size of a fresco, by itself, is not in every case an indication of date. As early as 1690–5, at *St Florian*, we find *Georg Anton Gumpp* and *Melchior Michel Steidl* greatly increasing the size and importance of the fresco; while, on the other hand, we sometimes find much later frescoes remarkably small and tentative in size (e.g. *Ochsenhausen*, 1725–7, or *Lucerne*, *Jesuit Church*, 1749–50).

Middle Period (*c.* 1710 to *c.* 1730)

Of principal importance were the following artists:
Johann Michael Rottmayr (1654–1730). Fifteen years a pupil of

FRESCO-PAINTING

Carl Loth in Venice. Chief works: *Breslau, St Matthias* (1704–6, his masterpiece); *Vienna, Peterskirche* (1712–13); *Melk* (1712– 18); *Vienna, Karlskirche* (1725); *Klosterneuburg Stiftskirche* (1729). In addition, many important frescoes in secular build- ings, especially in Vienna and Salzburg. One of the earliest to break with the tradition of one painting to a bay and to link up the bays in a single great fresco (*Breslau*; at *Melk* archi- tectural stipulations prevented this, but even here there is a tendency in the frescoes to run over the transverse arches). Forward-looking also in showing greater interest in colour, atmosphere and the grouping of figures than in details of illusory architecture. Of architectural motifs he made in general little use; those in the *Melk* church are by another hand (*G. Fanti*) and in the later *Vienna Karlskirche* the great fresco opens up directly without conventional parapet or balustrading or other form of architectural transition.

Cosmas Damian Asam (1686–1739). Study in Italy, 1712–14. Chief works: *Munich, Dreifaltigkeitskirche* (1715); *Michelfeld*, 20 m. N.W. Amberg (1716); *Amberg, Mariahilf* (1717); *Weingarten* (1717 f.); *Aldersbach* (1720); *Weltenburg* (1721 f.); *Innsbruck, St Jakob* (1722–3); *Freising Cathedral* (1723–4); *Einsiedeln* (1724–6); *Fürstenfeldbruck* (choir 1722–3, nave 1731); *Regensburg, St Emmeram* (1732); *Osterhofen* (1733); *Ingolstadt, St Maria de Victoria* (1732–6); *Munich, St John Nepomuk* (1733); *Straubing, Ursulinenkirche* (1737 f., un- finished at his death). Almost no work on secular buildings. As with his brother, his study in Italy left deep and recurrent in- fluences, e.g. a tendency to sombreness of colour and a fondness for architectural motifs. Unfortunately very few of his works are in a really good state of preservation (*Ingolstadt* one of the most brilliant). Like his brother, chiefly concerned to produce an effect of real and supernatural, earthly and heavenly merg- ing and blending (*Weltenburg*, the Nativity fresco at *Einsiedeln*). He had a great feeling for atmosphere and this lent him un- usual sensitivity in the decoration of existing churches (e.g. *Freising, Aldersbach*). His virtuosity in perspectival illusion was remarkable (let the visitor wander about the church at *Ingolstadt* and study the ceiling as he goes!).

Paul Troger (1698–1762). Spent three years studying in Italy. Chief works: *Salzburg, St Kajetan* (1728); *Melk, Marmorsaal* (1731) and *Library* (1733); *Zwettl,* 26 m. N. Melk, *Library* (1732–3); *Altenburg, church* (1733), *Marmorsaal* (1737), *Hauptstiege* (1738), *Library* (1741); *St Andrä-an-der-Traisen,* 8 m. N. St Pölten (1739); *Seitenstetten,* 25 m. S.E. Linz, *Library* (1741); *Brixen,* S. Tyrol, *cathedral* (1748–50); *Dreieichen,* 5 m. E. Altenburg (1752). Probably the greatest Austrian fresco painter of the Baroque period. His work seems to illustrate in itself the entire development of Baroque fresco painting in its main phases. With him the first turning point seems to have come with the great dome fresco in the *church* at *Altenburg* (see also pp. 223–5), which, in comparison with earlier work, shows great boldness and freedom of conception, a loosening-up of any rigid symmetry (the main scene is enacted at one end of the painting), profound and brilliant feeling for contrasts of light and atmosphere, fine colour harmony and intense dramatic power (note in this last respect the figures of the Dragon, the Woman and the headlong-swooping Archangel Michael). A second turning-point is represented perhaps by the *library* frescoes at *Altenburg* where a quieter note is felt in spirit, design and colour. At *Altenburg,* indeed, the visitor has a remarkable opportunity of studying in a series of major frescoes the development of the work of one of the greatest fresco-painters over a number of years.

Bartolomeo Altomonte (1702 Warsaw–1783). Chief works: *St Florian, Marmorsaal* (1724); *Spital-am-Pyhrn,* Pyhrn pass (1739–41); *Wilhering* (1741); *St Florian, Library* (1747); *Herzogenburg* (1751–6), *Library* (1753); *Admont,* upper Enns valley, *Library* (1753); *Engelszell,* Danube below Passau (1759–62); *St Pölten,* church of the *Englische Fräulein* (1769). A brilliant but apparently somewhat uncertain talent whose creative period covered, rather than reflected, the later as well as the middle phase of fresco development. To the end he retained a certain heaviness and lack of delicacy. There is a tendency to restlessness of design and grouping (*Wilhering*) and to a certain smokiness in his colours, particularly in the darker hues. He made little or no use of architectural designs and where these are present (e.g. *Herzogenburg*; *St Florian, Marmorsaal* and *Library*) they are by another hand (*Spital-am-Pyhrn* is the great exception). Though in his later work (*Engelszell*) a certain lightening of design and colour is observable he shows on the whole little (less than *Troger*) of that greater grace and serenity brought in in the second half of the century by the Rococo as it developed and passed over into Classicism.

(A note must be added on that fine artist *Daniel Gran* (1694–1757), the teacher of *B. Altomonte*. He is not referred to here at greater length as his works are mostly in palaces and other secular buildings, his masterpiece in this field being the ceiling of the *Vienna Hofbibliothek* built by *Fischer von Erlach*. His important church frescoes are those in the church on the *Sonntagberg* (1743) and in *St Pölten Cathedral*. Others are in the *Vienna Annakirche* (1747–8) and in the *Kapuzinerkirche* at *Stein-an-der-Donau* (next to Krems, 1756). At *Herzogenburg* (1751–6) he co-operated with *Altomonte* in the designs of the choir frescoes. He has so much in common with *Altomonte* that it is sometimes difficult to tell their work apart; but on the whole his colours are clearer and his spirit less restless.)

Later Period (from *c.* 1740)

Johann Baptist Zimmermann (1680–1758). The brother of the architect Dominikus. At first, a stucco artist; after the age of fifty, developed into a fresco-painter with astonishing rapidity and maturity. Chief works: *Steinhausen* (1731, plate 39), *Berg-am-Laim* (1739); *Landshut-Seligenthal* (1750); *Die Wies* (1750–4, his masterpiece); *Freising-Neustift* (1751–6); *Andechs* (1754); *Schäftlarn* (1754–6). His work has a lyrical, idyllic character that represents a complete break with earlier tradition. Not a breath of formalism, no obtrusive architectural motifs, no noticeable external influences. His atmosphere is quite his own, serene and gracious, nowhere threatening or eruptive. Even in the Last Judgment painting at *Die Wies* we feel somehow that mercy will prevail! His earthly scenes are light and charming landscapes (*Steinhausen*). His colouring throughout brilliant and mellow; an ultramarine blue characteristic on garments here and there. He has the golden brilliance of an early autumn evening sky.

Johann Georg Bergmüller (1688–1762). In 1730 became Director of the recently founded academy in Augsburg which, mainly through his work, came to exercise a great influence on S. German fresco painting. Chief works: *Diessen* (1736, his masterpiece); *Steingaden*, near Die Wies (1740 f.); *Fulpmes*, Stubai valley (1747). Of his various frescoes in *Augsburg* churches most were destroyed by air-raids in the last war; those in the church of the *Karmeliterkloster S. Anna* may be mentioned. An academic artist of the highest quality who combines generosity of conception with careful attention to grouping and detail and brilliance of colouring. Architectural motifs, where introduced (*Diessen*, esp. the choir fresco), are related to the theme and never serve merely to heighten perspective illusion.

Franz Josef Spiegler (1691–1757). He is included here with some hesitation because the works through which alone he is well known and which are his greatest achievements, the series of frescoes at *Zwiefalten* (1747–9), have, despite their date, certain qualities suggesting kinship with earlier years. They are compositions of the first order and of an extraordinary ecstatic power and movement, depth of composition and variety of colouring. Particularly notable are those over nave and crossing in which the figures (in the latter case over 200 in number) seem, by a kind of vortex, to be being veritably sucked up into the depth and height and light of heaven. For an earlier series of his works that affords an interesting comparison the visitor is referred to the church of *St Peter* in the Black Forest, E. of Freiburg (1724–7, see p. 132).

Matthäus Günther (1705–88). Pupil of *C. D. Asam*. In 1762 elected Director of the Augsburg Academy in succession to *Bergmüller* on the latter's death. Chief works partly in Bavaria and partly in Tyrol: *Rottenbuch* (1738 and 1742); *Mittenwald* Pfarrkirche (1740); *Oberammergau* Pfarrkirche (1742); *Fiecht* (1743–4); *Amorbach* (1744–7); *Schongau* Pfarrkirche, choir (1748); *Würzburg, Käppele* (1750); *Gossensass (Colle Isarco,* Brenner Pass), Pfarrkirche (1754); *Innsbruck-Wilten* Pfarrkirche (1754); *Indersdorf* (1754–5); *Schongau,* nave (1761); *Rott-am-Inn* (1767); *Götzens* (1774). He represents the zenith of S. German late Baroque fresco painting. The frescoes at *Fiecht* show a first development towards a freer, more asymmetrical composition; those at Würzburg the inspiration of *Tiepolo's* work in the *Residenz* there. The *Wilten* paintings first, perhaps, show his full range; the different themes are given remarkably varied treatment in respect of general design, lighting effects and colour gradation. A characteristic feature of his mature designs is an elevated stone platform or terrace, sometimes running forward to a sharp corner with great plastic and perspectival effect, on which he sets his chief figures (e.g. the frescoes of Judith at *Würzburg* and *Wilten,* or that at *Götzens* showing the Apostles Peter and Paul routing the demons). His colours always of a delicate, almost pastel quality, often with a prevailing greyish undertone.

Gottfried Bernhard Götz (1708–74). Augsburg school. Known chiefly for the frescoes at *Birnau* (1749) which are excellent works in the academic tradition, even though the architectural element in them may be felt to be somewhat conventional and heavy and the colours (at least in their present state) rather dull for so delicate and brilliant an interior.

Johann Evangelist Holzer (1709–40). A native of S. Tyrol with a fine, full-blooded sense for colour, atmosphere and humanity. He first painted many S. German house-fronts (e.g. the Pilatushaus in Oberammergau). His most characteristic and best-known work is the fresco in the little church of *St Anton* above *Partenkirchen* (1739), which combines admirable draughtsmanship and colour with a vital and homely yet dignified realism.

Johann Jakob Zeiller (1708–83). The most important member of a very productive fresco-painting family. His chief works are at *Ettal* (finished 1752) and *Ottobeuren* (1763). The Ettal dome, with its 70 ft. span and its 400 figures thronging endlessly on the clouds of heaven is, despite a certain duskiness of colour, his greatest achievement and notable by any standards. At *Ottobeuren* it may be felt that the frescoes, in common with the rest of the decoration, are somewhat too lightweight for the vast proportions of the church. In his art, as in that of his contemporary, though to a less extent, we see the tendency of the time in loosening structure, lightening technique and dissolving masses of figures into small groups or even isolated individuals.

Christian Wenzinger (1710–97). A native of Freiburg. Studied in Rome and Paris. His masterpiece the frescoes at *St Gallen* (1757–60) which show a quite remarkable looseness of composition and airy serenity. The great fresco in the central dome (plate 43) opens up the visionary world to us immediately above the stone cornice and portrays figures of saints and angels hovering, almost like large butterflies, singly or in loose groups on clouds against an abyss of light.

Franz Anton Maulbertsch (1724–96).A native of Langenargen (Lake of Constance). Active in Hungary and Bohemia as well as in Austria. Chief works: *Vienna Piaristenkirche* (1753); *Heiligenkreuz-Gutenbrunn*, 9 m. N.E. St Pölten, *Pfarrkirche* (1758); *Korneuburg*, 9 m. N.W. Vienna, *Augustinerkirche* (*c.* 1770); to which should be added *Schloss Halbthurn*, Burgenland, 30 m. S.E. Vienna, E. of Neusiedler See, *Mittelsaal* (1765) and the *Innsbruck Hofburg*, *Riesensaal* (1776). A somewhat mysterious genius about whose personality, antecedents and teachers it would be interesting to know more. His range can be seen if we compare the apocalyptic drama and intensity of the central fresco of the *Piaristenkirche* with the intimacy of the side paintings (Christ and the woman of Samaria, and in the house of Martha and Mary) or the almost classicist serenity of the Festsaal fresco at *Halbthurn*. The influence of Rembrandt seems unmistakable in his earlier works. Great range and variety and change of mood seem to reflect a restless, problematic personality.

Martin Knoller (1725–1804). Studied with *Troger* in Vienna. In 1755 made the acquaintance of *Winckelmann* and the classicist painter *Anton Raffael Mengs* in Rome. Chief works: *Volders* (1766, plate 41); *Ettal, choir* (1769); *Gries* (1771); *Neresheim* (completed 1775, his masterpiece, plate 42). An artist of great brilliance but a typical transitional figure. To follow his work through from *Volders* to *Neresheim* is an object-lesson in tracing the transition from the waning power of the late Baroque to the classicist calmness of form and clearness of light.

Christian Wink (1738–97). A natural painter-talent who blossomed with little training. Chief works: *Starnberg* (1760), *Inning*, N. end of Ammersee (1767); *St Leonhard, Dietramzell*, 16 m. S. Munich (1772); *Bettbrunn*, 8 m. N.E. Ingolstadt (1777). His treatment is broad, his tone and atmosphere popular, warm, bucolic; he included actual portraits among his figures. He has something in common with *J. E. Holzer*, but on a larger scale and more delicate, and with the greater looseness of texture and lightness of the later date (*Bettbrunn*).

APPENDIX I

Some common attributes and symbols of Apostles and Saints

Anchor	St Nicholas, St Clement
Angel (or man)	St Matthew, Evangelist
Angel (or organ, or both)	St Cecilia
Arrows (in the hand)	St Ursula
Arrows (in the body)	St Sebastian
Axe	St Matthias, St Jude
Axe in tree root	St Boniface
Bear (and baggage)	St Corbinian
Beehive	St Ambrose, St Bernard (plate 64), St John Chrysostom
Bread	St Antony the Great
Bread (in apron)	St Notburga
Bridge	St John Nepomuk
Chain(s)	St Leonard
Chalice (with snake)	St John Evangelist, St Benedict
Cloak	St Martin of Tours
Club	St James the Less, St Jude
Cock	St Peter
Cross saltire (X)	St Andrew
Crucifix (in hand)	St John Nepomuk, St Francis Xavier (plate 52)
Dish (with breasts)	St Agatha
Dove	St Scholastica
Dove (on or near shoulder)	St Gregory the Great
Eagle	St John, Evangelist
Fire in house (or bucket pouring water, or both)	St Florian
Fish (and keys)	St Peter
Fish (on book)	St Ulrich
Fish (tied to crozier)	St Zeno

280

APPENDIX I

Goose	St Martin of Tours
Gridiron	St Lawrence
Hat (cardinal's)	St Jerome (plates 44, 48, 56), St Peter Damian (plate 51), St Charles Borromeus, St Bonaventura
Hat (shepherd's) and wallet	St Wendelin
Head (on dish)	St John Baptist
Head (in hand)	St Dionysius, St Alban
Heart (flaming)	St Augustine
Heart (with crown of thorns)	St Ignatius Loyola, St Francis de Sales, St Catherine of Siena
Jug	St Notburga
Keys (crossed in hand, or hanging; often one gold, one iron)	St Peter
Knife (flayer's)	St Bartholomew
Lance	St Thomas
Lily, or flowering rod	St Joseph
Lion	St Jerome (plate 56), St Mark, Evangelist (usually winged)
Monstrance	St Norbert, St Clare of Assisi
Organ	St Cecilia
Ox (or bull)	St Luke, Evangelist
Pen (in hand)	St Gregory the Great, St Thomas Aquinas, The Evangelists
Plague-spot (on leg)	St Rochus
Ploughshare	St Kunigunde
Saw	St Simon Zelotes
Serpent (in chalice)	St John Evangelist, St Benedict
Ship	St Nicholas
Sickle	St Notburga
Skin (his own)	St Bartholomew
Skull (in hand)	St Jerome (plates 44, 48, 56), St Peter Damian (plate 51), St Charles
Stag (between antlers a crucifix)	St Hubert

Stars (round head)	St John Nepomuk
Stigmata	St Francis of Assisi, St Catherine of Siena
Stones	St Stephen
Sword	St Paul, Apostle (plate 47), St Barbara, St Catherine of Alexandria
Sword and scales	St Michael
Tongs (or pincers)	St Agatha
Tongue	St John Nepomuk (plate 66), St Placidas
Tree as staff	St Christopher
Tree stump	St Sebastian
Wallet (and staff)	St James the Great
Wheel	St Catherine of Alexandria
Winch	St Erasmus

APPENDIX II

Symbolic Colours

White — Purity, holiness. Liturgical use: Feasts of Christ not connected with the Passion; Corpus Christi; Trinity Sunday; festivals of the Virgin, of Angels, and of Saints who were not martyrs.

Red — (1) Blood (sacrifice, martyrdom). Liturgical use: festivals of Martyrs and Apostles.
(2) Fire. Liturgical use: Whitsunday.

Green — Gladness, hope. Liturgical use: Sundays after Epiphany; between Trinity Sunday and Advent, both excluded.

Purple — (1) Penitence. Liturgical use: Advent, Lent, Vigils. (2) Royalty.

Black — Mourning. Liturgical use: Good Friday, All Souls' Day, Requiem Masses.

Blue — Fidelity, humility. Regularly used for the robes of the Virgin.

Yellow — Envy, jealousy. Frequently used for the clothes of Judas Iscariot. Distinguish carefully the *golden* yellow of the robes of St Peter and other saints.

Brown, grey — Penitence.

APPENDIX III

Short Glossary of Terms

Technical terms have as far as possible been avoided in this book, but a few brief explanations are here added.

Antependium — Altar frontal.

Apse — Rounded, or polygonal (as distinct from square-

283

ended) termination of some part of a church, usually the E. end (choir, sanctuary q.v.) or a chapel. Apsidal: like, or having the form of, an apse.

Basilica   A church in which the middle aisle rises higher than the side aisles, the upper walls usually pierced on each side by a row of windows for the admission of light (clerestory q.v.). The opposite form of church, in which all the aisles are of equal height, is termed in German architecture 'Hallenkirche' ('hall church'); this type is rare in England. (Bristol cathedral choir is an example.)

Bay   Vertical compartment of a church interior between the columns or pillars and comprising the ground arch together with the orders above it (gallery or triforium q.v. and clerestory window q.v.). Also used of the compartment of a ceiling or vault between two transverse arches.

Capital   Head (plain or carved) of a column or pillar that effects the transition to the springing of the arch.

Cartouche   Originally an ornamental shield for an inscription. Later a roughly shield-shaped ornament (of stucco or other material) irregular in design and with scroll-like edges or other surrounding decoration.

Clerestory   Upper wall of central aisle (above side aisles) pierced with windows. Cf. basilica.

Corbel   A bracket (usually of stone), plain or ornamented, projecting from a wall to support a weight such as an arch, a statue or a cornice.

Crossing   That part of a church at which the transepts (q.v.) cross the axis of nave (q.v.) and choir. Above it is usually in the interior a square or circular vault compartment, externally sometimes a dome or tower.

Cruciform   Cross-shaped, having the form of a cross. By a

cruciform church is meant a church whose ground-plan and/or elevation has this form. It should be noted that a church may be cruciform in elevation, yet not in its ground-plan. This is the case when (as is found more frequently on the Continent than in England) the transepts (q.v.) cut across the side-aisles of nave (q.v.) and choir without projecting beyond the outer walls of the church.

Entablature   The superstructure that is above, and rests upon, a row of pillars or columns, including cornice, frieze, etc.

Fillet   A narrow strip (often sharp-edged) running down a shaft or column, or along a moulding.

Finial   Carved decoration, usually in the form of foliage, flowers or flames, at the top of a pinnacle, a gable or even a pew end.

Fresco   Wall or ceiling painting executed on plaster that is still wet ('fresh'=Italian *fresco*).

Helm   A term used for the steeple-like, sometimes several-storeyed superstructure of a Baroque church tower. Usually it is of lead, copper or shingles covering an inner wooden framework, but it may be of stone. One very characteristic form is the 'onion', found widely in S. Germany; towers bearing these are commonly termed 'Zwiebeltürme' ('onion towers' i.e. of bulbous form). This form is more akin to the pointed dome than to the steeple and doubtless has an eastern origin.

Impost   The section of a pillar or column (also a bracket on a wall) from which an arch springs.

Lunette   (German: *Stichkappe*). An arched, inward-curving aperture in a concave ceiling or vault resulting from the insertion of a vertical window for the admission of light.

Monstrance (Latin *monstrare*=to show.) A liturgical vessel used for the exposition of the Host at the service of Benediction and other devotions. It consists of a glass receptacle set in a more or less elaborate gilded or golden frame upon a stem and base, the whole often of detailed ornamentation and costly workmanship.

Nave The main body of a church extending from the W. wall to the transepts (q.v.) or choir. It may consist of one aisle only or may have centre and side aisles separated by arcades; if the centre aisle rises above the side aisles the nave has basilical form (q.v.).

Pendentive A spherical triangle (or spandrel q.v.) formed by two arch curves springing, and diverging, from the same point, and leading up to the base of a dome.

Pietà Seated statue of the Virgin mourning with the dead Christ on her knee.

Pilaster A shallow, strip-like pillar attached to a wall or, as facing, to another pillar.

Putto (Plur. putti; Italian=boy.) Small angel or cherub in the form of a plump, chubby-faced, curly-headed child, sometimes winged, and always of symbolic significance.

Rotunda A circular or oval building; or the circular or oval central part of a building.

Sanctuary That part of a church where the high altar stands.

Saucer dome The more or less shallow domed ceiling of one compartment (or bay q.v.) of a church, often painted with a fresco.

Spandrel The triangular space either between the curve of an arch and the rectangular corner framing it, or between the curves of arches springing, and diverging, from the same point. Cf. pendentive.

Stilted (arch)	An arch heightened by its vertical sides below the curve being raised.
Stucco	A fine plaster composed of various elements used for ornamentation of ceilings, walls and other surfaces, for cornices, columns and even statuary.
Tabernacle	Receptacle in the form of a shrine (or cupboard) for the consecrated Host, standing in the centre and at the rear of an altar. Usually of elaborate craftsmanship and enriched with ornament, figures and statues.
Transept	The transverse section of a cruciform (q.v.) church crossing the main axis of nave (q.v.) and choir. Also either arm of this section (N. and S. transept).
Triforium	Internal arcaded wall passage in a church above side aisle level running between the main arches below and the clerestory (q.v.) above. In a Baroque church replaced sometimes by gallery.
Volute	A scroll ornament found e.g. on the Ionic type of Greek capital (q.v.) and widely used in the sixteenth-eighteenth centuries as a decorative motif. Found in very varying sizes, sometimes against flat surfaces, sometimes projecting without background.
Wall pillar	Translation of the German term *Wandpfeiler*. A buttress taking part of the stress of a ceiling or vault but projecting inwards into a church instead of outwards from the outer wall (as in a Gothic church). Wall pillars usually form the walls of side chapels; if deep enough they are found pierced by arches whereby a kind of side aisle is formed. See further p. 54 and plates.

GROUND PLANS

(By kind permission of the Deutscher Kunstverlag)

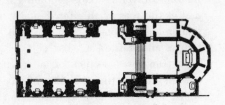

1. *St Michael, Munich.* Modelled on Il Gesù in Rome. Prototype of many S. German wall-pillar churches (length 250 ft.)

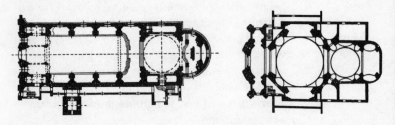

2. *Diessen* (length 215 ft.)   3. *Berg-am-Laim* (length 190 ft.)

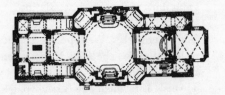

4. *Rott-am-Inn* (length 160 ft.)

Plans 2, 3, 4 (*J. M. Fischer*) show varying treatments of the axial problem (the relation of lengthways axis to transverse)

GROUND PLANS

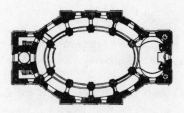

5. *Steinhausen* (length 145 ft.)

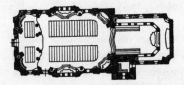

6. *Günzburg* (length 165 ft.)

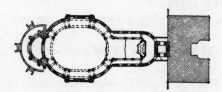

7. *Die Wies* (length 180 ft.)

The above three plans offer a study in the development of the designs of a single architect (*Dominikus Zimmermann*).

SELECT BIBLIOGRAPHY

1. GENERAL

BELLARMINE, Cardinal R. *De Potestate summi Pontificis in rebus temporalibus*, 1610.

BIBIENA, G. G. *Architteture e Prospettive*. Augsburg, 1740.

v. BOEHN, M. *Rokoko. Frankreich im xviii Jahrhundert*. Berlin, 1921.

BORROMEO, St C. *Instructiones Fabricae et Supellectilis Ecclesiasticae*, 1572.

BRIGGS, M. S. *Baroque Architecture*, London, 1913. (German translation: *Barockarchitectur*, Berlin, 1914).

BURCKHARDT, J. *Der Cicerone, eine Anleitung zum Genuss der Kunstwerke Italiens*, 1855 (English translation of part 1873).

CROCE, B. *Storia della età barocca in Italia*, Bari, 1929.

DEJOB, C. *De l'influence du Concile de Trente sur la littérature et les beaux arts chez les peuples catholiques*, Paris, 1884.

ESDAILE, K. A. *English Monumental Sculpture since the Renaissance*, London, 1927.

FEIBUSCH, H. *Mural Painting*, London, 1946.

FISCHER VON ERLACH, J. B. *Entwurf einer historischen Architektur*, Vienna, 1721.

FREYBERGER, L. *Die religiöse Deutung des Barocks*, Regensburg, 1949.

FÜRST, V. *The Architecture of Sir Christopher Wren*, London, 1956.

GOODHART-RENDEL, H. S. *Nicholas Hawksmoor*, London, 1924.

GUNNIS, R. *Dictionary of British Sculptors 1660–1851*, London, 1953.

GURLITT, C. *Geschichte der neueren Baukunst*, vol. 5, Stuttgart, 1889.

HAUSENSTEIN, W. *Vom Genie des Barock*, Munich, 1956.

SELECT BIBLIOGRAPHY

LEES-MILNE, J. *Baroque in Italy*, London, 1959. *Baroque in Spain and Portugal*. London, 1961.

LIEB, N. and DIETH, F. *Die Vorarlberger Barockbaumeister*, Munich (Schnell & Steiner), 1960. (The latest, fullest and best account).

LILL, G. *Deutsche Plastik*, Berlin, 1925.

LOYOLA, St I. *Spiritual Exercises*: edition by H. Keane, S. J., (5th ed.) London, 1952.

LÜBKE, W. and SEMRAU, F. *Die Kunst der Barockzeit und des Rokoko*, Stuttgart, 1905.

MAYER, A. L. *Liturgie und Barock*; Jahrbuch für Liturgiewissenschaft, vol. xv (1941), pp. 67–154.

MERRIFIELD, Mrs M. *The Art of Fresco-Painting* (1846); new edition by A. C. SEWTER, London (Alec Tiranti), 1952.

MOLESWORTH, H. D. *Baroque Sculpture*; Victoria and Albert Museum, H.M. Stationery Office, 1954.

MRAZEK, W. *Ikonologie der barocken Deckenmalerei*; Österreichische Akademie der Wissenschaften, vol. 228, No. 3 (1953). (Has a good bibliography of primary and secondary literature.)

PEVSNER, N. *European Architecture*, London, 1947; new ed. 1956. *An Outline of European Architecture*, Penguin Books, 1960 (Jubilee ed.) *Gegenreformation und Manierismus*, Repertorium für Kunstwissenschaft, vol. xlvi (1925), pp. 243–62.

PIGLER, A. *Barockthemen*, 2 vols., (E) Berlin, 1956.

POWELL, N. *From Baroque to Rococo. An introduction to Austrian and German Architecture from 1580 to 1790*, London, 1959.

POZZO, A. *Perspectiva Pictorum et Architectorum*, Rome, 1693–1700 (English translation: *Rules and Examples of Perspective proper for Painters and Architects*, by J. James, London, 1707).

ROEDER, H. *Saints and their Attributes*, London, 1955.

RIEGL, A. *Die Entstehung der Barockkunst in Rom*, Vienna, 1908.

SANDNER, O. *Vorarlberger Bauschule. Die Entwicklung der kirchlichen Raumform 1650–1780*, Innsbruck, 1950.

SCHÜRER, G. *Katholische Kirche und Kultur in der Barockzeit*, Paderborn, 1937.

SCOTT, G. *The Architecture of Humanism*, 2nd ed., reprint of 1935.

SELECT BIBLIOGRAPHY

SITWELL, S. *British Architects and Craftsmen*, 1600–1830, London, 4th ed., 1948.

SCHMARSOW, A. *Barock und Rokoko*, Leipzig, 1897.

STAMM, R. (editor). *Die Kunstformen des Barockzeitalters*, Berne, 1956.

SUMMERSON, J. *Architecture in Britain* 1530–1830 (Pelican History of Art), Penguin Books, 1953.

TAPIÉ, V-L. *Baroque et classicisme*, Paris, 1957 (English translation: *The Age of Grandeur. Baroque and Classicism in Europe*, London, 1960).

WATKIN, E. I. *Catholic Art and Culture*, London, 1942.

WEISSBACH, W. *Der Barock als Kunst der Gegenreformation*, Berlin, 1921.

WÖLFFLIN, H. *Renaissance und Barock*, Munich, 1907.

ZENDRALLI, A. M. *Graubündner Baumeister und Stukkatoren in deutschen Landen zur Barock- und Rokokozeit*, Zurich, 1930.

2. SOUTHERN GERMANY

BARTHEL, W. and HEGE, W. *Barockkirchen in Altbayern und Schwaben*, Deutscher Kunstverlag, Munich and Berlin, 1953.

BAUMEISTER, E. *Rokokokirchen Oberbayerns*, Strassburg, 1907.

BENZ, R. *Deutscher Barock*, Stuttgart, 1949.

BOECK, W. *Die Frühzeit des kirchlichen Barocks in Schwaben* (in the volume: *Aus der Welt des Barock*, Metzler, Stuttgart, 1957).

v. BOEHN, M. *Deutschland im xviii Jahrhundert*, Berlin, 1921.

BRAUN, J. *Die Kirchenbauten der deutschen Jesuiten*, 2 vols., Freiburg, 1908–11.

BUCK, K. *das Bauernleben in den Werken Bayerischer Barockprediger* (a collection of characteristic village sermons), Munich, 1953.

ESCHWEILER, J. and STADE, G. *Die Kuppel über dem Kreuz*, Stuttgart, 1954. (A study of Steinhausen, Weingarten, Neresheim and Wiblingen with good photographs).

SELECT BIBLIOGRAPHY

FEULNER, A. *Bayerisches Rokoko*, Munich, 1923. (A massive, authoritative, splendidly illustrated work that has not been superseded). *Ignaz Günther*, Munich, 1947.

FLEISCHHAUER, W. *Barock im Herzogtum Württemberg*, Stuttgart 1954.

v. FREEDEN, M. *Balthasar Neumann, Leben und Werk*, Deutscher Kunstverlag, Munich and Berlin, 1953.

FREYBERGER, L. *Baiwarisches und Barockes*, Munich (3rd ed.) 1949.

GIEDION-WELCKER, C. *Bayrische Rokokoplastik: J. B. Straub*, Munich, 1922.

GUBY, R. *Die niederbayerischen Donauklöster*, 2 vols., Süddeutsche Kunstbücher.

GUNDERSHEIMER, H. *Matthaus Günther*, Augsburg, 1930.

HAGEN-DEMPF, F. *Der Zentralgedanke bei Johann Michael Fischer*, Munich, 1954.

HAGER, C. *Die Bautätigkeit in Kloster Wessobrunn und die Wessobrunner Stuccatoren*, Oberbayerisches Archiv, vol. 48 (1894).

HAGER, W. *Die Bauten des deutschen Barocks*, Jena, 1942.

HALM, P. M. *Die Künstlerfamilie Asam*, Munich, 1896.

HANFSTÆNGL, E. *Die Brüder C. D. und E. Q. Asam*, Deutscher Kunstverlag, Munich and Berlin, 1945.

HARTIG, M. *Die Oberbayerischen Stifte*, 2 vols., Munich, 1935. *Kirche und Klöster*, in the series *Bayern Land und Volk in Wort und Bild*, Munich, 1953.

HAUTTMANN, M. *Geschichte der kirchlichen Baukunst in Bayern, Schwaben und Franken* 1550–1780.

HEGEMANN, W. *Deutsches Rokoko*, Königstein/Taunus (Die Blauen Bücher), 1953.

HEILBRONNER, P. *Johann Michael Fischer*, Munich 1933.

HOFFMANN, R. *Bayerische Altarbaukunst*, Munich, 1923.

LIEB, N. *Barockkirchen zwischen Donau und Alpen*, Munich, 1953. *Müncher Barockbaumeister*, Munich, 1941.

OSWALD, J. (editor). *Alte Klöster in Passau und Umgebung*, Passau 1954.

SELECT BIBLIOGRAPHY

PEST, M. *Die Finanzierung des Süddeutschen Kirchen- und Kloster-baus in der Barockzeit*, Munich, 1937.

PINDER, W. *Deutscher Barock*, Königstein/Taunus (Die Blauen Bücher), 1953

POPP, H. *Die Architektur der Barock- und Rokokozeit in Deutsch-land und der Schweiz*, Stuttgart, 1913.

REUTHER, H. *Die Kirchenbauten Balthasar Neumanns*, Berlin, 1960.

RUPPRECHT, B. *Die Bayerische Rokokokirche* (Münchener histor-ische Studien; Abt. Bayerische Geschichte, vol. 5), Kallmünz, 1959.

SCHAFFER, X. *Leidenschaftliches Rokoko. Die Plastik des Ferdinand Tietz*, Augsburg, 1958.

SCHMOHL and STÄHELIN. *Barockbauten in Deutschland*, Leipzig, 1874.

SCHNELL, H. *Der baierische Barock*, Munich, 1936.

SCHONBERGER, A. *Ignaz Günther*, with photographs by M. HIRMER, Munich, 1954.

SITWELL, S. *German Baroque Art*, London, 1927. *German Baroque Sculpture*, with descriptive notes by N. PEVSNER, London, 1938.

TINTELNOT, H. *Die Barocke Freskomalerei in Deutschland*, Munich, 1951.

ESSENTIAL HANDBOOKS AND GUIDES FOR THE VISITOR

DEHIO, G. (revised and re-edited by GALL, E.): *Handbuch der deutschen Kunstdenkmäler*, Deutscher Kunstverlag, Munich and Berlin. Volumes available to date for the S. German area are: *Oberbayern* (1952); *Östliches Schwaben* (1954); *Westliches Schwaben* (1956).

RECLAMS KUNSTFÜHRER: I BAYERN by A. von REITZENSTEIN and H. BRUNNER, Stuttgart, 1957. Includes all central and northern Bavaria not yet covered by the Dehio/Gall volumes. II BADEN-WÜRTTEMBERG by H. BRUNNER, 1957. (These are the first of four volumes planned to cover W. Germany and Berlin.)

KLEINE KUNSTFÜHRER, Verlag Schnell und Steiner, Munich.

SELECT BIBLIOGRAPHY

Each of these admirable little illustrated booklet-guides, of which there are now many hundreds, gives in some fifteen pages a succinct yet detailed account, historical, architectural and artistic, of some one ancient monument (church, palace, castle). Obtainable at any bookshop and almost always in the buildings to which each relates (1.50 D-mark). They cover many buildings in Switzerland and Austria also. Many of the latest include colour photographs.

3. SWITZERLAND

DONNET, A. *Walliser Kunstführer*, Sitten, 1954.

GYSI, F. *Die Entwicklung der kirchlichen Architektur in der deutschen Schweiz im 17. und 18. Jahrhundert*, Aarau, 1914.

LANDOLT, H. and SEEGERER, T. *Schweizer Barockkirchen*, Frauenfeld, 1948.

REINHARDT, H. *Die kirchliche Baukunst in der Schweiz*; vol. 3 of the series *Schweizer Kunst*, Basel, 1947.

ESSENTIAL GENERAL HANDBOOK

JENNY, H. *Kunstführer der Schweiz*, 4th ed., Berne, 1945. Small-size, full and reliable, with many illustrations and covering the whole country.

4. AUSTRIA

DECKER, H. *Barockplastik in den Alpenländern*, Vienna, 1943. *Meinrad Guggenbichler* (in the *Sammlung Schroll*), Vienna, 1949.

FISCHER VON ERLACH, J. B. Catalogue of Exhibition held in Graz, Vienna and Salzburg, 1956–7, in commemoration of the tercentenary of his birth.

FREY, D. *Johann Bernhard Fischer von Erlach*, Vienna, 1923.

FRODL-KRAFT, E. *Tiroler Barockkirchen*, Innsbruck, 1955.

GRIMSCHITZ, B. *Johann Lukas von Hildebrandt*; new and expanded edition, Vienna, 1959. *Johann Michael Prunner*, Vienna, 1960. With FEUCHTMÜLLER, R. and MRAZEK, W. *Barock in Österreich*, Vienna, 1960.

KLEINER, S. *Vera et accurata delineatio omnium templorum et coenobiorum quae tam in Caesarea urbe ac sede Vienna Austriae*, Augsburg 1724.

MANN, A. *Meinrad Guggenbichler*, Berlin, 1935.

MAYR, A. *Die Werke des Plastikers Johann Thaddäus Stammel*, 1912.

OTTMANN, F. and POHORECKI, F. *Barockes Wien in Bildern*, Vienna, 1948. The extensive and useful descriptive text in English as well as German.

RIESENHUBER, M. *Die kirchliche Barockkunst in Österreich*, Linz, 1924.

SANDNER, O. *Vorarlberger Bauschule. Die Entwicklung der kirchlichen Raumform* 1650–1780. Innsbruck, 1950.

SEDLMAYR, H. *Österreichische Barockarchitektur* 1690–1740, Vienna, 1930. *Johann Bernhard Fischer von Erlach*; new and greatly expanded edition, Vienna and Munich, 1956.

ULMER, A. *Die Gotteshäuser Vorarlbergs in Wort und Bild*, Dornbirn, 1934.

WEINGARTNER, J. *Die Kirchen Innsbrucks*, 2nd ed., Innsbruck, 1950.

ESSENTIAL GENERAL HANDBOOKS

DEHIO-HANDBUCH, *Die Kunstdenkmäler Österreichs*, revised editions Vienna, 1953 ff. Volumes available to date: *Wien, Salzburg, Oberösterreich, Niederösterreich, Steiermark*.

RECLAMS KUNSTFÜHRER: I WIEN, NIEDERÖSTERREICH, OBERÖSTERREICH, BURGENLAND, Stuttgart, 1961; II SALZBURG, TIROL, VORARLBERG, KÄRNTEN, STEIERMARK, 1961.

CHRISTLICHE KUNSTSTÄTTEN OESTERREICHS, pub. Rupertuswerk Erzabtei St Peter, Salzburg. A new series of illustrated booklet guides similar to the *Kleine Kunstführer* of Schnell & Steiner but less detailed.

INDEX OF PERSONS

INDEX OF PERSONS

INDEX OF PERSONS

INDEX OF PLACES

INDEX OF PLACES

INDEX OF PLACES

INDEX OF SUBJECTS